MICROCOMPUTER
APPLICATIONS

IN HEALTH EDUCATION

MICROCOMPUTER
APPLICATIONS
IN HEALTH EDUCATION

Robert S. Gold
University of Maryland

Wm. C. Brown Publishers

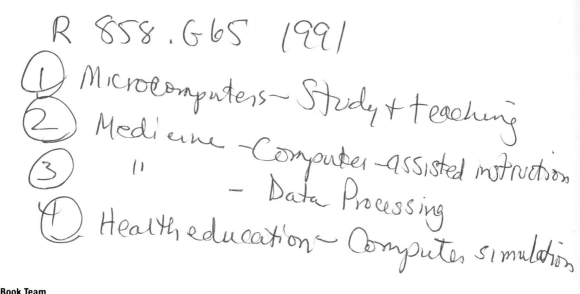

R 858 .G65 1991

1. Microcomputers ~ Study & teaching
2. Medicine ~ Computer-assisted instruction
3. " ~ Data Processing
4. Health education ~ Computer simulation

Book Team

Editor *Chris Rogers*
Developmental Editor *Sue Pulvermacher-Alt*
Production Coordinator *Kay Driscoll*
Photo Editor *Carrie Burger*

WCB

Wm. C. Brown Publishers

President *G. Franklin Lewis*
Vice President, Publisher *George Wm. Bergquist*
Vice President, Publisher *Thomas E. Doran*
Vice President, Operations and Production *Beverly Kolz*
National Sales Manager *Virginia S. Moffat*
Senior Marketing Manager *Kathy Law Laube*
Marketing Manager *George H. Chapin*
Executive Editor *Edgar J. Laube*
Managing Editor, Production *Colleen A. Yonda*
Production Editorial Manager *Julie A. Kennedy*
Production Editorial Manager *Ann Fuerste*
Publishing Services Manager *Karen J. Slaght*
Manager of Visuals and Design *Faye M. Schilling*

Cover design by Kay Dolby Fulton

Cover image © Pete Turner/Image Bank, Chicago

The credits section for this book begins on page 281, and is considered an extension of the copyright page.

Library of Congress Catalog Card Number: 90–80269

ISBN 0–697–10628–4

Printed in the United States of America by Wm. C. Brown Publishers, 2460 Kerper Boulevard, Dubuque, IA 52001

10 9 8 7 6 5 4 3 2 1

CONTENTS

List of Figures

Contents

List of Tables

List of Exhibits

FOREWORD

One gropes for metaphors to capture the essence and historical significance of recent events. In both the health field and in technology the term *revolution* seems almost a cliché. Used to describe the second epidemiological revolution and the computer revolution, the word now pales in the face of the momentous political changes in Eastern Europe, the Soviet Union, South Africa, and some Third World countries. But the parallels among these three revolutions suggest some fascinating relationships.

Most of these uses of the revolution metaphor correctly suggest a certain redistribution of power. The second epidemiological revolution produced the self-care movement and the health-promotion policies and programs that transferred control and responsibility from professionals to patients, consumers, and lay citizens. The computer revolution made high technology readily accessible in the form of PCs, laptops and user-friendly software. The global democratic revolutions at the turn of the decade achieved a redistribution of political power.

The metaphor breaks down, however, when applied to the resources created by the new public health and the new computer applications. Political revolutions typically achieve a redistribution of existing resources, but they seldom in themselves create new resources. The new public health, with its greater emphasis on health education for the masses, citizen participation in planning, and individual empowerment to control the determinants of one's own health, has unleashed enormous resources for individual and community action to improve health. The old medical hierarchy remains largely intact, if somewhat reorganized and refinanced, but a parallel system of lay-health initiative and community-health promotion has emerged, involving multiple sectors beyond the health establishment.

Similarly the computer revolution has multiplied exponentially the power, speed, and accessibility of computing resources, as Robert Gold points out in the opening chapters of this book. The affordability of computers for the vast middle-income populations of Western and Pacific Rim societies with market economies has opened untold advantages to these people and to their nations. "Information is power," was stated as early as the creation of the Federalist Papers. James Madison argued the idea as a founding principle for the United States constitutional democracy, justifying a free press to arm the people with the information they needed to balance their voting power against the unfair advantage of the elite and privileged classes, with their greater access to sources of information. Some of the widening gap between the poor and the non-poor in Western societies in the 1980s might be attributed to the differences in their access to computers for retrieving, storing, and processing information. One of the tasks of the educational professions today is to "democratize" computers, making them still more accessible and user-friendly for the disadvantaged, and for those who serve them, to prevent a further widening of the information gap. This book addresses that need.

In health, as in other needs and aspirations susceptible to socioeconomic and information advantages, the poor of Western societies and the masses of most Eastern European, Soviet, and Third World countries have not had the full advantage of the computer revolution. Most of them have yet to experience the full advantage of the first epidemiological revolution, much less exposure to the health benefits of the second epidemiological revolution. The computer and its related technologies of information processing, printing, communications, and automation had not brought the fruits of modern health knowledge to these other countries. As the life expectancy of Western nations and Japan continued to improve dramatically after 1970, that of the Soviet Union actually declined. Something more than coincidence traces to the same era the explosion of microchip technology in the United States and Japan. Something more than happenstance accounts for the fact that the protection and pirating of that technology has been one of the most jealously contested commercial secrets of these nations and an object of CIA and Soviet spying in the last years of the Cold War. The microchip has made much of the difference between the haves and the have-nots within and among countries in the last two decades.

The World Health Organization has made "technology transfer" and "health education" two of the pillars of its global strategy of "Health for All by the Year 2000." But its caveat with respect to technology transfer is that the transfer must involve "appropriate technology," meaning technology that can be applied and managed locally to analyze and solve a people's own health problems. The caveat with respect to health education is that it must involve and enable people to take control of the determinants of their own health. These, then, are the challenges for computer applications in health today. This book offers hope that the challenge will be met.

Lawrence W. Green

PREFACE

Microcomputer Applications in Health Education is a book designed to provide an introduction to the potential uses of microcomputers in the field of health education. It was written for students preparing for a career in health education, and for those already practicing, who consider themselves novices in the professional application of computers. Experienced users may also find some new ideas and a worthwhile review of existing skills. The book covers a broad range of hardware and applications and has been written in an attempt to provide some new material to all health professionals.

Chapter 1 is a historical overview of technological developments in computer hardware and an examination of the ways in which computer technology has been applied to health education in the past. Chapters 2 and 3 examine various applications of what is often called personal-productivity software—database, word processing, spreadsheet, graphics, and communications. Chapters 4 and 5 provide specific applications of microcomputer technology to the practice of health education, including instructional uses and health assessments such as health-risk appraisal, dietary analysis, fitness assessments, and stress appraisals. Chapter 6 contains a brief overview of research and statistical applications, and of artificial intelligence. Chapter 7 describes some of the legal and ethical issues related to the use of technology in health education. Chapter 8 provides answers to some additional questions that are commonly posed by health educators, and concludes with an examination of developments on the horizon. Appendix A, perhaps the most important chapter in many respects, is a list of twenty-two exercises that can be used to teach or learn all the applications mentioned in the book. This chapter may be used as a guidebook or workbook for a course on microcomputer applications in health.

Each chapter provides a list of chapter objectives, key words, discussion questions, and recommended readings. A key feature of many of the applications chapters is a list of currently available software in that area. It is my hope that this book will answer some questions and provide some motivation for those not yet using this technology, and at the same time provide some new twists and information to those already involved with computers in the practice of health education.

Any book such as this requires the cooperation and assistance of others. I would like to thank Mim Kelly, Simon Priest, and William Montelpare for their contributions to chapter 6, Lisa Gilbert for her work on the graphics section in chapter 2, and Glen G. Gilbert for his contributions to chapters 1, 2, and 4. A special thanks goes to the reviewers for their helpful comments and suggestions: Blair Irvine, University of Oregon; Bethany Shifflett, San Jose State University; Gerald Graf, San Diego State University; Ross E. Vaughn, Boise State University.

I would especially like to thank HT and Caitlin for their patience during this project, but most of all I would like to thank Barbara for her love and support. Without that support, this project could not have been completed.

Robert S. Gold, Ph.D. Dr. P. H. FASHA

1

AN OVERVIEW
OF COMPUTING

By the completion of this chapter, the student will be able to

- understand basic terminology related to computer hardware and software;
- describe the major historic events leading to the availability of today's modern computers;
- summarize some events of historic significance in the application of microcomputers to health education;
- compare the characteristics of supercomputers, mainframe computers, minicomputers, and microcomputers;
- list the major capabilities and limitations of microcomputers for health education;
- identify the principal concerns regarding the use of computers in health education;
- summarize the range of potential health-education applications available to health educators.

K E Y   W O R D S   &   P H R A S E S

Application software: Computer programs created for a specific purpose, such as word processing or data analysis.

Byte: The primary storage unit in the memory of a computer. One byte of memory holds the equivalent of one character of information (e.g., any letter, number, or symbol).

Computer: A general-purpose machine that processes data based on some instructions.

Hardware: A computer and all the physical equipment that is part of a computer system.

Mainframe computer: Large-scale computer system capable of storing hundreds of millions of bytes of information. Mainframe computers have the capacity to handle as many as several thousand users simultaneously.

Microcomputer: A small desktop-size computer, often called personal computer. Although capable of doing many of the same things as other computers, it is designed for use by one person. Generally costs less than ten thousand dollars.

Minicomputer: A midrange computer between mainframe and microcomputer. Minicomputers can support up to several hundred users. Cost in the range of twenty thousand to two hundred thousand dollars.

RAM: Random-process memory in a computer system. RAM is the primary memory in which information is stored by a user.

ROM: Read-only memory. ROM is memory that contains information that cannot be changed by the computer user. It generally contains information needed by the computer system to operate.

Software: Set of instructions that the computer follows. A series of instructions designed to serve a particular purpose or solve a particular problem is called *software program* or *program*.

Supercomputer: The fastest computers currently available. Capable of executing hundreds of millions of instructions per second supercomputers are used only for solving complex problems.

3

HISTORICAL OVERVIEW OF COMPUTING

When we consider the evolution of both communication and the use of information, several landmark events come to mind that have changed the course of human history. These events include

- the development of the spoken word;
- the development of the written word;
- the invention of the printing press;
- the invention of the telegraph machine;
- the invention of the typewriter;
- the invention of the telephone;
- the invention of the computer; and
- the development of microwave and satellite communications.

Many people consider these events revolutionary changes in our ability to manage and manipulate information and to communicate ideas. As we examine the history of computers and information management, we find it striking how many different events needed to occur before our present-day levels of communication could be achieved. Perhaps even more important is the notion that throughout history there have been many powerful machines available for these purposes.

Simkin (1987, p. 10) defines *computer* as any "electronic device with the ability to (1) accept user-supplied data; 2) input, store, and execute programmed instructions; 3) perform mathematical and logical operations; and 4) output results according to user specifications." At the current time there are at least four functioning types of computers, including *microcomputers, minicomputers, mainframe computers,* and *supercomputers.* Table 1.1 is a chronological list of some of the major events in the history of computers. Examine this chart with an eye toward several things: (1) the early availability of powerful computational devices; (2) the sequence of events that build upon one another; and (3) the rapid progression in technological advances made in your own lifetime.

It was not until the beginning of World War II that breakthroughs in technology speeded up—probably as a direct result of the need to ensure the rapid analysis of data necessary to fight a modern global war. It was during this time that *mechanical* and *electrical* components yielded to *electronic components.* Many notable milestones followed. Two worthy of particular note are

- 1943: John W. Mauchly and J. Presper Eckert developed ENIAC (the electronic numerical integrator and calculator). ENIAC contained eighteen thousand vacuum tubes and seventy thousand resistors, weighed more than thirty tons, and occupied a room eight hundred square feet in size. Dorf (1974) suggests that ENIAC could multiply two ten-digit numbers in three-thousandths of a second. This represented a remarkable breakthrough in computational power.

Pictured here is the full range of stand alone computers. The Cray Supercomputer, capable of executing more than 100 million instructions per second; the CYBER 960 mainframe computer by Control Data Corporation with operator's console, CPU, disk and tape drives; a Micro VAX 3100 minicomputer from Digital Equipment Corporation—a desktop computer with multi-user capabilities; a PS/2 series microcomputer from IBM—designed to provide powerful desktop computing to an individual user; and a Macintosh Portable Computer from Apple—one of many laptop computers that provides individual computing power as well as mobility.

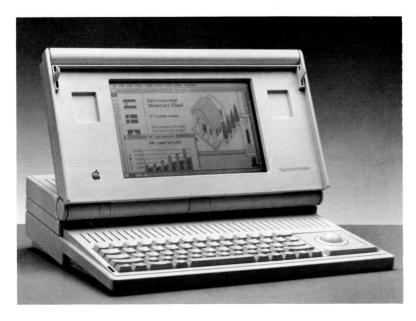

Table 1.1

Chronological History of Computing Devices

DATE	EVENT/ADVANCE
?	Finger counting
1600 B.C.	Stonehenge
1000 B.C.	Abacus
	Clay tablets
	Roman and arabic numeric systems
1300 A.D.	Double-entry bookkeeping
1400	Quipu beads
1617	Napier's bones
1620	Slide rule
1642	Pascal's calculator
1801	Jacquard's loom
1822	Babbage's difference engine
1890	Hollerith's code and punched card tabulator
1911	Monroe calculator
1930	Electrically activated calculators
1937	Aiken's Mark I: first-generation computer
1940	ENIAC: electronic numerical integrator and calculator
1945	UNIVAC: universal automatic computer
1954	UNIVAC II: commercially available second generation
1960s	Third-generation computers, multiprogramming, teleprocessing, time-sharing
1970s	Fourth-generation computers, microprocessors
1980s	Fifth-generation computers, very large-scale integration

- Mid-1940s: John von Neumann demonstrated the final technological breakthrough necessary to produce the dramatic development that followed the 1940s. A mathematician at Princeton University, von Neumann proved that both computer programs and the data necessary for their functioning could be stored together in the same format in a computer's memory. This seemingly simplistic idea provided proof that programs could be encoded and stored in computer memory which mixed both instructions and data. This was the beginning of the stored program in computers.

Sullivan, Lewis, and Cook (1985) suggest that at this point further development of computer technology took two different paths: (1) development directed by East Coast companies interested in applications of computers to commercial data processing, specifically useful to government and financial institutions; and (2) development by West Coast companies driven mostly by the engineering and scientific needs of the military and space programs. The former resulted in the dramatic increase in power and size of computers commonly found in most business and industry settings through the 1970s. These mainframe computers were the standard for administrative and financial computing. The latter path, shaped by the need to develop small, lightweight controlling mechanisms for critical equipment, resulted in *microelectronics*. The

An Overview of Computing

Table 1.2
Mainframe Computer Generations

	FIRST 1951–58	SECOND 1958–64	THIRD 1964–71	FOURTH 1971–82	FIFTH 1982–?
Technology	Vacuum tube	Transistor	Integrated circuits	Large-scale integration	Very large-scale integration
Instructions per second	250	30,000	200,000	500 million	> 1 billion
Speed	Milliseconds	Microseconds	Nanoseconds	Picoseconds	Gigaseconds
Memory in characters	< 10,000	< 64,000	< 4 million	32 million	Virtual/unlimited
Storage	Punched cards	Magnetic tape	Disk	Mass storage	Optical
System characteristics	Single user, manual scheduling	Single user, automatic scheduling	Multiple user, time-sharing	Multiple user, local area networks	Multiple user, multi-processing, global networks

Note: Adapted from *Computing Today: Microcomputer Concepts and Applications* (p. 14) by D. R. Sullivan, T. G. Lewis, and C. R. Cook, 1985, Boston: Houghton Mifflin.

mainframe history is often described in terms of four or five generations of computers, whereas Sullivan, Lewis, and Cook suggest that the smaller microcomputers (personal computers) coming out of the West Coast developments have passed through four stages. A summary of these generations and stages is provided in tables 1.2 and 1.3

We see from table 1.2 the rapid developments in the field of mainframe technology. We now hear many references to *fifth-generation machines.* While there is still some difference of opinion as to what a fifth-generation machine will do, these as-yet-unavailable computers do have some predictable characteristics. They will probably be capable of executing 100 billion instructions per second. They will have enormous storage capacity measured in gigabytes (billions of characters of information), with external storage based on some form of optical technology. They will be not only multiuser systems but multiprocessing systems as well (i.e., able to conduct several different tasks simultaneously) and will heavily utilize *artificial intelligence* in their operation. These are the machines of the 1990s and beyond.

As with mainframe computers, certain technological events and milestones had to exist to make innovations possible in the personal-computer industry. Some of those developments include the following:

- 1956: The Nobel Prize winning development of the *transistor* by William Shockley, John Bardeen, and Walter Brattain. The transistor replaced the vacuum tube and allowed for the initial miniaturization of computer machinery with comparable improvements in reliability.
- Robert Noyce, a student of Shockley, later developed the *integrated circuit*—a microprocessor chip that contained several components of a *computer system.* Noyce started Intel

Corporation, which was later responsible for the development of large-scale integration—the building of miniature chips with many thousands of computer circuits.

- Bill Gates, a young Harvard University dropout, developed a microcomputer version of the programming language BASIC (beginner's all-purpose symbolic instruction code). This programming language became standard on almost all microcomputers through the 1980s. In 1974 Bill Gates joined with Paul Allen to form Microsoft Corporation, a company responsible for major software running on all microcomputer systems today.

- 1973: Gary Kildall, working as an Intel Corporation consultant, developed a mechanism for controlling eight-bit *microprocessors*. He started his own company, Digital Research, in 1975 and marketed CP/M (control program for microprocessors), which became the industry standard eight-bit *operating system* on microcomputers.

- 1977: Steve Jobs and Steve Wozniack sold preassembled Apple computers out of a garage. This *open-architecture machine* (a microcomputer that could be opened by the owner in order to add new components and capabilities) became the standard for microcomputers to follow. They subsequently founded Apple Corporation.

- 1977–79: A business student, Dan Bricklin got tired of doing repetitive computations in columnar pads and wrote a program for an Apple computer which would automate the process. Later known as Visicalc, this was the first major program to sell microcomputers.

- 1981: IBM introduced its PC and legitimized the personal-computer industry.

- 1982: *Time* magazine named the personal computer as its "Man of the Year."

- 1984: Apple computer introduced the Macintosh, the first commercially available microcomputer with a *graphical user interface* (using visual displays rather than text-oriented displays for controlling the activities of the system).

- 1985: Aldus Corporation introduced a program called Pagemaker for the Apple Macintosh and created the era of "desktop publishing."

- 1988: Introduction of the NeXT computer by Steven Jobs. The NeXT computer contained many technological advances not available on other computer systems, such as erasable optical memory.

These events and others spurred the growth of the personal/desktop computer industry, its major stages of development outlined in table 1.3. To put these events into perspective, let's look at some comparisons.

Table 1.3
Personal Computer Stages

	DEVELOPMENTAL 1974–77	EARLY ADOPTERS 1977–81	CORPORATE 1981–84	INTEGRATED SYSTEMS 1984–89	KNOWLEDGE MACHINES 1989–?
Primary target and availability	Hobbyist kits, mail order	Full systems in retail stores	Full systems from corporate sales forces	Personal productivity tool for individuals	Productivity for individuals and groups; artificial intelligence
Technology	8 bit	8 bit	16 bit	32 bit	64 bit
Memory	< 32,000	< 64,000	< 256,000	> 1 million	16 million+
Uses	Hobby, programming	Games, word processing	Productivity software	Integrated systems and networking	Decision assistance
Storage	Cassette tape	5.25 floppy	5.25 floppy	3.50 microfloppy, hard disks	Laser optics
Operating	CP/M	Single user, standardized	Enhanced single user, many standards	Graphical interface	Enhanced user interfaces, alternative input devices
Cost in dollars at time	$2,500	$3,000	$3,500	$3,000–7,000	$5,000–10,000

Note: Adapted from *Computing Today: Microcomputer Concepts and Applications* (p. 14) by D. R. Sullivan, T. G. Lewis, and C. R. Cook, 1985, Boston: Houghton Mifflin.

1. ENIAC was fifteen hundred square feet, contained eighteen thousand vacuum tubes, cost several million dollars, and kept a horde of technicians busy so that it could operate for a few minutes per day. Today microcomputers occupy one to two square feet, cost thousands of dollars, and have more computer power than ENIAC.

2. In 1960 rapid access memory cost ten thousand dollars per million characters and operated at clock speeds in the hundreds of milliseconds. Today 100 million characters of storage can be bought for several hundred dollars.

3. The computational ability of computers is measured in millions of instructions per second. The most advanced supermicrocomputers can execute nearly 10 million instructions per second, with supercomputers nearing the 1-billion-instructions-per-second barrier.

We have come a long way from the abacus and Stonehenge. The speed with which innovations occur today is increasing at the same time that the cost of technology continues to decline. We have not yet reached the stage at which computers are as user friendly as telephones, but there are already more functioning computers in this country than there are people. Only our imagination limits us in our application of this technology in the health fields.

GENERAL CAPABILITIES AND LIMITATIONS OF COMPUTERS AND COMPUTER SYSTEMS

Computers have been available now for several decades, and microcomputers are becoming more familiar to many of us. However, there are many elementary terms that may still be confusing to the novice. A review of some basic terminology follows, much of which is common to all classes of computer (e.g., microcomputers, minicomputers, mainframe computers, and supercomputers).

Microcomputer Systems

Simkin and Dependahl (1987) suggest that any microcomputer systems contain at least five major components. The way they are related is called the system *configuration.*

- Hardware: including processing, communications, input, output, and storage equipment
- Software: including operating systems, application programs, and documentation
- Data: including numbers, words, files, and formulas
- Procedures: including log-on procedures and security procedures
- Users: including professionals, specialists, experts, and novices

Hardware

In discussion of microcomputer hardware, some of the most commonly heard terms include *microcomputer system, microprocessor, ROM, RAM, bits, bytes, Ks, input/output, memory,* and *peripherals.* Fortunately, most of these terms are easily demystified.

Any microcomputer system is a general-purpose group of components much like a stereo system. As illustrated in figure 1.1, the system is composed of at least four major components: a control unit or brain (*microprocessor*), some built-in memory (both *ROM* and *RAM*), some means of communicating with that control unit (*input/output devices*), and some auxiliary storage devices (e.g, diskettes).

Microprocessor

The microprocessor is the brain of any system. It controls all of the system's resources and executes all commands. Some microcomputers have two microprocessors (coprocessors), but most have only one. There are many microprocessors available, but only a handful are used in most major systems. Microprocessors have two major components, an *arithmetic logic unit* and a *supervisory or control unit.* The arithmetic logic unit is responsible for computational tasks like addition, subtraction, multiplication, and division—as well as logical operations such as comparing numbers to determine which is larger. The control unit is responsible for overseeing the execution of instructions: it determines order of execution, access to system resources, and input/output in general. Today's microprocessors are capable of executing instructions as rapidly as many mainframe computers of just a few years ago. Table 1.4 compares the *clock speed* of some of the more common microprocessors.

Figure 1.1. Graphic of microcomputer system and its components.

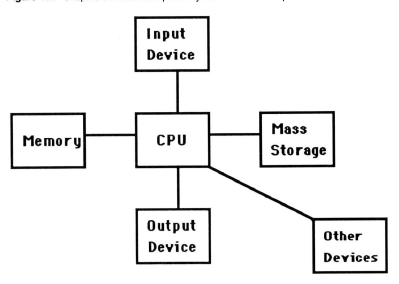

The power of modern microprocessor gives the impression of a large piece of equipment. Pictured here is an IBM microprocessor passing through the eye of a needle.

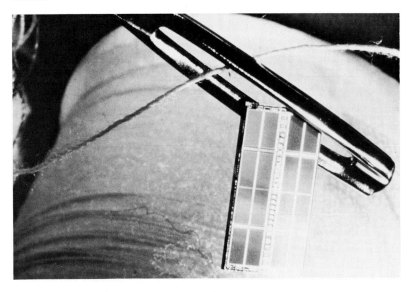

Microprocessors are marvelous devices, able to execute several hundred thousand instructions per second. However, they do have one major shortcoming: they have no memory and therefore cannot store information. In order to overcome this deficit, microcomputer systems usually contain components that act as a storage medium for instructions and data. This type of built-in memory comes in two major forms—ROM (read-only memory), and RAM (random-access memory). Both types of memory are very important to the system.

Table 1.4

Clock Speed of Some Common Microprocessors

MICROCOMPUTER	MICROPROCESSOR	CLOCK SPEED*
Apple II (1978–85)	Motorola 6502	1.5 megaherz
IBM-PC (1982)	Intel 8088	4.7 megaherz
Apple Macintosh (1984)	Motorola 68000	7.8 megaherz
IBM-PC AT (1984)	Intel 80286	up to 25 megaherz
IBM-PS/2 (1986)	Intel 80386	up to 33+ megaherz
Apple Macintosh IIc	Motorola 68030	up to 25+ megaherz

*A clock is the internal timing device that governs the speed at which the computer can process instructions: the faster the clock speed, the faster the computer can operate. Clock speed is measured in cycles per second, and the term *megaherz* is million cycles per second.

Memory

ROM contains instructions and data that may be read and used by the system, but that cannot be changed by the user of the system. ROM often contains instructions that direct one's system to perform specific actions that save the user a good deal of time and effort. For instance, the ROM contains the series of instructions the computer needs to execute when the power to the system is turned on, or when the computer is *booted* (started up). The ROM may also contain computer languages. An important characteristic of ROM is that the stored information is not lost when the power is turned off. This is not the case with RAM.

The term *read and write,* or *random-access memory,* means that the user of a microcomputer system can change the contents of memory at will. It is here, in RAM, that information entered by the user is kept by the microcomputer. Therefore, one can store in RAM whatever information is desired. However, the other distinguishing characteristic of RAM is that it loses the information when the power is turned off. When the power is turned back on the RAM is blank.

Now that the difference between ROM and RAM is clarified, one can consider the storage capability, or memory, of the computer at one's disposal. The easiest way to understand a computer's memory is to visualize it as a mass of pigeonholes, each one capable of storing some information Each individual hole is divided into smaller parts called *binary digits* (or bits). These parts are called binary digits because they are capable of only two operational states—being turned "on," or being turned "off."

A single bit does not contain very much information, but when at least eight of them are combined into a *byte,* they can symbolize each of the letters from *A* to *Z*, the numbers from 0 to 9, and any special characters found on a computer keyboard (e.g., #, $, %, and &). A byte, then, is the equivalent of one pigeonhole of memory in a computer system, and it is capable of storing the equivalent of one character of information. How much memory does a computer have? The answer is that each system is different. Some systems may have approximately 256,000 bytes of memory, or 512,000 bytes, or 640,000 bytes. However, computer

Figure 1.2. Graphic representation of computer memory. This illustrates graphically the logical organization of computer memory. Each cell (byte) has a locations address and the capacity to store approximately one character of information.

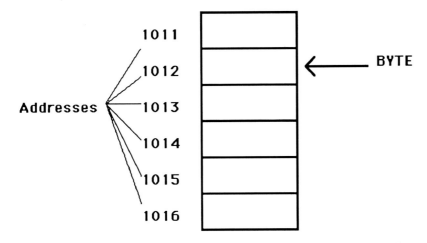

memory is often described in *kilobytes* or *Ks*. One kilobyte (*K*) of memory is equivalent to 1,024 bytes. So when one hears that a computer has 256K of memory, it really means 256 times 1,024 bytes or 262,144 bytes of memory. This means that the system has the capacity to store 262,144 characters of information, or the amount of information on approximately 150 typed double-spaced pages. Figure 1.2 is a graphic description of the organization of a microcomputer's memory.

Input/Output Devices

The next component of the system is the *input/output* device. This term refers to the mechanisms by which one communicates with the microprocessor. Input devices are used to transmit information to the system, and output devices constitute the means by which the system communicates with users. There are many types of input/output devices: computer keyboards, mice, light pens, punch-card readers, optical scanners, and game paddles are examples of input devices, while computer monitors, television screens, and printers are examples of output devices. Some devices (e.g, disk drives) actually serve both input and output capabilities. Figure 1.3 illustrates several of these different devices.

Auxiliary Memory

The final basic component of most systems is a form of auxiliary memory. Remember, when the computer is turned off, everything stored in RAM is lost. If one wants to save information for longer periods of time, one needs to find some other mechanism to do this. The most frequently used auxiliary storage mechanism in today's microcomputer systems is floppy diskettes, but this storage medium is changing rapidly and is being augmented by other, more sophisticated technology. We should not forget,

Figure 1.3. Input to computer systems may be provided by such devices as the (a) Apple Macintosh keyboard, (b) Microsoft mouse, (c) IBM bar code reader, or (d) Apple graphic and character recognition scanner. Output is provided by the computer system through video display devices such as (e) the Princeton High Resolution Monitor, (f) the Hewlett-Packard Laserjet IIP printer, and the (g) CalComp 1044 GT Pen Plotter.

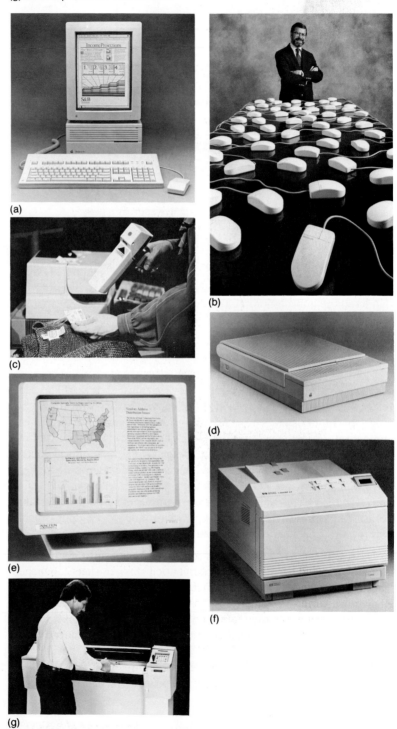

(a)

(b)

(c)

(d)

(e)

(f)

(g)

There are several storage mediums available. Shown here are (a) Three sizes of floppy disks. The 8-inch, 5¼-inch, and 3½-inch. (b) A 5½-inch compact disk. (c) A 12-inch laser disk.

(a)

(b)

(c)

however, that there are many other common mechanisms for storing information, including IBM-type examination answer sheets, punched cards and tape, and cassette tapes. Figure 1.4 illustrates the most common scheme for storing information on floppy diskettes.

A summary of the more common peripheral storage mediums used in today's microcomputers appears in table 1.5. When comparing floppy, microfloppy, hard disk, and CD-ROM storage systems, several issues become clear: (1) as the recording density increases (storage capacity grows), the reliability of the medium seems to increase as well; (2) as

Figure 1.4. Graphic images of storage scheme on floppy diskettes. Regardless of which type of floppy diskette is used, the general storage scheme is the same. This is a magnetic medium that stores information in concentric circles called *tracks*. The entire platter is divided into pie slices called *sectors*. A specific number of bytes of information is stored in each sector per track: if each sector contains 256 bytes of information, the diskette is called *single density;* 512 bytes *double density;* 1,025 bytes is called *quad density*. Usually, one of the tracks serves as a *volume table of contents*—a listing of all the file names on the diskette and the specific starting address on the diskette where the file can be found.

One reason diskettes from one machine cannot be used in another vendor's machine is because information is stored in a different pattern of tracks and sectors, and a different track is used for the volume table of contents.

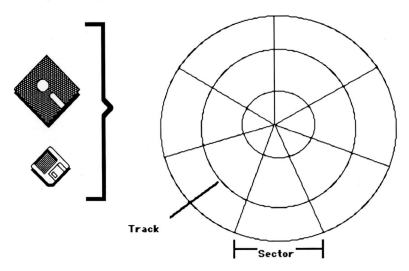

Track

Sector

the recording density increases, the cost per byte of storage decreases; and (3) as the recording density increases, the technological requirements also increase.

Software

The term *software* refers to the programs that run on any computer. A program is nothing more than a series of instructions to be executed by the *central processing unit* (CPU). Some people divide software into two broad categories—*system software* and *applications software*. Figure 1.5 is a graphic representation of the relationship between different types of software.

Systems Software

Besides having a knowledge of several different classes of computers (microcomputer, minicomputer, mainframe computer, supercomputer), the reader should also know by now that there are many different capabilities among microcomputer systems. These differences are mostly due to the different ways that the microprocessors are used by the computer system. One thing, however, that is the same in all computer systems, whether mainframe or micro, is the necessity for software designed to guide the activities of the system. This software is different for each

Table 1.5
Peripheral Storage Devices for Microcomputers

TYPE	PHYSICAL SIZE	MEMORY CAPACITY	ADDITIONAL COMMENTS
Floppy diskette (personal computers) (many business computers)	5.25 inches	Up to 1,000K 8 inches	Magnetic medium, most frequently used, fragile, up to 2 million K.
Microfloppy	3.50 inches	Up to several thousand K	Housed in stiff plastic cases, becoming very popular especially in new machines, less fragile than floppies.
Hard disk	Varies	Up to 100,000K (100 megabytes)	Made of one or more rigid platters, can store information more densely than floppies or microfloppies, access time shorter than floppies or microfloppies.
CD-ROM (Compact disk, read-only memory)	5.25	Up to 600,000K (600 megabytes)	Newest technology, similar to audio-disks. Information stored by creating pits in surface of platter with laser beam. Most now have only read-only, or write-once, read-many-times, capacity. Used to store massive amounts of information.

computer type and is called *systems software*. Systems software refers to any program that is necessary for the operation of the computer system or for the management of its resources. *Operating systems* are used to manage all the components of a computer system and to ensure adequate communication capabilities between the various components. In today's microcomputer environment there are several important operating systems in use, including MS-DOS/PC-DOS; OS/2 in the IBM and compatible world; PRODOS; the Macintosh OS on Apple II and Macintosh computers; and UNIX used on *workstations* (computers with a great deal of memory and very rapid processing capabilities) for *multiprocessing* and/or *multiuser* capabilities. In addition to operating systems, there are other types of systems programs such as various utility programs for performing necessary system tasks outside the operating system itself. Examples of utility programs include special programs that recover damaged files from disks or that reorganize the data stored on a diskette to improve its utilization.

Figure 1.5. Relationship between software applications.

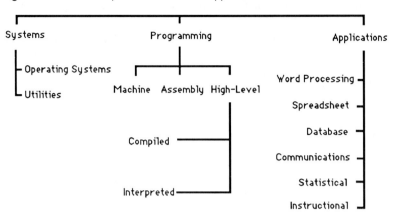

Programming Software

There are three main types of programming languages found on computer systems today: *machine languages, assembly languages,* and *high-level languages.* Both machine and assembly languages are considered low-level languages because they contain instructions that are in a form that is very close to what the computer can understand directly (i.e., the instructions are written in numeric codes).

Machine languages use commands that consist only of binary numbers (0 and 1) and theoretically represent the way information is ordinarily stored in computers. All numbers, letters, characters, and special symbols (e.g., punctuation marks) can be represented as a set of at least eight binary numbers. For those who remember binary arithmetic, the number 9 can be represented in the following way: 0000 1001. There are several different numbering systems used today which set a specific code to represent all possible symbols used on a keyboard. One of these systems, ASCII (American Standard for Computer Information Interchange), uses the binary equivalent of the number 65 (0010 0001) to represent the capital letter *A,* 66 (0010 0011) to represent the capital letter *B,* and so on. In order to enter any code into a computer in machine language, every character must be translated into its binary equivalent and then entered one at a time.

Assembly languages use abbreviations called *mnemonic codes* to represent key terms that have meaning to a computer. Although also low-level language, assembly languages were developed to remove some of the tedium and difficulty associated with programming in machine language. In assembly language the mnemonic codes are entered rather than the binary codes for each character of a data point or command. However, once an assembly-language program is entered into a computer, it must be translated by another program into machine code so the instructions can be understood by the computer. The programs that translate assembly language into machine code are called *assemblers.*

Programming in assembly language is quite difficult for most people, so attempts have been made to develop programming languages that more closely resemble English.

High-level languages have instructions that often read like English and can make computer programming easier. As with assembly languages, the computer systems cannot understand these higher-level languages directly, so programs written in these languages must be translated into machine code. For the higher-level languages there are two primary types of translator programs—*compilers* and *interpreters*. These two types of programs use different strategies in their translation. Interpreters translate instructions one by one as the program is being executed. This means that as a program is run, each instruction is examined for grammatical errors (*syntax errors*) and then translated. Compilers translate the entire program prior to its being executed, and a new version of the program is created. This new version is translated into machine code (executable code), so when the program is run, it runs very rapidly. This process is called *compilation,* and compilers check for syntax errors in this process. These apparently minor differences cause two major differences when running programs: (1) compiled programs run more rapidly than interpreted programs because all the translation is completed before the program is executed; (2) compiled programs have already been checked for syntax errors when the program is executed, which means that an interpreted program will "crash" (be interrupted and end unexpectedly) in the middle of operation if a syntax error is found. These crashes should not happen with compiled programs (though logic errors and poor programming style can also cause programs to crash).

When selecting a high-level language to use in program development, programmers consider these differences between interpretation and compilation. Some examples of compiled languages include FORTRAN, COBOL, PL/1, PASCAL, and C. The most notable example of an interpreted language is BASIC (beginner's all-purpose symbolic instruction code), although there are now BASIC compilers to improve execution efficiency. It is important to note, however, that programming a microcomputer involves basically the same process as programming a mainframe computer. But most computer users, and in particular microcomputer users, need not worry about the differences between programming languages or their intricacies, because the needs of most users can be easily satisfied by using existing programs designed to meet just about any need. These programs are called *applications software.*

Applications Software

Applications software refers to programs designed to help *end users* solve problems or perform specific tasks. Today, major applications software in microcomputers includes word-processing packages, spreadsheets, database management applications, communications software, graphics software, statistical software, and instructional software. There are, however, many other types of applications software. Most of the first five of these types of applications are collectively known as *productivity software*—applications designed to improve the personal productivity of professionals. Although designed for users who are not computer programmers but who want to use the power of the computer to solve problems, each of these applications are written in one or more computer languages.

HISTORICAL OVERVIEW OF COMPUTING IN HEALTH EDUCATION

In 1977 Apple™ and Radio Shack™ computer companies made consumer-oriented microcomputers a reality. However, it was not until the development of Visicalc™ in 1979 by two graduate students at MIT that people bought computers to run an existing piece of software. The microcomputer marketplace changed dramatically again in late 1980 when IBM™ introduced its first personal computer. With these two very powerful computers, many applications were developed that improved individual productivity. The most frequently used applications continue to be word processing and spreadsheet and database applications. However, in 1981 when Lotus Corporation™ introduced 1-2-3™, sales of microcomputers again took a geometric upswing. It was the introduction of the first truly functional *integrated package* (software containing more than one application—e.g., word processing, spreadsheets, and database capabilities) that assisted the collective use of this individual power for the first time. It is important to recognize the power of these stand-alone applications and to look for ways to apply them to personal and professional needs.

Today there are many powerful health-education applications for microcomputers. Examples of these applications include health-risk appraisals, dietary analyses, and simulations, all providing sophisticated analyses regarding health status and skills. However, if the outcome is to move beyond the level of sophistication of Visicalc™ and toward the utility of Lotus 1-2-3™, a method by which to integrate these stand-alone packages must be developed. The critical criterion of success lies with a whole that provides a greater level of understanding than the sum of the individual applications. The technology already exists for accomplishing these ends; but only when the full potential of *artificial intelligence* and *expert systems* is explored will this goal finally be achieved.

Milestones in Health-Education Computing

By the 1980s many health-education applications were being developed for microcomputers, and several milestones are worth noting. Gold and Duncan (1980a, 1980b) outlined the potential of computers in health education as instructional devices—as aids to instruction, as teachers, or as management devices. In 1983 the National Health Information Clearinghouse produced the first of three HEALTHFINDERS, or information packages on computer applications in health education. The first was a list of computer software for health promotion, the second described computer health-risk appraisals, and the third provided sources of on-line information for health educators.

In the same year the journal *Health Education,* a publication of the Association for the Advancement of Health Education, was entirely devoted to the topic of microcomputer applications in health education (14[6], 1983). At that time Bailey and Pigg (1983), Chen (1983), and McDermott and Belcastro (1983) first warned about problems that might result from the unplanned incorporation of computers into health-education programming and identified the need for training of health educators. Randolfi (1985) soon proposed that health educators could use computers for the transmission of information, to complete personal and community health assessments, to motivate appropriate health decisons, and as a management tool.

In 1985 and 1986 two special issues of professional journals targeted this area. The *Journal of Nutrition Education* (1985), produced the first comprehensive review of state-of-the-art computer applications in the field of nutrition education. In addition, it published the first series of software reviews for nutrition education. *Family and Community Health* (9[2], 1986) devoted an entire issue to technological advances in community health. Several articles in this issue were seminal in the field:

- Hawkins, Duncan, and McDermott (1986) suggested the use of "high technology" to promote self-care;
- Hahn and Nicholson (1986) and Randolfi, Irvine, and Davis (1986) proposed the need to provide specialized training for all health educators in this field; and
- Anderson, Needle, and Mosow (1986) provided the results of a major study on the use of microcomputers as promotional tools incorporated into the curriculum of middle schools.

In 1986 Randolfi provided the most comprehensive examination of the diffusion of microcomputer courses at the university level for health educators. As a result of this study, Randolfi (1986) made the following recommendations:

- An increasingly greater number of health-education preparation programs should require completion of an undergraduate course in microcomputer applications in health education (p. 102).
- Although content will be somewhat generic, all health educators should be exposed to health-risk appraisals, nutrition-analysis programs, and the use of database management software (p. 103).
- In spite of some controversy, introductory and advanced courses need not include a high degree of instruction of computer programming (p. 104).

Although these developments focused mainly on instructional issues, many other events were occurring simultaneously in other areas of health education. Brown, McDermott, and Marty (1981a) demonstrated how computers could be used for employee health monitoring and in surveillance of toxic environments (1981b). Tom (1981) indicated the utility of a microcomputer in maintaining and updating pupil health records, thus maximizing access for nurses and other appropriate school health personnel.

Recent Technological Advances

We have seen in the last decade a tremendous growth in the technology that might be applied to health education. The most notable of those advances have been in the following areas:

- Mass data storage devices
- Better and more varied input devices
- Graphical interfaces
- Voice recognition/output
- Local and global communications
- Laptop computer capability

Because of these and other advances, we have seen greater application of microcomputers to health-related fields. We have seen much greater use of computers for self-assessments in the areas of dietary analysis, stress reduction, health-hazard appraisals, fitness profiles, body-composition profiles, smoking assessments, assessments of diabetic patients, and storytelling.

THE CHARACTERISTICS OF COMPUTER SYSTEMS AND HEALTH EDUCATION

The experience we have had for the past twenty years in health education and related fields suggests that there are many characteristics that make the use of computer systems (particularly microcomputers) desirable. Among the more important to be identified are the following.

Desirable Characteristics of Microcomputer Systems

1. Ability to store and retrieve data. Because of the increasing memory capacity of microcomputers, enormous amounts of information can now be stored in quite a portable and accessible format. With hard disks capable of storing twenty to several hundred megabytes of information easily, or optical CD-ROMs able to store more than six hundred megabytes of information, our capacity may seem almost unlimited. But in order to make this information worthwhile to practitioners, it must be organized in such a way that it can be accessed easily, and microprocessors have to operate at increasing speeds. With the recent availability of sophisticated applications software and very fast microprocessors, all of these criteria are satisfied—and we genuinely have the capacity to manage information even in the face of rapid proliferation. In summary, there are some important related features that make this capacity a reality with today's microcomputer systems:

- Sophisticated applications software
- Availability of massive amounts of memory
- Very rapid microprocessors

2. Reliability. Unlike computer systems of the past in which mean time between failure rates was charted in minutes, today's microcomputer systems are very reliable electronic components. Although it is rare for a modern system to fail, it is possible, and the most common components of the system to fail are the mechanical devices. Disk drives and printers are the most likely features of the system to "go down" today.

3. One-on-one interaction. Because of the speed of operation of systems in a time-sharing or networking environment, and the nature of the interaction between the user and a microcomputer, a person may feel as if individual attention is being given. This is a very desirable characteristic, particularly if someone is dealing with sensitive information about which they feel uneasy when conversing with health professionals. This ability is particularly important in several different situations, including those times

- when the user requires immediate feedback;
- when the application is particularly sensitive.

4. Inherent challenge and interest. The work by Ellis, Raines, and Hakansan (1982) in the waiting room provides substantial evidence that individuals working with a microcomputer system can feel challenged and attain some genuine satisfaction from interaction with a microcomputer. The key element that often determines such a result is the quality of the software being used.

5. Numerous potential technological capabilities. Because of the rapid advances in computer technology, a great many new capabilities become available at a dramatic pace. Among the newest currently available are

- access to computers worldwide through satellite telecommunications;
- numerous new pointing devices reducing the need to use keyboards (e.g., mouse, trackball, touch-sensitive screens);
- speech synthesis and voice recognition, both of which increase the potential for use by a wider range of individuals, particularly among handicapped populations;
- optical scanning devices, allowing users to input vast amounts of both character and graphical information directly into a computer from a printed page.

There is, however, another side to this coin: a number of undesirable characteristics must be considered as we search for ways to apply computer technology to health education and related fields. Among the more important are the following.

Undesirable Characteristics of Microcomputer Systems

1. Cost. Although the cost of computer technology has decreased greatly in the last decade, it is still a concern for some very important reasons:

- Computers are still beyond the economic reach of many disadvantaged populations.
- Some of the costs of a computer system are hidden—for instance, the cost of software, maintenance, repair, and related outlays over the life of a system.

2. System incompatibilities. Although we often think in terms of components in a microcomputer system, the term *component* here does not carry the same connotation as it does with a stereo system. Printers, keyboards, monitors, and other system components must be quite carefully matched. There are no universal linkages, cables, or communications protocols as in the stereo world. Perhaps more important than this type of incompatibility, however, is our inability to transfer programs and information easily from one type of computer system to another. Even if similar diskettes are used, a diskette formatted in an IBM cannot under normal circumstances be used in an Apple—and the reverse is true as well. There are a number of reasons for this lack of compatibility, including the following:

- The microprocessors utilize different instruction sets and do not understand the commands of those in other machines.
- Different computer systems store information in different formats, making it difficult for a disk drive from one machine to understand the information on a disk formatted for a different system.

3. Computer's inherent lack of intelligence. Although capable of executing instructions many thousands of times per second, and able to store enormous amounts of information for easy access, the brain of a microcomputer system is incapable of thought or reason. Microprocessors are capable only of executing instructions as given—and if the wrong instructions are given, the system will make mistakes. While computers can be programmed to make conditional decisions, they are not yet capable of judgment or intuition as humans are. Because of this, computers are capable only of doing exactly what they are told to do.

4. Potential for invasion of privacy. With the increase in networked computer systems, particularly those with telephone access, enormous amounts of health information on a particular population raise the specter of invasion of privacy. There are already many cases of computer users with too much skill for their own judgment breaking access codes to large computer systems in hospitals, banks, and government installations. Because these invasions are possible, the information in these systems is accessible. Much is being done to minimize these threats, but there are still those who seem capable of short-circuiting most protection schemes. This is a serious problem and raises the concern of whether or not large amounts of personal information should be linked in networked systems.

5. Computer's inability to react to moods. Computer systems can do many things, but one of the vital skills that health educators develop with training and experience is a skill that today's computer systems do not have—the ability to react to the mood changes of clients. This is often a vital part of work with clients in health education, and though we often suggest that computer systems can be used on a one-to-one basis, the ability to modify actions or words based on mood is not yet possible for computers.

6. Threat of dehumanization. Today's modern computer systems can do many things for health educators, but if we rely too heavily on their capabilities and minimize the interaction between health educator and client, we run the risk of dehumanizing the health-education encounter.

I would like to conclude this section with several specific concerns regarding the use of computers to affect health and health behavior.

1. Software quality. Good instructional applications require expertise in learning theory, program planning, context, and software design. All too often these skills are not brought together to a project and we are left with technically good programming and weak organization, content, and educational impact, or the reverse—good educational material weakly presented in the form of an electronic pamphlet.

2. Software design. There are many capabilities of interactive computers that make them unique for health-education settings; however, many programs are designed to provide little more than information in the form of an electronic page or pamphlet. Unless we use these capabilities to their fullest, we may find that the more cost-effective approach is to provide such information in printed form.

3. Access. We should recognize the fact that the vast majority of computer users are male. Is there some gender bias involved? If computers become the principal method of providing information in health-education settings, we do not yet know the extent to which women would be excluded from benefiting from these applications.

4. Evaluation of software. We are quite accustomed to carefully evaluating printed and audiovisual materials before distributing them widely. We must guard against a tendency to distribute electronic material without careful evaluation to meet the high demand for computerized applications.

I have expressed here some general concerns regarding the use of computers in instruction, concerns that cross many instructional disciplines. However, there are two additional points that are specific to health information and education, and they are perhaps the most important concerns of all.

5. Difficulty of interpretation. There are indications that some health behavior may be changed as a result of some interaction with computers, but that has been tested only in settings where health professionals have been available to interpret results, explain their implications, answer questions, and provide some follow-up. It certainly appears that computer applications can provide high-quality, self-paced, individualized instruction, but the question remains whether they should be used by themselves without some human element involved.

6. *Liability issues.* There is a growing concern that as health-related software becomes more widely used and more sophisticated, problems of liability and malpractice will emerge. There have already been proposals in the United States for the U.S. Food and Drug Administration to regulate health-related software in the same way that medical devices are regulated. There are really two related concerns here: (1) whether such regulation will occur and what effect it would have on further development; (2) the impact of legal decisions on the continued use of computerized applications in public health.

POTENTIAL USES OF MICROCOMPUTERS IN HEALTH-RELATED FIELDS

Table 1.6 contains a summary of some of the potential applications of microcomputers in health-education-related fields. Many of these applications areas will be more fully explained in later chapters.

SUMMARY

A great many events link the development of the spoken word to the modern computer. Today's computers fall into four types, ranging from desktop models (microcomputers) to very large and powerful supercomputers; however, there are several characteristics that are common to all types of computer systems: a central processing unit, memory, input and output devices, and a mechanism for permanently storing information on some medium external to the computer itself. There are many capabilities of microcomputers that lend themselves to health-related computing, including storage and retrieval of data, reliability, "personalized" interaction with users, the capacity to challenge a user, and the many technological capabilities. These capabilities allow microcomputers to be used for administrative, instructional, specialty, and research applications in health education.

DISCUSSION QUESTIONS

1. The rapid development of computer technology in our lifetimes has been dramatic. What developments have occurred in the health fields that could not have happened without this technology?
2. Will computers ever completely replace health professionals in some settings?
3. Given the speed and the computational power of modern computers, how do you think this technology can be applied to health education?
4. Should all health professionals be computer literate?
5. What does computer literacy mean to you?
6. Consider the potential capabilities of each of the classes of computers. How could these capabilities be applied in different health-related settings?

Table 1.6

Potential Applications of Microcomputers in Health Education

ADMINISTRATIVE MANAGERIAL

Routine record keeping	Budget accounting	Cost projections
Inventory control	Management of events	Word processing
Electronic mail	Database applications	

INSTRUCTIONAL

Aid to instruction
    Self-assessment
    HRA'S   Dietary analyses   Stress measures
    Application of knowledge
    Simulation   Problem solving

As a teacher
    Drill and practice   Tutorials   Dialogue

Educational management
    Record keeping   Database management   Test scoring   Decision assistance

SPECIALTY APPLICATIONS

Computer-assisted decision making
    Improved accuracy of diagnoses
    Assessment of appropriateness of interventions
    Improved decision support for health professionals
    Elimination of unnecessary clinical/diagnostic tests
    Educational tool
    Intelligent interface to medical databases
    Improved understanding of the structure of knowledge

Control of laboratory subsystems

Physiologic monitoring systems

Signal acquisition and pattern recognition
    Signal acquisition—analog to digital conversions
    Pattern recognition
    Feature extraction (data reduction)
    Classification and analysis

Aids to the handicapped

RESEARCH APPLICATIONS

Acquisition of data
    Analog to digital conversion   Survey/telephone applications

Management of data

Analysis of data

---

7. In different health settings we need to consider the capabilities and limitations of the populations we are working with. Sometimes we deal with people who are handicapped in a variety of ways. In what ways can the needs of physically handicapped individuals be considered in selection of input and output devices?

8. How can the capacity of CD-ROM be applied to health-education needs?

9. What health-education potential does portability add to a microcomputer?

10. Are computers inherently limited in their potential application to health-education settings?

11. Should health professionals be trained to utilize computers in their professional settings?

12. What do you think is the potential of some of the newer hardware and software developments?

RECOMMENDED READINGS

Saba, V. K., & McCormick, K. A. (1986). *Essentials of computers for nurses.* Philadelphia: J. B. Lippincott.

Simkin, M. G., & Dependahl, R. H., Jr. (1987). *Microcomputer principles and applications.* Dubuque: Wm. C. Brown.

Sullivan, D. R., & Lewis, T. G., & Cook, C. R. (1985). *Computing today: Microcomputer concepts and applications.* Boston: Houghton Mifflin.

2

PRODUCTIVITY APPLICATIONS APPLIED TO HEALTH EDUCATION

By the completion of this chapter, the student will be able to

- understand basic terminology related to personal-productivity applications;
- demonstrate how databases, word processing, spreadsheets, and graphics software can be applied to health-education activities;
- describe the major characteristics of each of the types of productivity software;
- assess the capabilities and limitations of each type of application.

K E Y   W O R D S   &   P H R A S E S

Cursor: Any blinking character on a computer screen that indicates where the next character typed at a keyboard will appear.

Database: Any collection of information.

Database management software: A program that allows a user to store, manage, manipulate, and retrieve data from a database.

Desktop publishing: Production of publication-quality output from a personal computer.

File: Any collection of information electronically stored.

Graphics software: Any computer program capable of creating or processing pictures or images.

Productivity software: A group of software-applications programs that enhance the speed and capabilities of individual professional activities (e.g., word processing, database management).

Spreadsheet software: An application program that mimics a table with columns and rows. Any operations on numbers or text that can be performed in such a table can be done electronically in spreadsheet software.

Word processing: An application program that allows a user to enter, store, manipulate, and print text information.

INTRODUCTION

Aside from accounting packages used to ensure that most businesses and institutions have adequate control of their daily transactions and payroll activities, database, word-processing, spreadsheet, and graphics applications are the most frequently used software. For individual productivity these are the four most frequently used microcomputer applications packages. Each is a general-purpose application that has the potential for adaptation to many personal and professional needs.

Database-management software permits the storage and manipulation of data of any type—whether numeric, textual, or a combination. Users can create databases, view their data in a variety of ways, and produce reports to meet individual needs. *Word-processing* applications are used to create documents consisting primarily of text. These documents may then be edited, formatted, and printed in a variety of forms selected by the user. *Spreadsheet software* consists of electronic columnar pads with many rows and columns. Any information that an individual would ordinarily put in rows and columns can be managed and manipulated electronically in spreadsheet software. *Graphics applications* refers to software that permits the creation of tables, figures, diagrams, charts, and maps with substantial assistance from the software itself. The use of most graphics software does not require that the user be an accomplished artist or graphics designer. This chapter is intended to provide only a brief overview of the potential of database-management systems, word processing, spreadsheets, and graphics for health educators. It is not intended to suffice as a general tutorial on all the uses of these applications.

DATABASE-MANAGEMENT TECHNOLOGY

Any collection of data is essentially a database. If you look around your home or office, you will easily find many such depots of data—file cabinets, drawers in desks, bookshelves, and shoe boxes are all common locations for a wide variety of data. Conklin, McCormack, Andersen and Libenson (1987, p. 1) suggest that evidence of attempts to collect and maintain information on patients has been discovered in ancient Greek temples. Names of patients, descriptions of their medical conditions, and dispositions were recorded by physicians. Since that time the maintenance and use of information in the health sciences has been a critical component of professional practice. Although initially practiced primarily in clinical settings, the accumulation of information on the recipients of health programs of any kind, including education, is becoming more important.

Hammond and Stead (1988) define a database as any "collection of related elements, together with the hardware and software necessary to record or retrieve a datum." Although the terms *hardware* and *software* imply that databases can be created only in a computerized environment, this is clearly not the case. A more global perspective suggests that any collection of information, in any medium, that is fundamental to a specific purpose is a database. In this context any file drawer filled with

EXHIBIT 2.1

DISTINCTION BETWEEN DATA
AND INFORMATION

In an information system, data are distinguished from information, the end product (Shoderbek, Shoderbek, & Lefales, 1980). *Data* is derived from the Latin verb *do, dare,* meaning "to give," and refers to unstructured raw facts. These facts, even though they lack structure, are accepted by the computer as input in preparation for processing.

The term *information* is derived from the Latin verb *informo, informare,* meaning "to give form to." Information is data that have been given form or structure and are organized. Thus, unstructured data (facts) are processed to produce a structured form (information) as the result of processing (Yovits, 1983).

(Saba & McCormick, 1986, p. 105).

patient records is a database, as is a box containing reprints of professional articles, or a collection of census-tract maps for any geographic area. Databases can be maintained on paper or electronically.

Conklin et al. (1987) suggest that the following objectives are the most important when creating databases:

- Attention to the design to ensure that the database will serve as a useful repository of information.
- Identification and development of procedures and safeguards to ensure consistency and integrity of the information collected.
- Systematization of data collection, entry, and access to information within the database.
- Elimination of redundancy in data collection and data entry.
- Development of procedures and safeguards to ensure access to the information by all those individuals who require it.
- Attention to design issues that will result in simplification of data access, management, and control.
- Attention to procedures and safeguards that will protect sensitive data from inappropriate access.

Today's modern database technology is a descendant of early applications of information systems. In health-related applications this usually meant the application of computerized technology to the storage and selective access of information in a patient record in a clinical setting. The earliest such information systems were often found in hospitals for the purpose of collecting, processing, and communicating patient and administrative information to enhance patient care (Collen, 1983). Such hospital information systems provided support to many different departments in a hospital and have emerged today into sophisticated, multipurpose systems such as that depicted in figure 2.1.

Figure 2.1. The structure of a hospital information system. In this type of system a main computer with its secondary storage maintains all files (records), data, and programs. Each of the different units in the hospital will have separate needs but may need access to common records.

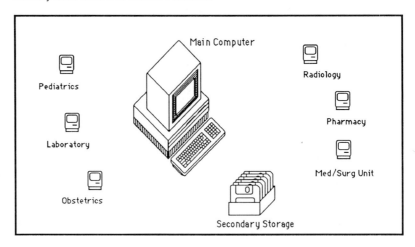

There are many information systems in use in health settings today. The breadth of application becomes apparent upon examination of the subjects of selected papers presented at the 12th Annual Symposium on Computer Applications in Medical Care (SCAMC) and the 166th Annual Meeting of the American Public Health Association. Table 2.1 is an abbreviated list of subjects and authors.

As information-systems technology developed and became adapted to the microcomputer ennvironment in the form of database-management systems, the potential of the technology has grown. It is important to examine here some basic concepts of database applications. What follows is a brief fictitious illustration regarding the technology that can be applied to a health-related database.

A DATABASE PROBLEM

THE WELLSPIRIT HEALTH PROMOTION PROGRAM (WSHPP) is initiating a worksite wellness program designed to focus on four risk factors for heart disease—weight (WGT), cholesterol (CHOL), systolic blood pressure (SBP), and diastolic blood pressure (DBP). The plan is to conduct an initial needs assessment, do preliminary screening for these risk factors, and then conduct programming targeted at maintaining acceptable levels of these risk factors, or reducing the client's risk. A follow-up was to be conducted one year later. The initial intake screening occurred in November 1988 with follow-up in November 1989.

Table 2.1

Selected Current Application of Information-Systems Technology in Health Settings

SUBJECT	AUTHOR(S)
Decision Making	
Improved quality of care	Shippey
Liability in HMO/PPo	DeFuria
Public health data management	Woodbury
Public health nursing interventions	Shirley et al.
Quality assessment/assurance	Slack
Hospital Information Systems	
Methodology for success	Jacobs
System selection	Mandell & Rothenberg
User satisfaction	Bailey & Rollier
Laboratory Information Systems	
Competency	Friedman
Development and operation	Miller et al.
Management Information Systems	
Improved environ. health services	Serata; DeRoos & Bonifield; Eastwold
Primary care information	Bruegge & Spear
Primary care (international)	Campos-Outcalt (Papua, New Guinea)
	Foreit et al. (Ecuador)
	Inam (Aga Khan University)
Medical Records	
Alcohol treatment unit	Chang et al.
Ambulatory geriatric record	Hammond et al.
Cardiology applications	Kiely
Evaluation	Payne et al.; Campbell et al.; Tape et al.
Nursing	
Computer-aided research	Chang & Gilbert
Home-care nursing	Brennan
Improved productivity	Mason
Scheduling	
In vitro fertilization	Cahill & Bailey
Surgical Information Systems	
Development	Olund

Descriptions available in the *Precedings of the Thirteenth Annual Symposium on Computer Applications in Medical Care*, New York: IEEE, 1988.

An Overview of Database Concepts

The focus here is not on what kind of programming is to be conducted but on how the project data will be managed and utilized. Figure 2.2 is a WSHPP data form. The purpose of this form is to provide a medium for recording data on clients and storing those data for later use. Table 2.2 contains a summary of the data collected. Seventeen workers volunteered to participate in the program, but follow-up data were collected on only sixteen. Because this is a small number of records, it is reasonable to maintain this database on paper. However, if the objective is to manipulate the data, analyze or use the data in a variety of other ways, or if there were 170 rather than 17 workers, a computerized database would be a preferable choice.

Figure 2.2. Sample data form.

Wellspirit Health Promotion Program

Client's Name _____

Street Address _____

City _____

State _____

Zip Code _____

Telephone _____

Intake Date _____

Age _____   Gender_____   Hgt_____

Wgt_____   Cholesterol_____   SBP_____   DBP_____

Follow Up Date _____

Wgt_____   Cholesterol_____   SBP_____   DBP_____

Table 2.2 allows us to describe here some important vocabulary related to database systems. The column headings in the table (Name, Date, Age, etc.) are sometimes called variables, but in database terminology these are *fields*. A field is a location reserved for a specific type of data, including text, numbers, or special characters. This database has fourteen fields. Each row represents the data collected on a person (e.g., Allen Smith, Bobby Becker) or the *records* in database terminology. A record is a collection of fields specific to one person, or entity. The term *entity* is preferable to use in a general sense, because some databases may contain records in units other than people (e.g., housing units, communities, census tracts). In this example table 2.2 contains seventeen records. The entire collection of seventeen records is called a *file*. In more general terms, a *database* is one or more files specific to a given purpose. In this example the WSHPP database is made up of one file containing seventeen records—and each record contains data in fourteen fields.

We can compare these terms with others that we are more familiar with. Imagine a four-drawer filing cabinet. The top drawer contains the records for all the clients in the WSHPP. If we open the top drawer, we see a file folder for each client, and on opening one of these folders, we see several sheets of paper containing information about the client. There may be a sheet containing the results of a cholesterol screen when the client began the program, another slip of paper containing the results of a cholesterol screen done one year later. Each of these sheets of paper

Table 2.2
Raw Data Collected by WSHPP

Name	Date	Age	Gender	Hgt	Wgt	Chol	SBP	DBP	Date	Wgt	Chol	SBP	DBP
				INTAKE					**FOLLOW-UP**				
Allen Smith	11/22/88	36	male	69	150	350	195	100	11/20/89	150	220	150	90
Bobby Becker	11/22/88	18	male	72	195	240	115	75	11/20/89	180	180	118	80
Kathryn Nye	11/22/88	26	female	62	115	170	120	70	11/20/89	115	170	120	75
Barbara Tice	11/22/88	38	female	68	135	180	110	60	11/21/89	130	190	110	60
Debby Webb	11/23/88	49	female	65	140	200	130	90	11/21/89	140	170	120	80
Scott Webb	11/25/88	52	male	74	215	260	150	95	11/21/89	220	160	130	80
Andrew Webb	11/24/88	19	male	74	200	220	130	80	11/22/89	205	160	120	70
Sarah Webb	11/22/88	21	female	68	120	140	100	65	11/22/89	125	150	100	65
Becky Fyfe	11/23/88	43	female	65	135	340	140	95	11/22/89	128	220	110	85
Bob List	11/21/88	29	male	68	197	320	130	85	11/22/89	170	160	115	75
Cheryl Dent	11/23/88	22	female	62	112	170	115	75	11/23/89	115	—	—	—
Liz Jones	11/25/88	15	female	73	95	300	125	90	11/23/89	98	210	120	90
Eve Scott	11/24/88	23	female	66	123	170	120	87	11/23/89	125	150	120	80
Gail Ice	11/25/88	50	female	58	160	250	130	89	11/23/89	155	220	120	80
Glen Christo	11/24/88	43	male	74	223	195	123	100	11/24/89	188	190	120	90
James Deveney	11/21/88	53	male	75	195	300	150	90	11/24/89	192	180	120	80
Steve Study	11/21/88	29	male	72	156	220	115	75	11/24/89	160	170	115	80

contains selected information about an individual. These sheets of paper are the same as fields in the electronic database. The collection of information in each file folder is a record for one client, and the collection of all the file folders is a database on the WSHPP.

When setting up a database, whether computerized or manual, there are certain things that should be done. Perhaps the most important step that must be taken before setting up a database is to establish the purposes that the database will serve. The purposes of the database define how the data should be recorded. What follows is a list of questions, adapted from Hammond and Stead (1988, p. 12), that demonstrates the complexity in adequately planning for a database structure if one is interested in statistically analyzing a set of data. Will the database be used to

- statistically analyze a defined set of data to answer specific research questions?
- replace paper records used for maintaining information on program clients?
- address both program content as well as administrative management?
- serve as a needs-assessment device, or help to answer subsequent questions about target populations?

The answers to these questions influence the complexity and structure of any database. For the current problem related to WSHPP, there are a number of specific needs that the sample database must address. Among them are the following:

1. The database must be able to be sorted on any of the fourteen primary fields (variables). This particular problem has three different types of data—text, numeric, and chronological. Our database will need to *sort* on each of these field types (e.g., alphabetize the records by last name; sort the list chronologically by date of intake; sort the list numerically by cholesterol levels).

2. Because our primary purpose is to assess intake and follow-up differences, we will need to have the capacity to create summary statistics of the pertinent fields.

3. Because it is likely that most database systems will not be able to conduct complex statistical analyses, it is important to be able to *export* (or move) the data to another application package in a format usable by that package (e.g., SPSS, SAS).

4. Because it is probable that the program will want to communicate with its clients, there is the need to set up the database in such a way as to allow the generation of form letters directly from the database (see the word-processing section of this chapter). For example, form-letter generation generally requires the separation of first and last names.

These are issues that need to be considered in designing the structure of a database. In the current example, figure 2.3 illustrates what the intake form might look like in a computerized format.

As depicted in figure 2.3A, the input format contains a location for entering data into each of the fields of one record. However, it is important to note that the name field has been made into two fields—first name and last name. Therefore, the database now has fifteen fields. In this particular record it can be seen that Allen Smith is thirty-six years of age and has a cholesterol of 350 milligrams. Each of these pieces of information is called a datum, or *element*. An element is the information in a field that is specific to a record.

Once data have been entered into a database structure, the structure begins to take form. In this case we have what is called a *flat-file* database. A flat-file database is one in which the entire database consists of only one file. In addition to flat-file databases, there are also *relational databases*. A relational database is one made up of more than one file, with the relationship between the files described so that records in one of the files may be linked to the appropriate records in another file. An example will serve to distinguish between these two types of databases.

Reexamine table 2.2, the listing of data collected on each of the clients. You will notice that there are four people whose last names are Webb. If these four individuals are family, and living in the same household, they will each have the same address. In a flat-file system, each record will contain all pertinent information. In this example, therefore, four records will contain exactly the same information—a specific address. In a small database such data redundancy will not be costly in

Figure 2.3. Computerized Input Format.

A. Initial input format containing just the fields collected on the data entry form.

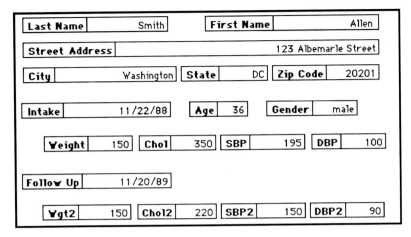

B. Database modified to compute two new fields: Change in cholesterol from intake to follow-up, and percent change: Once entered into the database structure, these two new computed fields are automatically calculated by the system.

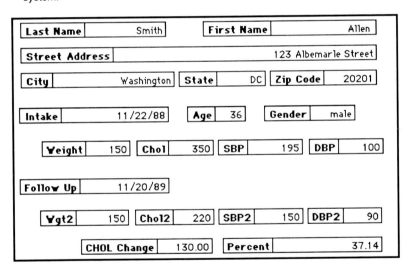

terms of storage (e.g., amount of memory required to hold the database) and efficiency (e.g., the time to search through the database for specific information is in part tied to the amount of information in that database). But in a large database of thousands of records, the cost in terms of storage capacity and lost efficiency might be dramatic. Removing this redundancy might be absolutely necessary in order to have a functional database. This removal might be accomplished by setting up a relational system in which one file contains a list of the client names and raw data, and a second file contains a list of client addresses. In this case the client data file will contain seventeen records with fifteen fields, and the ad-

Figure 2.4. Flat-file and relational databases.

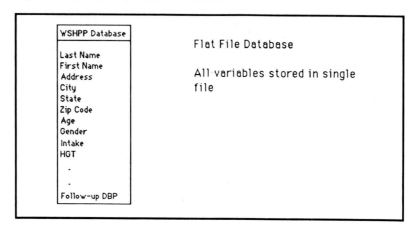

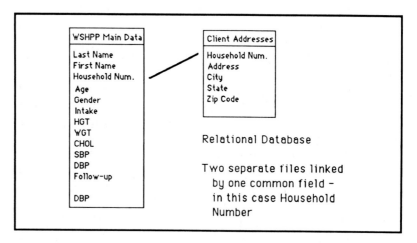

dress data file will contain fourteen records with six fields. There will need to be a linkage defined between the files in the relational database—and that linkage is often a key field or several key fields, such as client name or number. That linkage will identify for the computer how each record in one file relates to a specific record in the other file. Figure 2.4 illustrates this difference graphically.

A third form of database structure is called a *hierarchical database*. In a hierarchical database a treelike structure is created in which data are organized into levels so that each level has a single higher-order owner. Figure 2.5 illustrates how the database would be organized in a hierarchical structure. Using this type of structure, the WSHPP data could be ordered by groups of related variables.

Figure 2.5. Hierarchical database structure.

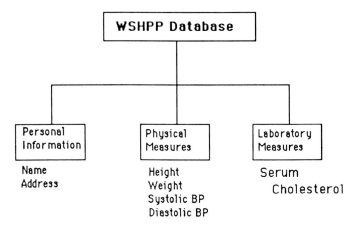

Once a database has been created, its more powerful capabilities include manipulation of the data to answer questions pertinent to the program. In this simple database there are many questions that could easily be answered. Table 2.3 contains a partial list of these questions and a brief strategy on how they can be answered. Although several of these questions appear to be similar, each one illustrates a different and important capability of database technology. Questions number 1 and 2 in table 2.3 are based on the capacity to selectively sort a database to gather information. A database can ordinarily be sorted on any field. In this case we find that the highest cholesterol level on intake among these workers is for Allen Smith at 350 milligrams (SBP 195; two workers have a DBP of 100). Question number 3 implies that more than one *sort key* (a sort key is the field on which the database will be sorted) can be used to examine a database. Here gender and cholesterol (or SBP, DBP) will be used as sort keys. After conducting these sorts we find, for example, that Becky Fyfe has the highest cholesterol at intake among the women.

Question 4 in table 2.3 is somewhat different. It does not utilize sort keys, but instead requires global searches for records satisfying specified criteria. The best way to describe this process is to relate it to electronic searches through bibliographic databases. *Medline* (a list of references in the medical literature), ERIC (a compilation of education resources) and *Dissertation Abstracts International* (a collection of completed doctoral dissertations in abstract) are three such examples. Whenever a bibliographic search is done through *Medline,* ERIC, or *Dissertation Abstracts International,* a *search strategy* is constructed. All the appropriate citations satisfying the search strategy are then provided to the person making the query. A search strategy is a concise description of the characteristics of the records that a person wants to identify. Search strategies can be simple (using a single field), or complex (using two or more fields). To answer question 4, a complex strategy is required, asking

Using the Database

Table 2.3
Using the Database

QUESTION	STRATEGY FOR ANSWERING QUESTION
1. What is the highest cholesterol (SBP, DBP) level among clients in the program?	Sort the database on any field (CHOL, SBP, DBP) and examine the results.
2. Who have the highest cholesterol (SBP, DBP) levels among the clients in the program?	Examine the name fields of the sorted database.
3. Among the men (women), who have the highest cholesterol (SBP, DBP) levels in the program?	Sort on gender and cholesterol (SBP, DBP) and examine the results.
4. What are the names of all those workers who have a cholesterol greater than 180 milligrams and who are hypertensive?	Do a global search for cholesterol > 180 and SBP > 140 or DBP > 90. The records satisfying the search strategy will be identified.
5. Who are the workers who have reduced their cholesterol level by more than 20 percent during the course of the program?	Create two new computed fields: one that computes absolute change in cholesterol levels over the course of the year, and a second that computes the percent change based on intake levels. After these two fields are created, then a search may be conducted to find all those records whose percent change is greater than 20.

the computer to examine three fields and conclude if a record satisfies the search strategy. The search strategy for this inquiry is stated in general terms: find all those records in which the cholesterol level is greater than 180 and whose SBP is greater than 140 or DBP is greater than 90. In shorthand terminology this search strategy would be written as follows:

$$\text{CHOL} > 180 \text{ AND (SBP} > 140 \text{ OR DBP} > 90).$$

Question 5 in table 2.3 depends upon the ability of the database system to do computations. In this case the computer will have to assess the relationship between two or more fields and then determine if the relationship satisfies the criteria established. Here the program is interested in finding those people who started with cholesterol levels higher than 180 and who reduced their cholesterol levels by at least 20 percent during the course of the program year. This can be accomplished by creating one or more computed fields in a database. Most database systems allow this to be done. A new field is created containing a formula for that field rather than data. The formula describes how the computer is to enter data into that field (see figure 2.3b). In this case the following general formula would be necessary for two new fields:

Field 1 (CHOL Change) Subtract CHOL at follow-up from intake
Field 2 (% CHOL Change) CHOL Change divided by CHOL at intake
Search Strategy: Select if % CHOL Change > 20

Fig. 2.6. Reporting function of database systems. A report such as the one in this figure can be produced very easily in any database system. The report template can then be stored for future use with other subsets of data.

Last Name	First Name	Chol	Chol2	CHOL Change	%Change
Becker	Bobby	240	180	60.00	25.00
Christo	Glen	195	190	5.00	2.56
Dent	Cheryl	185	170	15.00	8.11
Deveney	James	300	180	120.00	40.00
Fyfe	Becky	340	220	120.00	35.29
Ice	Gail	250	220	30.00	12.00
Jones	Liz	300	210	90.00	30.00
List	Bob	320	160	160.00	50.00
Nye	Kathryn	170	170	0.00	0.00
Scott	Eve	155	150	5.00	3.23
Smith	Allen	350	220	130.00	37.14
Study	Steve	220	170	50.00	22.73
Tice	Barbara	180	190	-10.00	-5.56
Webb	Scott	260	160	100.00	38.46
Webb	Debby	200	170	30.00	15.00
Webb	Sarah	140	155	-10.00	-7.14
Webb	Andrew	220	160	60.00	27.27

When the results of these different requests are available, the last major function of all database systems may then be used to print special reports. Virtually all systems allow for the creation of report templates that can be stored and used as needed for interim or final reports or administrative purposes. Figure 2.6 contains a report listing the clients alphabetically with information about their initial and follow-up cholesterol levels.

Another Example of Database Technology

Although we most often think of bibliographic retrieval systems as the purview of libraries, it is possible to utilize database technology to effectively maintain and utilize personal reference material. Graves (1987) describes how microcomputers can be used for personal-library management within both word-processor and database technology. However, she concludes that the advantages of database technology far outstrip the potential in this area for word-processing software. What follows is another illustration of how this technology may be used in a health-related setting.

Although most people think of databases in terms of numeric data, there is no reason to limit the technology to that domain. It is well within the capacity of most modern database systems to manipulate text as well as numbers. If a health-education program provides referrals for clients to agencies in a geographic area, a database could be created containing a list of all the agencies in the area and their pertinent characteristics. Each class of characteristics would be entered in a fixed field. If a client wanted a list of all agencies that provided patient-education services to adults with arthritis, a search strategy could be created to identify the names of agencies satisfying these criteria.

EXHIBIT 2.2

CASE EXAMPLE OF DATABASE TECHNOLOGY

As Director of Graduate Studies for the Department of Health Education at the University of Maryland, I am responsible for maintaining records on 220 active graduate students, advising all of them on general program requirements, reviewing all requests for program waivers and substitutions, signing off on all program statements and applications for degree completion, signing off on all M.A. and Ph.D. proposal meetings and defenses, addressing inquiries of all prospective students, and overseeing the implementation of comprehensive examinations for M.A. and Ph.D. students twice yearly. I can receive as many as fifty or more telephone inquiries per week from students, and requests for half that many appointments. This does not include the program advising I do for my own specific advisees, or advising on graduate-student research for those students whose committees I serve on. These expectations can make for a very busy day, and some difficulty in keeping track of requests for action.

One of the first things I did when coming to the University of Maryland was to computerize all active and alumni student records. At the time we were using Apple IIe's™ in the Department with Appleworks™ integrated software (word processing, spreadsheet, database). This process took approximately three months. Then I created several support databases—a telephone database, a student-encounter database, a graduate-actions database, and a correspondence database. I would make and answer phone calls with a headset on, leaving my hands free to type while I was talking. All pertinent information about the phone call was

If an agency offered a service in which citations for reading materials about specified topics were provided, all the citations the agency regularly dealt with could be entered into a database. Clients could create search strategies, and the database could provide a list of references as a report. Many other potential applications exist, but exhibit 2.2 provides a real-life example of how I have used database technology in my own work.

One of the more intriguing and recent developments in this area is *hypertext* and *hypermedia* technology. The term *hypertext* implies that linkages between words, phrases, ideas, or concepts may be established in a document of any form. An illustration will serve to clarify what this means. Imagine reading a journal article about a very difficult topic in health behavior. There are many health-behavior models, but some of the more common include the health belief model, social learning theory, Fishbein's theory of reasoned actions, and Triandis's theory of social behavior. Each of these theories is built on a very complex and large research base, and each contains references to many concepts that are derived from several different disciplines.

stored in a single database record (caller's name, phone number, date and time, subject of call, disposition). The last five minutes of every student appointment I had was spent summarizing the session, and a copy was given to the student before leaving. The pertinent details of each meeting were recorded in a single database record. Every time I signed a form—either approving or disapproving a request—the details were logged in the graduate-actions database. Finally, every time I wrote a letter, the subject was entered into a correspondence file.

These files were always active on my computer during working hours. If someone called me to inquire about something, I immediately searched each of these databases to review every discussion I might have had regarding the request. Before a student would come to a meeting, I would review each database for all pertinent information I should know about the student or the student's program.

These searches literally took less than fifteen to twenty seconds to complete, and the information made me look a lot smarter than I really am. I was also able to use these databases to answer questions for the chairman, Dr. Glen Gilbert, or faculty members, or students. For example:

- How many students are being advised by Dr. _____ ?
- Has anyone ever done a study on the health effects of hatha-yoga?
- How many students requested waiver of requirement _____ ?

As you read this article, you see many references to other articles and research efforts. If you are unfamiliar with the literature base, it might be helpful for you to review some of these original studies. Imagine being able to point to a phrase in the article, push a button, and then instantly see an explanation of that phrase; or push a button and see a copy of the original research; or push a button and be able to see a graphic image of the relationships between the original concepts and those referred to in the paper. This is exactly what hypertext allows.

Hypertext is a way of linking information, in any form, with any other information. Hypertext is essentially a free-form database that allows any words, phrases, concepts, ideas, graphics, or sounds (i.e., information in any format) to be linked so that anyone can ask for more information at any time. We are just beginning to realize how important this technology is, and how it can be applied. Yet this technology is already available. Apple Computer was the first to introduce a commercial product with these capabilities, called Hypercard™. Hypercard runs on

EXHIBIT 2.3

ILLUSTRATION OF HYPERTEXT TECHNOLOGY

Imagine you are interested in finding out some information about the distribution of AIDS cases in the United States. As you look at a map of the United States on the screen of an Apple Macintosh™, you could move a mouse to any state and double-click on the mouse button, and a window would open up and provide you with a list of certain statistics for that state. Then you would see on the screen several boxes labeled "More Information." You move the mouse and click in one of the boxes, and a new window opens on the screen with a list of centers where AIDS patients may receive counseling and other treatment. You click on another box to get a list of AIDS-information hotlines in that state, and another button for a list of locations where you can be tested for the presence of the virus that causes AIDS.

All of this information may be contained in a book, or in other form. However, hypertext allows the immediate linkage of this information at the click of a mouse. The potential is tremendous, and very exciting.

Macintosh computers and is now distributed with every one sold. In essence, Apple Computer has stated that Hypercard (hypertext) is so important that it should be in the hands of every computer user. We are now beginning to see comparable applications for other computer systems as well. Exhibit 2.3 contains an illustration of the potential of this technology.

See the case study describing how this technology can be brought together in one project.

Summary of Database Technology

Although the preceding discussion is not intended to be a complete review of all the capabilities of a database system, it should serve to provide a general overview of the potential for enhancing the productivity of any professional. When properly used, database systems allow for the creation of simple to very complex databases, with the capacity to add, delete, or modify records as needed. There is also the capability to sort records on single or multiple sort keys, to create simple or complex search strategies to identify records satisfying specific criteria, and to prepare reports based on individual or programmatic needs.

This type of technology possesses both advantages and disadvantages. Simkin and Dependahl (1987, p. 198) suggest that the most important advantages include (1) the capacity to use a single file for many different purposes without having to replicate the file, thereby reducing data redundancy in any setting; (2) the ability to create subset databases

The Maryland Database on Drug Treatment Programs

We recently engaged in a cooperative statewide project with our governor's Office of Justice Assistance. The notion was very simple. There are numerous drug treatment and prevention programs in the state, but it is often very difficult to match the correct one with a client and almost impossible to determine the extent of services available statewide in an efficient manner. We wondered why we could not conduct one major statewide survey, computerize the information, update it regularly, and provide a toll-free system to access the information, and we were surprised to find that, to the best of our knowledge, no state provides such a service.

Pursuing this straightforward goal, then, we decided early on that we wanted the system to be PC-based, thereby allowing us to provide the entire database, when appropriate, to government agencies or researchers via disk or telecommunications. We had set ourselves a formidable task: we estimated that we might be inputting information on 750 agencies, and that the survey questionnaire would contain 75 items.

Because we are for the most part an Apple office, we reviewed Macintosh database systems. After trying multiple pieces of software, we decided on a system called 4th Dimension, which is a rather powerful relational database system designed to allow programming within the system.

The relational structure allows for a common core of questions with branches of different items. Unless one uses a system designed this way, it can be incredibly slow to make changes or to print out information with large databases. Even with this software we found it slow and eventually upgraded our Macintosh to a Macintosh IIx, which is faster and has five megabytes of RAM. We needed a system that could respond in fairly prompt fashion to phone inquiries and also print a quality output for a directory.

This system has met all our needs and can be run on a PC system. It is a valuable system at a relatively low price.

Note. Contributed by Dr. Glen G. Gilbert, Chairperson, Department of Health Education, University of Maryland.

to specifications by selecting only those records that meet certain criteria; and (3) the ability to organize data into efficient structures, thereby reducing storage-capacity needs. Among the principle disadvantages are (1) a restrictive dependence on machines (database applications are generally designed to run on a single vendor's hardware, and it becomes difficult to use databases on more than one system); and (2) the costliness of sophisticated database software.

Aside from these constraints, the potential of database technology for health professionals is virtually unlimited. By organizing data and storing it in a way that it can be selectively changed, manipulated, and used, the professional can change data to information that is meaningful.

WORD-PROCESSING TECHNOLOGY: AN OVERVIEW

The term *word processing* refers to the entry of textual information into a computer for storage, manipulation, and printing. As with the database section of this chapter, this overview is not intended to be a thorough tutorial on word processing, but rather an introduction to some of the capabilities, and an explanation of how those capabilities may be applied to health-related settings.

As a personal-productivity device, word processing probably is the most frequently used microcomputer application today. If one considers nothing more than the quantitative comparisons between handwriting, typewriting and word processing, the potential increase in productivity becomes obvious. If a person handwrites at a rate of fifteen words per minute but types at a rate of thirty words per minute, then typewriting results in a 50 percent reduction in time spent. If a person uses a typewriter and subsequently wishes to modify the text of a document, then the document or portions of it will have to be retyped. If that same person uses a word processor to enter the document into a computer, modification of the document takes only a short period of time and eliminates the need to retype the entire document. Using word-processing capabilities results not only in a tremendous savings of time, but in many other benefits as well.

There are three different types of word-processing systems: *Dedicated word-processing systems, word-processing software,* and *time-shared word-processing systems.* Dedicated word-processing systems operate on specific computer hardware and do little or nothing else (e.g., Wang). These systems often contain little more than a keyboard and a monitor, and the hardware is generally low in cost compared to general-purpose computers with comparable capabilities. The keyboards of these systems are often specialized in terms of word-processing functions, and the systems are generally easy to use. They can come in many configurations, including single- or multistation systems in which several workstations are networked to a single processor. The biggest disadvantage of these systems is their inability to function as general-purpose computers. Word-processing software is designed specifically to run on general-purpose microcomputers and is often purchased to run on available microcomputer systems. There are a wide variety of capabilities available, with prices ranging from less than one hundred dollars to more than five hundred dollars for some packages. The major benefit of these packages is that they run on general-purpose microcomputers with many additional capabilities, that a user may already be familiar with. Time-shared word-processing systems are designed to run on mainframe computer systems. As with microcomputers, some organizations already have access to large mainframe computer systems and terminals. These systems are also able to provide many functions beyond word processing. When an organization needs to provide word-processing capabilities to many people, using the mainframe system may prove the most economical and efficient choice.

Each of these approaches to word processing has both advantages and disadvantages. In this chapter I will focus on word-processing capabilities of general-purpose microcomputer systems.

There are many word-processing systems available for microcomputers. I will focus here not on the capabilities of a specific package, but on a general overview of capabilities that should be available on most systems, then I will demonstrate how the data stored in the database created in the first part of this chapter may be used in a word-processing environment with mail-merge capabilities.

The four general functions provided by all word-processing applications are *document creation and text entry, editing, formatting,* and *printing.* Figure 2.7 contains a sample letter created in a word-processing environment. Although this letter clearly does not differ in substance from a letter that could be produced on any typewriter, the benefits of using word-processing capabilities will become obvious as we proceed.

Figure 2.7 is the kind of memorandum that would be appropiate to send to participants in the Wellspirit Health Promotion Program after the one-year follow-up. Some key information appears in this letter. For example, the letter is written specifically to Allen Smith, and it contains pertinent information regarding his cholesterol levels at intake and at his follow-up visit, and the percentage change over that period of time. A letter such as this could easily be prepared for each of the participants of the WSHPP.

The strengths of word processing, however, come from its ability to edit, manipulate, and print text material. Editing text involves not only corrections for spelling and grammar errors, but also global changes executed with just a few keystrokes. For example, suppose that the WSHPP program director decided to change the word *cholesterol* to the phrase *blood cholesterol* in the sample letter found in Figure 2.7. This could easily be done by changing each occurrence individually, or by simultaneously using *global-search-and-replace* functions found on every major word-processing package. With global-search-and-replace functions, the computer is instructed to change all occurrences of the word *cholesterol* to the phrase *blood cholesterol.* Figure 2.8A illustrates the result of this function.

Another very powerful editing procedure found in many word-processing programs is the ability to *cut and paste* material, and to physically move text from one portion of a document to another. In the WSHPP sample letter, the director may decide to change the text by switching the second and third sentences of the first paragraph. Once again, in a short document this can easily be accomplished by retyping; however, cutting and pasting is much more efficient and requires only a few keystrokes. The results are found in figure 2.8B.

Figure 2.7. Sample letter produced in a word-processing environment.

Wellspirit Health Promotion Program

November 29, 1989

Allen Smith
123 Albermarle Street
Washington, DC 20201
Dear Allen:
The purpose of this correspondence is to congratulate you for the work
you have done in the Wellspirit Health Promotion Program. You may
remember that your cholesterol level at the beginning of the program
was 350 mg, and that represented a significant risk factor for
cardiovascular disease. After one year in the program your cholesterol
level has been reduced by 37.14 percent to 220 mg.
It is our pleasure to congratulate you and to extend our wishes for
your continued success. Best of luck to you.

Sincerely,

Allen Rudolph, Program Director

Figure 2.8. Section of modified letter to WSHPP participants.

A. *Global search and replace*—blood cholesterol replaces cholesterol.

The purpose of this correspondence is to congratulate you for the work
you have done in the Wellspirit Health Promotion Program. You may
remember that your blood cholesterol level at the beginning of the
program was 350 mg, and that represented a significant risk factor for
cardiovascular disease. After one year in the program your blood
cholesterol level has been reduced by 37.14 percent to 220 mg.

B. *Cut and paste*—switch second and third sentences.

The purpose of this correspondence is to congratulate you for the work
you have done in the Wellspirit Health Promotion Program. After one
year in the program your blood cholesterol level has been reduced by
37.14 percent to 220 mg. You may remember that your blood
cholesterol level at the beginning of the program was 350 mg,
and that represented a significant risk factor for cardiovascular
disease.

In short documents, such as this sample letter, the importance of global-search-and-replace, and cut-and-paste capabilities is minimized. However, as a document gets significantly longer, the power of these editing features becomes more important. Imagine having a final report on a major project prepared, and then because of a change in current usage of a term hundreds of occurrences of a phrase need to be changed. This is not unusual, but with the capacity to do global-search-and-replace editing, only a few keystrokes are needed to make such changes.

Table 2.4

Page Composition in a Word-Processing Environment

TECHNIQUE	DESCRIPTION
Spacing	Number of spaces between each line in the document: e.g., single, double, triple
Justification	Describing how the print will be aligned with respect to the page: e.g.,
	left justified: All new lines begin flush at left margin as in these sample lines.
	right justified: All lines are flush to right margin as in these sample lines.
	center justified: All lines are centered on the page as in these sample lines.
	full justified: All lines appear to be flush to both the left and right margins as is found in books and newspapers, and as in these sample lines.
Headers	Specific text that appears at the top of each page printed from the document
Footers	Specific text that appears at the bottom of each page printed from the document
Highlighting	Setting off a section of text by changing its appearance: e.g., boldface, underlining, changing the type style or size
Margins	The left and right margins are specified for the entire document, including any modified for subsections of the document
Text alignment	Used to line up columns for tables

Or imagine that after the report is typed, someone decides that the summary should be prepared as an executive summary and placed at the beginning of the document rather than at the end. Cut-and-paste capabilities allow even large amounts of text to be moved with a few keystrokes.

The term *formatting* refers to page-composition techniques, including spacing, justification, headers, footers, making specific text unique, setting margins, and aligning text for tables. Table 2.4 contains a brief description of each of these techniques. As can be seen from this table, many options for page composition are provided in a word-processing environment. These kinds of options, however, should not be confused with the page-composition capabilities of *desktop publishing* applications.

Formatting Capabilities

Desktop publishing is a specialty application that provides even more sophisticated page composition and layout techniques than most word-processing packages. Figures 2.9A and B illustrate how a few changes in the letter add emphasis to different elements of the message. Figure 2.9A is done entirely with a word processor, whereas figure 2.9B was created using DTP capbilities.

EXHIBIT 2.4

DESKTOP PUBLISHING

As the demands for production of high-quality printed materials increase, we find that there are a number of tasks that must be accomplished: (1) creation of document design; (2) creation of text, photographs, and graphics; (3) composing the documents by combining text, photographs, and graphics with attention to design elements; (4) preparing the document for publication. The purpose of desktop-publishing technology is to put as many of these capabilities into the hands of individuals, and to automate as many of these tasks, as possible. Whether producing a newsletter, business or project report or manual, annual report, or information flyer, many will find that word-processing software will suffice. However, DTP software adds greater flexibility, design capabilities, and sophistication to the final document.

Figure 2.9A. Modified letter with addition of page composition in word processor.

Wellspirit Health Promotion Program

November 29, 1989

Allen Smith
123 Albermarle Street
Washington, DC 20201

Dear Allen:

The purpose of this correspondence is to congratulate you for the work you have done in the **Wellspirit Health Promotion Program**. You may remember that your cholesterol level at the beginning of the program was **350** mg, and that represented a significant risk factor for cardiovascular disease. After one year in the program your cholesterol level has been reduced by 37.14 percent to **220** mg.
It is our pleasure to congratulate you and to extend our wishes for your continued success. Best of luck to you.

Sincerely,

Allen Rudolph, Program Director

Figure 2.9B. Modified letter with addition of page composition with desktop-publishing capabilities.

*W*ellspirit Health Promotion Program

November 29, 1989

Allen Smith
123 Albermarle Street
Washington, DC 20201

Dear Allen:

The purpose of this correspondence is to congratulate you for the work you have done in the *Wellspirit Health Promotion Program*. You may remember that your cholesterol level at the beginning of the program was **350** mg, and that represented a significant risk factor for cardiovascular disease. After one year in the program your cholesterol level has been reduced by <u>37.14</u> percent to **220** mg.

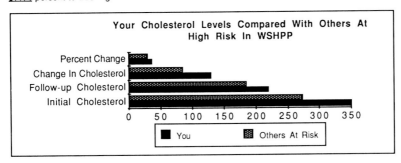

As you can see in the chart that accompanies this letter, you began at higher risk than others in the program. Although your current cholesterol levels still indicate some increased risk, you have made a greater change in both absolute levels (130 mg compared with 86 for others) and in percent change (37% versus the average of 30%).

It is our pleasure to congratulate you and to extend our wishes for your continued success. Best of luck to you.

Sincerely,

Allen Rudolph
Program Director

So far I have focused principally on how to create, edit, and modify a single document. However, one of the capacities of word-processing systems that may be most useful to program managers who wish to dispatch personalized mass mailings is *mail merge*. The term *mail merge* refers to the creation of a form letter with embedded variables that will change as each letter is printed. With the increasing sophistication of word processors on any type of microcomputer, the production of form letters with any number of personalized messsages becomes an easy process. Figure 2.10 illustrates how a form letter may be produced in a word-processing environment.

Mail Merge

Figure 2.10. Mail-merge form letter.

Wellspirit Health Promotion Program

«DATE»

«FIRST NAME» «LAST NAME»
«STREET ADDRESS»
«CITY», «STATE» «ZIP CODE»

Dear «FIRST NAME»:

The purpose of this correspondence is to congratulate you for the work you have done in the *Wellspirit Health Promotion Program*. You may remember that your cholesterol level at the beginning of the program was «CHOL» mg, and that represented a significant risk factor for cardiovascular disease. After one year in the program your cholesterol level has been reduced by «PERCENT CHANGE» percent to «CHOL2» mg.
It is our pleasure to congratulate you and to extend our wishes for your continued success. Best of luck to you.

Sincerely,

Allen Rudolph, Program Director

Not all word-processing environments use the same syntax to produce mail merge or form letters, but there are enough commonalities to describe the process in a general way. When mail merge is performed, both the form letter (figure 2.10) and a database containing the information for the form letter must be available. You will recall that a flat-file database for the WSHPP program was created earlier. That database contained seventeen records, each with twenty fields. The form letter illustrated in figure 2.10 uses the field names as variables (e.g., first name, last name, CHOL, CHOL2). There are predefined *delimiters,* in this case double-arrow brackets (« ») that alert the program as to which words are field names from the database. Whenever the word-processing program sees these delimiters, it looks to the database for the specific information to merge into the form letter. As a result, a personalized letter will be produced for each record in the database. In this case, however, we do not want a letter of congratulations to go to everyone in the database, because only a few of the seventeen individuals had greater than a 20 percent reduction in cholesterol. This is easily dealt with by creating a subset of the database using a search strategy designed to select only those records in which greater than a 20 percent reduction in cholesterol was achieved. What has been done, therefore, is to merge the capabilities of a database system to manage, manipulate, and retrieve selected records, thereby allowing the word-processing system to print personalized letters to those individuals whose records were selected.

This type of technology is useful for producing tables, form letters, bibliographic and other listings, and any other document with repetitive typing in which the information can be maintained in a database. Exhibit 2.5 contains a brief description of how this type of technology was applied to the production of parts of this book.

In addition to the capabilities described so far, there are many other available components that can be included. Among the more important are (1) spelling checkers, which provide on-line access to enormous standard dictionaries to assess the spelling accuracy of each word in the document; (2) grammar assessments, which review an entire document and make recommendations on grammatical syntax; (3) style assessments, which make recommendations regarding such things as sexist language, weak sentence construction, overusage of phrases, or dependence on vernacular; (4) word counters, which provide a precise count of the number of words found in a document; (5) reading-level assessments that apply any of several standard measures for reading level and provide the results—some with recommendations for how to change the text for readability; and (6) on-line thesauruses, which allow a user to enter a word and look for synonyms or antonyms. Each of these utilities is designed to provide a unique contribution to an individual's ability to write. At the current time Microsoft Corporation™ has a CD-ROM (a compact laser disk: see chapter 1 for an explanation) available called Bookshelf™, which is a compendium of ten of the most used writer's aids known (e.g., Roget's thesaurus and unabridged dictionary, *Bartlett's Familiar Quotations*). These ten aids can be accessed on-line by any writer with a word-processing program and a CD-ROM drive.

An important caveat: even with all this technology available, there are still many writing errors that fall through the cracks (a word that is spelled correctly but used incorrectly will not be flagged by a spelling checker: e.g., *thee* instead of *three*), and none will guarantee that a weak writer will become a strong writer. When used properly, however, writing aids become a set of very important productivity tools.

One last word of caution is worth mentioning. Unless a user takes the time to learn how to use the capabilities of the software available, and then uses those capabilities effectively, their potential benefits are lost.

Additional Word-Processing Utilities

For anyone whose professional position involves writing, word-processing software on microcomputers usually results in an increase in productivity. Creating, storing for later retrieval and editing, formatting, and printing documents are among the most frequently used capabilities of word processing. However, the integration of word processing with database technology in the context of form letters provides a very powerful tool to health professionals. Table 2.5 contains a list of some

Summary of Word-Processing Technology

EXHIBIT 2.5

USING MAIL-MERGE CAPABILITIES TO PRODUCE A REFERENCE LIST

This book was written on an Apple Macintosh SE™ micro-computer and a Toshiba 1200 HB™ laptop computer. Some of the typing for the manuscript was done on each of these computers. When I was traveling, the Toshiba™ was used for word processing and database work, but then all the text was moved to the Macintosh™ for formatting and composition. On the Macintosh™ I maintain a database (Reflex Plus™ from Borland International) of almost one thousand articles on computer applications in health-related settings, and each record contains at least the following fields:

a1	lead author	Volume	volume number
a2	second author	Number	number of issue
a3	third author	Pages	publication pages
a4	fourth author	Key1–4	four descriptors
Title	first line of title	Key5	publication type
Title2	second line of title	Abstract	abstract of publication
Journal	journal title	Year	year of publication

This database allows me to selectively access the literature on computer applications in health. Among the most important fields are the ''key'' fields—descriptors of the publication. It is here that each publication is described in key words that may be searched in the database. If I want to get a listing of all articles about the use of computers for instructional purposes in health-related settings, I set the search conditions as follows:

> Select if Key1 = ''CA1'' or Key2 = ''Patient Education''

This will produce a list of records containing citations for articles, books, dissertations, or monographs about computer-assisted instruction or patient-education applications. I can then print the results directly from the database.

Database applications, however, do not have the sophisticated page-composition capabilities of most word processors, so I export all the selected records to a mail-merge file and develop a "form letter" in Microsoft Word™ (the word-processing program used for this book). That mail-merge program is as follows:

«DATA export.CAI»

«a1» «IF a2»,«a2»«ENDIF»«IF a3», «a3»ENDIF»«1F a4», «a4»«ENDIF».
(«year»). «IF key5="book"»«title1» «ELSE»«title1»«ENDIF»«IF
key5="book"»«title2» «ELSE»«title2»ENDIF». «If
journal»«journal»«ENDIF»«If journal2»«journal2»«ENDIF»«If publisher».
«publisher»«ENDIF»«If volume», «volume»«ENDIF»«If number»,
«number»«ENDIF»«If pages», «pages»,«pages»«ENDIF».«next»

Although it is not important to be able to understand each of the components of this "form letter," there are a few characteristics worth noting: (1) It will look to the file "export_CAI" for its information; therefore, by changing just this one line, I can use the same program on any number of files. (2) A form like this one can be written for any publication-style manual. This particular one is APA, but it could just as easily be Chicago or AMA. (3) Microsoft Word™ allows for selective inclusion of fields; that is, if there is a second author ($<<$a2»), it is printed; if not, this space is left blank. This is a very powerful feature if the nature of the citation style changes for different types of publications. You will note that on line 2 the form looks to see if the publication is a book («IF Key5 = "book"»). If it is, one style is used; if not, a different style is used (see ELSE in subsequent lines). (3) This particular form will print separate citations for each record in the identified file (export_ CAI) in the appropriate format.

This made the production of the "Additional Readings" listed at the end of each chapter a little easier to produce. For each chapter the following steps were taken:

- the database was searched for any publications related to the chapter content;
- an export file was created for each of these searches;
- a single "form" was used to produce all of the listings in a text file;
- the text file was then merged with each chapter.

It is worth reporting also that I maintain a separate database of health-related software. Each table listing software in this book was produced in exactly the same way, though a different form was used.

Table 2.5
Selected Features of Word-Processing Software

AREA	FEATURE
Editing	Split-screen editing
	Insertion and overstrike capabilities
	Automatic hyphenation
Formatting	Headers and footers
	Page numbering
	Multiple-column capabilities
	Left, right, center, full justification
	Automatic pagination
	User-defined macros
	Temporary margins and indentations
	What you see is what you get (WYSIWYG)
Mail merge	Insertion from keyboard
	Multifile merging
Printing	Multiple-copy printing
	Envelope printing
	Print spooling
Spelling	Large dictionary
	Ability to add words to dictionary
	Automatic look-up of several alternatives
	Ability to use several dictionaries
	Access to thesaurus

Note. Adapted from *Microcomputer Principles and Applications,* by M. G. Simkin and R. H. Dependahl, Jr., 1987, Dubuque, IA: Wm. C. Brown.

of the more important features to be found in word-processing packages. These capabilities should be examined carefully when looking for software.

AN OVERVIEW OF SPREADSHEET TECHNOLOGY

Most professionals have used a columnar pad at one time or another to create a budget, do accounting, or create a table of statistics. In 1979 Visicalc™ became the first major spreadsheet and represented the first time people bought microcomputers in large numbers just to use a specific software application. Three years later, Lotus 1-2-3™ was introduced and has become the best-selling spreadsheet since 1982. What are spreadsheets, and how are they helpful to health educators? Answering these two questions is the purpose of this section of the chapter.

Anything that can be represented in a table of columns and rows can be manipulated electronically in a spreadsheet. A spreadsheet is nothing more than an electronic table with empty columns and rows. The importance of spreadsheet technology, however, comes from the capacity to enter formulas so that computations can be made on data. Figure 2.11 illustrates the anatomy of a spreadsheet. As the figure demonstrates, a spreadsheet by itself is really nothing more than a series of columns and rows. Today's software typically holds the potential for using several hundred to several thousand columns and rows, which provides the ability to develop very large applications.

Figure 2.11. Anatomy of an electronic spreadsheet.

A. Structure of a spreadsheet.

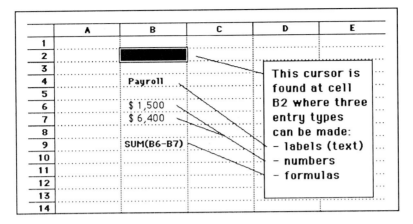

B. Illustration of different entries in a spreadsheet.

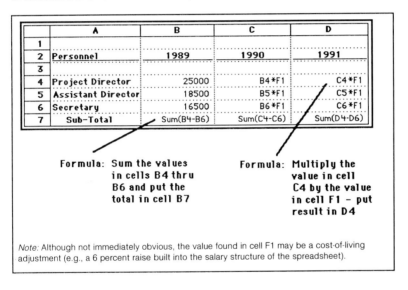

Note: Although not immediately obvious, the value found in cell F1 may be a cost-of-living adjustment (e.g., a 6 percent raise built into the salary structure of the spreadsheet).

Some key terms and concepts are important to understand. The intersection of any column or row is called a *cell*—a location where information can be stored. Cells in a spreadsheet are called by their *address*— the combination of the column heading and the row heading (e.g., cell B2 is the cell found at the intersection between column B and row 2). In general, three different types of information may be entered into any cell: *labels* (or text), *numbers,* and *formulas.* The *cursor* is the cell that is currently being addressed for data entry. In figure 2.11A the cursor is on cell B2.

Figure 2.12 contains a simplified budget that was prepared in a spreadsheet format for a survey research project. This figure helps to illustrate some of the potential uses of spreadsheets. Not seen in figure

Figure 2.12. A spreadsheet for a survey research project. This figure represents the full spreadsheet for a sample survey project, with all computations completed.

	A	B	C	D	E
1					
2	Personnel	1989	1990	1991	Total Project
3					
4	Project Director	$25000.00	$27000.00	$29160.00	$81160.00
5	Assistant Director	$18500.00	$19980.00	$21578.40	$60058.40
6	Secretary	$16500.00	$17820.00	$19245.60	$53565.60
7	Sub-Total	$60000.00	$64800.00	$69984.00	$194784.00
8					
9	Expenses				
10					
11	Mailing	$2500.00	$2625.00	$2756.25	$7881.25
12	Telephone	$12000.00	$12600.00	$13230.00	$37830.00
13	Supplies	$5000.00	$5250.00	$5512.50	$15762.50
14	Sub-Total	$19500.00	$20475.00	$21498.75	$61473.75
15					
16	Project Totals	$79500.00	$85275.00	$91482.75	$256257.75

2.12, cell F1 contains a single number that is used as a cost-of-living adjustment for personnel salaries (in this case it might be 1.08 for an 8 percent increase). Multiplying the data in any cell by F1 will therefore produce a number that represents an 8 percent increase in salary. A similar number is found in another cell to adjust for annual increases in expenses. An examination of figure 2.12 reveals that all of column A, from row 1 to 15, as well as all of row 2, columns A through E, consist entirely of labels—text that describes the content of the rows and columns. The numbers found in cells B4 to B6 are all raw data—numbers that have been entered into these cells that represent 1989 salaries for the project personnel. The same is true for the figures listed in cells B11 to B13—these are numbers that have been entered into these cells representing estimated expenditures in 1989 for mailing, telephone, and supplies. Less obvious is the fact that every other entry in this table is a formula. Because this is the area in which the greatest potential for spreadsheets exists, it is worth exploring how and why this was done.

Spreadsheet Formulas

Professionals who have done multiyear budgeting realize that incremental increases in salary and expenditures due to cost-of-living adjustments (COLAs) are necessary. This budget builds in incremental increases in salary and expenditures of 8 percent. Moreover, expenses other than personnel contain automatic adjustments of 5 percent per year. Doing these calculations by hand can be very tedious and time consuming for even very small budgets, and the potential for error is great. Spreadsheet software can mechanize this process by allowing for the entry of formulas into cells to do the calculations.

Most modern spreadsheet applications allow several different types of formulas to be entered into cells, including both custom formulas and predefined functions. A custom formula might direct the spreadsheet to add the value of two or more cells as follows:

$$B3 + B4 + B5 \qquad (2.1)$$

This formula would be placed in cell B6. Any legitimate mathematical formula may be entered into a cell of a spreadsheet for computation. On the other hand, formulas may be made up of predefined functions. Virtually all spreadsheets offer a "Sum" function, so the formula might be changed to:

$$Sum(B3–B5) \qquad (2.2)$$

Formulas 2.1 and 2.2 serve the same purpose. In either case, if any of the numbers in cells B3–B5 changed, the spreadsheet would automatically recalculate the sum of those cells. A similar formula is found in cell B13:

$$Sum(B10–B12) \qquad (2.3)$$

Finally, the formula in cell B15 need only direct the program to add the totals from B6 and B13 as follows:

$$Sum(B6, B13) \qquad (2.4)$$

The subject of formulas is very complex and requires a great deal of understanding. There are distinctions to be made in terms of absolute and relative references, and the use of constants in formulas versus references to cells containing constants. These issues are beyond the scope of this book and will not be explored here.

"What-If" Projections

Imagine that as a study is being planned, the initial figures estimated a 6 percent annual increase. Before start-up, however, new fiscal data indicate that the cost-of-living increase for the next year may be as high as 8 percent. In order to adequately plan for this difference, the study director simply changes the 1.06 found in cell F1 to 1.08, and the new budget estimates are instantly available.

The use of formulas wherever possible, rather than numbers, allows for the most important use of spreadsheets—"what-if" projections. A project planner might pose any of the following questions and get rapid answers from a correctly prepared spreadsheet model or template. In this case a model or template is a spreadsheet that contains the raw data and formulas necessary to do a variety of new computations based on changes in assumptions. For instance, in the personnel section of a spreadsheet, the model will contain a formula that multiplies the beginning salaries by a cost-of-living adjustment. To make other projections with different adjustments, only one number must be changed.

- What will be the effect on my three-year budget if I need to increase the initial salary offering of the project director from $25,000 to $28,000?

- What if the initial size of the survey mailing increases from 1,200 pieces of mail to 2,000 pieces of mail?
- What if the cost of living increases by more than 6 percent? less than 6 percent?

These and many other projections can be made with a properly constructed spreadsheet. In order to ensure a properly operating spreadsheet, the following steps can be taken:

1. *Plan your model before you go to the computer.* It is useful to fully describe all "knowns" and "assumptions" prior to entering anything into a spreadsheet.

2. *Label your spreadsheet extensively.* Recognize that spreadsheets, in professional settings, will sometimes have to be used by others. There will also be instances when a person will come back to a spreadsheet after an extended period of time has passed. In either case, a spreadsheet will have to be adequately labeled and documented to be used effectively.

3. *Identify all model parameters and group them separately.* A model parameter is an assumption used in the computations found in spreadsheets. For instance, one parameter of the examples accompanying this section of the text is that a cost-of-living adjustment will alter personnel salaries. As with this simple spreadsheet model, rather than using a constant (e.g., 1.08 for cost-of-living adjustments) in all formulas, it is more useful to have formulas that refer to a specific cell. However, it may be too simplistic to consider that all projections will be affected by the same constant. In this case salaries and expenses may not be expected to rise or fall at the same rate. Therefore, at least two parameters should have been used—an increment for salaries and an increment for expenses. In any case, avoid constants in formulas if possible.

4. *Work on small sections or modules that are clearly defined.* Divide your spreadsheet into logical modules. Develop and refine the operation of these self-contained modules rather than work on an entire model all at once.

5. *Pay attention to formatting.* Formatting is more than adequate labeling; it also refers to the appearance of a spreadsheet. Attention to formatting increases the readability and potential utility of models.

6. *Validate the model.* As with all mathematical models, spreadsheets should be thoroughly tested to ensure that they are providing accurate and adequate information. This may be accomplished by following some common tips for spreadsheet construction (Simkin & Dependahl, 1987, pp. 176–178):

- Use common sense: carefully examine all components of the model. Double-check all cells that don't "look right."
- Use known answers: when testing a model, use problems that have been completely worked out.
- Document formulas: this allows the user to review the process, make necessary changes, and replicate the model.
- Observe model responses to parameter changes: in the sample spreadsheet in figure 2.12, if the project director's salary was increased, an increase in all column totals would be expected. If this does not happen, then there is a problem in the model.
- Double-check foot totals: as is often done by hand when working on a budget, a person might double-check grand totals by summing all the numbers in that row, and then summing all the numbers in that column. This can easily be done in a spreadsheet by creating similar formulas in side-by-side columns—one to sum the numbers in the row, another to sum the numbers in the column. If the two cells do not match, then there is an error in the model.
- Check data and results with graphs: a graphic depiction of data sometimes allows for the rapid identification of errors in models. Many spreadsheet programs today offer graphing capabilities. These are useful not only for reporting and representing data, but for validation of the model as well.
- Have colleagues review and audit models.
- Use separate validation software.

7. *Backup models.* Create backup files of important models by copying the models onto several different diskettes.

The following case study will demonstrate how this technology is used in a department of health education.

Managing Office Budgets

As a good-sized university department of health education we must manage on average some twenty-five budgets totaling close to 2 million dollars annually. The university keeps official budgets on a mainframe computer and provides us with printouts each month. We must maintain parallel budget-entry procedures to double-check their system and to ensure that we know up to the minute where we stand in each account. This is vital because the university does make mistakes (usually not in our favor) and because as we approach the end of the fiscal year, the information becomes important to avoid going into the red or, even worse, turning back money we desperately need.

Until we computerized our office, all budgets were kept by hand, a laborious task. My secretary had to double as an accountant. The benefits derived from the use of electronic spreadsheets were well received by even my secretary, who was just being introduced to computers. I could quickly set up a spreadsheet with simple formulas that allowed her to fill in the blanks, and the computer would automatically do all the computations. With our current software we can even "link" spreadsheets so that the bottom line on one will automatically appear on the other.

This simple application has saved us countless hours and has insured much more accurate record keeping.

Note. Contributed by Dr. Glen G. Gilbert, Chairperson, Department of Health Education, University of Maryland.

Summary of Spreadsheet Technology

This concludes the brief introduction to spreadsheet technology. Any problem that involves the use of numbers, text, or some combination in tabular format can be addressed with a spreadsheet. The real power of the spreadsheet over manual manipulation comes from the use of formulas to describe relationships between cells, and to recalculate parameters automatically. The building of models in this way allows for the repetitive use of the spreadsheet for projecting outcomes of situations under different assumptions.

COMPUTER GRAPHICS IN HEALTH EDUCATION

The purpose of communication is to transmit ideas clearly and accurately. *Graphics* enhance communication by visually representing numerical data and reducing large amounts of data to digestible amounts of information. A graphic might include one or more of the following components: a visual representation of statistics; a key, legend, or explanation of the categories; a title; a source line. Each of these elements is described in this section.

With the ever-increasing sophistication of microcomputer software applications, professional quality graphics can be produced quickly, a development that has led to a proliferation of graphics, not all of which are necessary. This section provides basic information on the purpose, benefits, and effective uses of graphics, a partial listing of current graphic software available, and step-by-step guidelines on how to design and produce graphics on a microcomputer.

Engineers, scientists, and educators have used graphics for hundreds of years to record and transmit ideas, and though they have used computers for at least thirty-five years, it has only been in the last ten to twenty years that computer graphic systems have become less expensive and easier to use (Demel & Miller, 1984). The ease and availability of software for microcomputers has provided a vehicle for virtually anyone to produce high-quality graphics.

Functions of Graphics

The purpose of graphics is to communicate numerical information through visuals to enhance understanding. Text without graphics is tedious to read and less memorable. There are numerous benefits of using graphics in the field of health education. Graphics often command attention and involve the reader. They convey a message, illustrate a point, or clarify an issue. With large amounts of complex data, graphics are useful for simplification and summarization. *Demographics* (information about a sample population: e.g., gender, age, geographic location, annual income) are much more interesting and informative when they appear as graphics rather than in text. Relationships or proportions can be compared, correlations shown, conclusions drawn, and specific data emphasized. Graphics can describe or demonstrate a series of events in a process or show trends over time. The most important function of graphics is to communicate, to inform, or to educate a specific audience. Just as there are many benefits, there are also numerous uses for graphics.

Graphics are used in textbooks and educational materials, in newspapers, magazines, and journals. Projects, presentations, and proposals are more effective with graphic elements used to highlight information and to provide a visual respite from lengthy blocks of text. Graphics enhance research projects, theses, and dissertations. Almost any type of health-related information can be communicated more rapidly, and perhaps more effectively, with the aid of graphics. Pamphlets, brochures, booklets, and newsletters can be quickly and easily created with a variety of graphic-software applications.

Graphic Uses and Misuses

Graphics should not be used

- in excess, but rather to highlight specific findings;
- to distort or misrepresent information;
- when information is sketchy, incomplete, or inconclusive.

Graphics should be used for the purpose of enhancing communication.

The following list includes a sample of the types of software packages available. Many graphic images can be *imported* (moved from one application to another) into drawing or painting software, so that certain stylistic changes can be made. These may include type style, type and

Graphics Software Availability

Exhibit 2.6. Sample Graphics, Fonts and Type Sizes.

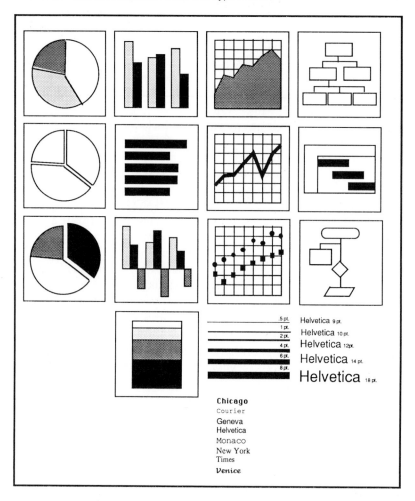

line-point size, and borders. See exhibit 2.6 for examples of type styles, point sizes, line-point sizes, and borders. Illustrations can usually be added only in drawing or painting applications. Some of the newer software (WingZ™ is an example) have charting and drawing capabilities. Some examples of drawing applications are listed in table 2.6. The final graphic can then be imported into a word-processing application or a desktop-publishing program, which is a powerful application providing the capacity to type and edit text and merge graphics. Examples of a variety of graphics and desktop-publishing applications are also listed in table 2.6.

As with any software purchase, determine what capabilities will be useful, examine the import and export capabilities, and predict what may be useful in the future. The following section will serve as a checklist of functions to help in the selection process for graphics software.

Table 2.6
Partial Listing of Currently Available Graphics Software

SOFTWARE NAME	FUNCTIONS	VENDOR	SYSTEM
WingZ	Spreadsheet 3-D capabilities	Informix	Macintosh
Harvard Graphics	2-D and 3-D extensive accessories	SPC	IBM
Lotus:			
Graphicwriterll	24 chart formats	Lotus	IBM
Freelance Plus	charts and graphs	Lotus	IBM
Cricket Graph	charts and graphs	Computer Associates	Macintosh
Xerox:			
Presents	charts and graphs	Xerox	IBM
Graph	charts and graphs	Xerox	IBM
Microsoft Excel	spreadsheet 42-choice gallery	Microsoft	Macintosh
Mac Draw	draw	Claris	Macintoch
Freehand	draw and paint	Aldus	Macintosh
Illustrator	draw and paint	Adobe	Macintosh
Pagemaker	desktop publishing	Aldus	Macintosh
Quark Express	desktop publishing	Quark	Macintosh

The first step in the production process is to identify the audience, or those who will read the information. Identifying your audience will help to define both the data included in the final document and the format selected to deliver the message. If your message is directed toward second-grade health students, select very basic information and present it in a clear, bold manner. If the receiving audience will be graduate students, a more sophisticated approach would be appropriate.

Producing Computer Graphics

STEP **1**

Identify the audience

The target audience to receive the data on the effectiveness of the wellness program is made up of stockholders of the Wellspirit Health Promotion Program.

The second step is to collect all of the statistics and accompanying information. In addition to data, typical elements include titles, key or legend information, and source lines, which identify the source of the statistics or analysis of the data. For some formats each axis must be labeled and numbers explained in percentages, thousands, billions, and so on.

STEP 2

Collect the information

The sample data includes statistics on the four risk factors: weight, cholesterol, systolic blood pressure, and diastolic blood pressure. In addition, demographic information will be shown.

Once the data to chart have been selected, the third step is to choose a *format,* or one of the four basic types of charts: pie, fever chart/line graph, bar/column chart, or table. In addition, diagrams are occasionally the best method to show a relationship between elements. Each format has specific attributes that make it desirable for use in specific situations.

STEP 3

Select chart formats

To show demographics, pie charts will be used. To show the overall change in the four risk factors over time, a fever chart will be used. To compare the men's and women's risk-factor changes, a bar-chart format will be used. A table will show all of the data collected for those wanting additional information.

Pie Charts

"The circle is a shape that is universally understood to represent a totality, a whole, a complete unit" (White 1984). The function of a *pie chart* is to show the relationship of parts to a whole. Usually reflecting percentages, the pie chart compares the amount of a section to the total amount.

Some examples of pie-chart usage include demographics, budget divisions, total services broken down by category, and the utilization of funds. Pie charts should not be used when there are more than eight segments or when there is too much information (they tend to look cluttered). They are less precise than other chart formats because there is no scale of measurement shown.

Pie charts typically begin with the largest segment at the top right quadrant. Segments are then shown from largest to smallest in a clockwise direction. Clearly label each section (use a short label and a number or percentage if necessary). Place the text information next to or within each segment. Differentiate segments with color or texture. Figure 2.13 is an example of a pie-chart format.

Fever Charts/Line Graphs

Fever charts, sometimes referred to as *line graphs,* show a trend over time, the relationship of two variables, or both. Examples of uses include

Figure 2.13. Sample ple-chart format.

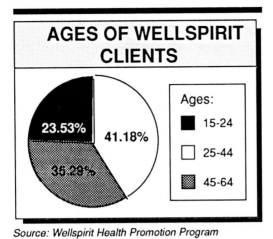

AGES OF WELLSPIRIT CLIENTS

23.53% 41.18% 35.29%

Ages:
■ 15-24
□ 25-44
▨ 45-64

Source: Wellspirit Health Promotion Program

the change in life expectancy each decade, trends in seat-belt usage, or the decline of smokers as a function of cigarette production in the past decade.

Fever charts should not be used when there are too many time segments, when there is too great a variation between the highest and the lowest numbers, or when the line is flat. If the numbers need to be shown as decimal points, a table is preferable. To begin, plot the time increments on the x-axis (the horizontal line) and the variables on the y-axis (the vertical line). Compare only consistent increments. For example, monthly statistics should not be mixed with yearly numbers. A fever chart is often shown on a grid to aid the reader in analyzing the numerical positions of the line. Grid design is discussed later in this section. Figure 2.14 demonstrates an application of a fever chart.

Bar Charts/Column Charts

Bar charts compare relationships between sets of numbers on a common scale at a particular point in time. Vertical or horizontal bars can also show a trend over time. One bar divided in sections can show parts of a whole (the same as a pie chart). A sample bar chart is shown in figure 2.15.

Bar charts, or column charts, can be created as 3-D, single, multiple, or illustrative graphics. Bar charts can be used to compare men's and women's smoking habits for the past ten years, or to contrast the amount of money spent on health care in different countries. Use vertical bars when long labels are needed. Use a fever or table format if there are too many numbers to show individually, or if the bars would be too thin or too close together.

Figure 2.14. Sample fever-chart format.

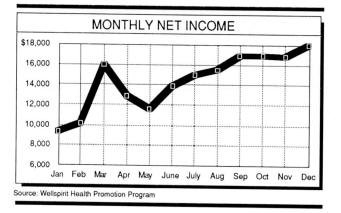

Figure 2.15. Sample bar-chart format.

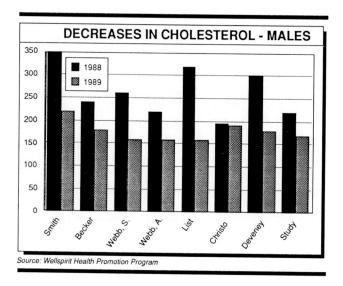

Tables

Tables include words or numbers arranged in columns or lists. Tables are used to organize information that cannot be charted in a pie, fever, or bar chart when the statistics are too complex, too lengthy, have too many variables, or when specific numbers must be shown (for example, when decimal points must be shown). Tables are used when the numbers are widely divergent, if the fever-chart lines are confusing, for calendars, or for other tabular information. Tables should not be used when statistics are chartable. Charts and graphs tend to be much more interesting than tables.

Table 2.7
Sample Table Format

DEMOGRAPHICS OF WELLSPIRIT CLIENTS					
Name	**Date**	**Age**	**Gender**	**Height**	**Weight**
Allen Smith	11/22/88	36	male	69	150
Bobby Becker	11/22/88	18	male	72	195
Kathryn Nye	11/22/88	26	female	62	115
Barbara Tice	11/22/88	38	female	68	135
Debby Webb	11/23/88	49	female	65	140
Scott Webb	11/25/88	52	male	74	215
Andrew Webb	11/24/88	19	male	74	200
Sarah Webb	11/22/88	21	female	68	120
Becky Fyfe	11/23/88	43	female	65	135
Bob List	11/21/88	29	male	68	197
Cheryl Dent	11/23/88	22	female	62	112
Liz Jones	11/25/88	15	female	73	95
Eve Scott	11/24/88	23	female	66	123
Gail Ice	11/25/88	50	female	58	160
Glen Christo	11/24/88	43	male	74	223
James Deveney	11/21/88	53	male	75	195
Steve Study	11/21/88	29	male	72	156

Source: Wellspirit Health Promotion Program

Tables can be used to show spreadsheet information or multiple variables, or to analyze the pros and cons of an intervention. In addition, charts can be useful for showing timetables, report cards, mileage tables, factorial tables, and other cross-factorial information. When designing tables, organize data efficiently and effectively. Carefully select type and leave only a small space between columns. Use rules, spaces, or screens to guide the reader's eye across the columns. Column headings should be kept short, and numbers aligned with the decimal points. The demographic breakdowns for the Wellspirit clients appear in table 2.7.

Diagrams

Diagrams "show pictorially how a series of activities, procedures, operations, events, ideas or other factors are related to each other" (Lefferts, 1981). "The elements are generally abstract and appear as symbolic shapes: squares, rectangles, circles, triangles or volumes" (Meilach, 1986).

Diagrams can demonstrate the stages in the development of a program, a disease, or a treatment. They can transform complex and lengthy information into visually simple segments. The audience can easily see the relationships between various segments of an operation. Diagrams can clarify issues, summarize lengthy procedures, and add coherence and unity to textual information.

The organizational chart is one diagram format with which everyone is familiar. Other format examples are flowcharts and time charts including PERT and Gantt. Figure 2.16 demonstrates how a diagram can explain a process.

Figure 2.16. Sample diagram format.

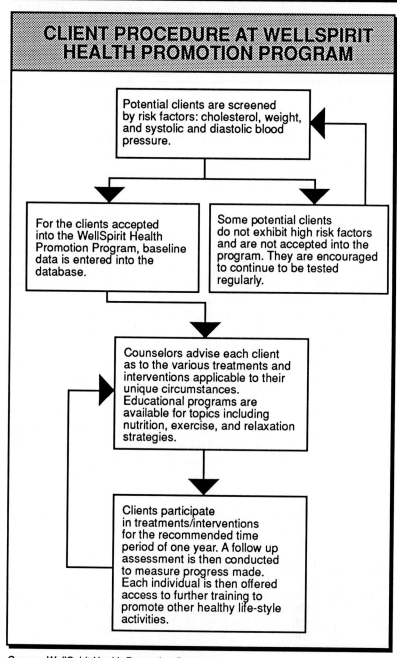

CLIENT PROCEDURE AT WELLSPIRIT
HEALTH PROMOTION PROGRAM

Potential clients are screened by risk factors: cholesterol, weight, and systolic and diastolic blood pressure.

For the clients accepted into the WellSpirit Health Promotion Program, baseline data is entered into the database.

Some potential clients do not exhibit high risk factors and are not accepted into the program. They are encouraged to continue to be tested regularly.

Counselors advise each client as to the various treatments and interventions applicable to their unique circumstances. Educational programs are available for topics including nutrition, exercise, and relaxation strategies.

Clients participate in treatments/interventions for the recommended time period of one year. A follow up assessment is then conducted to measure progress made. Each individual is then offered access to further training to promote other healthy life-style activities.

Source: WellSpirit Health Promotion Program

The next step in the production of graphic is to design a style to be used consistently throughout a project. *Design* is the process of taking all of the elements and arranging them in a pleasing, readable way. The design principles include unity, balance, contrast, and proportion. These four principles can be used as a checklist to avoid confusing, hard-to-read graphics.

Unity/Simplicity

For the total presentation or project, you should design one style and use it consistently. Select one type *font* (a style of type), and use only variations of that font. Some fonts are more decorative for use in titles (Chicago); some fonts are very readable and are therefore used for large amounts of text (Helvetica and Times). When several fonts are used in a graphic, the result is busy and confusing. Type is measured in *points* instead of in inches. There are seventy-two points in an inch. Limit the different point sizes to three per graphic. In other words, the title can be in eighteen-point, the chart labels in twelve, and the source line in eight-point type. See exhibit 2.6 for a visual presentation of fonts and point sizes. Attention should be focused principally on the graphic image itself, not on fancy type manipulation. Remember that the goal of graphics is clear, precise, and accurate communication.

For each chart a strong, readable title is required. The reader should immediately be able to determine the content of the graphic. Typically, the title is placed at the top, either centered or flush left, in type more bold than the rest of the text. Caps can be used to add emphasis. To achieve unity, select rules, a box, or a border to enclose every graphic. Choose a point size for the thickness of the box or rules. Choose a line thickness for the graphic information. Many applications allow the designer to select any point size of line (overriding defaults.) Simplicity is achieved by "showing trends not details" (Meilach, 1986). Break complex information into several charts. If there are more than eight categories in a pie chart, combine the smallest into an "other" category. Use patterns from darkest shade to lightest, and avoid placing loud patterns next to each other.

Selecting a uniform style to achieve unity/simplicity

The overall style will include a reversed (white letters on a black background), bold headline, a .5-point border box around each graphic, and use of Helvetica as the selected type font.

Balance

The second design principle is balance. Effective balance in a graphic creates equilibrium, as space is well utilized and distributed evenly. No area has too much or too little information in it. Balance requires objects to be placed in a pleasing composition.

Achieving balance

Balance is achieved in this example by centering the headline above the graphic and composing the visual and the text information to avoid awkward empty spots.

Contrast/Emphasis

The third design principle is contrast. Some elements in a graphic are more important than others. The title is more important than the source line. The visual image is more important than the legend. Contrast is achieved by using one elemlent as a focus in the graphic and minimizing all other elements. Use of size, the color black (or other colors), or exploding a portion of the chart are some methods of emphasizing certain elements within a graphic. The designer helps the reader to know what is most important by providing that information bigger or bolder than the rest.

Utilizing contrast for emphasis

Decide what should be highlighted and what can be diminished visually. The information that is the most important should be larger, bolder, and/or darker than the other information.

Proportion/Scale

The last design principle is proportion or scale. Scales should be consistent when comparing two sets of data. The space between bars should be smaller than the width of each bar. Proportion and scaling are critical if information is to be portrayed in an accurate manner.

Grid lines, when used correctly, allow the reader to compare numbers easily. They should not pass through bars, columns, lines, or areas that represent data, and they should correlate with the numbers. Keep grid lines simple enough to avoid conflict with the charted information. They should recede into the background and can be omitted altogether if trends or comparisons are shown.

STEP 7

Select scales to put data in proportion

Select accurate scales and utilize grid lines when they will aid the reader in comparing numerical information.

The preceding design principles are the building blocks for effective graphics. As illustrated in exhibit 2.7, creativity can play a big role in enhancing graphics. For example, charts can be shown in 3-D, or illustrations or photos can be added. The particular software program used will determine many of the design decisions. For example, some of the chart programs automatically select Geneva as the default font, but with a little patience and ingenuity, the graphics can be enhanced by importing the charts into drawing applications, and altered to fit your exact needs. One useful practice is to start a graphics file. Clip examples of graphics from newspapers and magazines to provide inspiration and ideas. You may also want to keep an eye on national publications to assess the current status of computer-graphic technology.

Summary of Graphics

This discussion on graphics is not meant to be conclusive but is, rather, an elementary introduction to basic computer-graphics usage. Each software program has various opportunities and limitations; with a little experimentation the limitations can be overcome. The sophistication of computer graphics increases exponentially each year, yet applications get easier and easier to use. It is impossible to predict the magnitude of the technological changes that will occur in the next ten years, but the future holds a great deal of potential in the arena of computer graphics, with expanded capabilities in input devices, hardware, software applications, and output devices.

Computers will become more powerful, have faster microprocessors, and memory will be cheaper. Input devices will be able to optically scan type. Imaging systems can and will alter images, and systems will be able to produce three-dimensional artwork, such as holographs. Ink-jet and laser printers with the capability to print in four colors, thereby producing the effect of full color, will be within the range of affordability.

SUMMARY

The ability to adapt a single software-application package to any problem is what makes spreadsheets, word processors, and databases so unique. However, the fullest utilization of these systems may come from the integration of their separate capabilities. Simkin and Dependahl (1987, p. 225) suggest several criteria essential to the evaluation of database software, including the following: (1) recognize the limitations of the program selected; (2) understand the storage considerations necessary to operate the application efficiently; (3) examine the user friendliness of the program; (4) look for those programs that provide the greatest

Exhibit 2.7. Sample graphic preparation

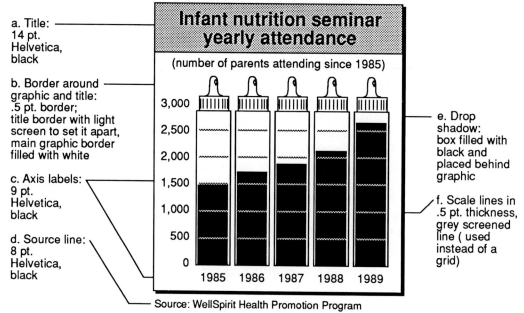

a. Title:
14 pt.
Helvetica,
black

b. Border around
graphic and title:
.5 pt. border;
title border with light
screen to set it apart,
main graphic border
filled with white

c. Axis labels:
9 pt.
Helvetica,
black

d. Source line:
8 pt.
Helvetica,
black

e. Drop
shadow:
box filled with
black and
placed behind
graphic

f. Scale lines in
.5 pt. thickness,
grey screened
line (used
instead of a
grid)

STEP ONE:
The audience is the stockholders of the Wellspirit Health Promotion Program.

STEP TWO:
The infant nutrition class was selected to highlight because it is a new program, and because it is increasingly well-attended

STEP THREE:
A bar chart format was selected to compare the yearly attendance increase, and to utilize the baby bottle motif. A fever chart would also have been an appropriate format to use because the data is in measures of time. The bar chart was created in Excel, then imported into MacDraw for type changes, baby bottle illustrations and graphic treatments (boxes, line width changes, etc.), then the image was imported into Microsoft Word to be merged with the text.

STEP FOUR:
The following design decisions are necessary to unify the information in order to present the information in a clear, concise, informative manner.
a. Title type size, style and color
b. Border type, thickness, and color
c. Type size, style and color for axis labels
d. Source line type size, style and color
e. Shadow behind graphic, or other rules or devices to add interest
f. Scale lines or grid pattern
Once these decisions are made, the same style should be utilized throughout the project.

STEP FIVE:
Balance is achieved by centering the title and explanatory information above the graphic and composing the visual information to avoid awkward empty spots.

STEP SIX:
The information bar located within the baby bottles is left in black to contrast the data from the illustration portion of the graphic.

STEP SEVEN:
The two most important elements of this graphic are the data and the title. The type size and font selected for this graphic give it emphasis. The large size of the baby bottles highlights the importance of the data. The text is shown in 9 pt. type because of its reduced importance, and the source line type size is even smaller.

degree of flexibility and adaptability for your needs; (5) evaluate the program's capacity for backup, recovery, and security; (6) understand the interface capabilities and limitations; and (7) assess the program's special features.

Virtually all of these programs allow for the creation, editing, manipulation, and reporting of data, including text and numbers. All provide some capabilities that others do not, and because of that, it is worth exploring how they can be used together.

1. What are the potential advantages and disadvantages of database, word processing, spreadsheet, and graphics software for health education?

2. What are the advantages of a flat-file manager? a relational database system?

3. Identify a specific health-education example that would be most appropriate for a flat-file manager, a relational database system, and a spreadsheet. How are these applications different? How does each use the unique advantages of the application?

4. Aside from budgeting and forecasting, what other examples of professional health-education needs can be satisfied by spreadsheets?

5. How can combinations of database, word processing, spreadsheet technology, and graphics applications be used in a complimentary manner in health-education settings?

Abernathy, W. B. (1979). The microcomputer as a community mental public information tool. *Community Mental Health Journal,* 15 (3), 192–202.

Conklin, G. S., McCormack, M., Andersen, E. G., & Libenson, D. D. (1987). Database management systems into the 1980's: A review. *Topics In Health Management,* 7 (3), 1–11.

Holmes, Nigel. (1984). *Designer's guide to creating charts and diagrams.* New York: Watson-Guptill.

Kline, N. W. (1986). Principles of computerized database management. *Computers in Nursing, 4* (2), 73–81.

Lunin, L. F., & Stein, R. S. (1987). CHID: A unique health information and education database. *Bulletin of the Medical Library Association, 75* (2), 95–100.

Meilach, Dona Z. (1986). *Dynamics of presentation graphics.* Homewood, Illinois; Dow Jones-Irwin.

Siemon, J. E., & Robertson, J. S. (1987). Databases and report writers: An introduction to basic concepts for health care professionals. *Topics in Health Records Management, 7* (3), 13–21.

Watzlaf, V. J. M. (1987). The medical record as an epidemiological database. *Topics in Health Records Management, 7* (3), 61–67.

Whyte, A. A. (1983, June). What's new in health information systems. *Occupational Health and Safety,* pp. 48–50.

Winters, D. M. (1988). CD-ROM and its application in the storage of health information. *Topics in Health Records Management, 9* (1), 24–31.

3

COMMUNICATIONS

By the completion of this chapter, the student will be able to

- understand the basic terminology related to computer-based telecommunications;
- describe the services available to health educators through telecommunications;
- compare the characteristics of different communications capabilities;
- identify the potential of telecommunications applications to health educators.

Communications: The exchange of information from one computer to another.

Communications software: An application that allows for transmission and receipt of information between computers.

Download: The receipt of information to a user's computer from a remote location.

Electronic bulletin board: A computer system that acts as a central location for storage of information.

Electronic mail: Transmission of information (letters, memos, reports) over a communications network.

Facsimile (FAX):   Communication of printed information between locations. A fax machine scans a printed page and converts the information on the page into information that can be transmitted over phone lines.

Local area networks (LAN):   A communications network that is confined to a small geographic area such as an office complex.

Modem: Modulator-demodulator. A piece of equipment that translates electronic information in one computer into signals that can be transmitted to another computer. At the other end of the transmission, another modem converts the signals back into electronic form.

Network: A communications path between computers.

Telecommunications: The communication of any form of information—data, text, video, and sound.

Upload: To send information from a user's computer to some other location.

Wide area networks (WAN):   A communication network between computers at remote locations. A WAN may be citywide, statewide, nationwide or worldwide.

INTRODUCTION

The computer revolution has been dramatically expanded by a number of developments in technology, but perhaps the most important has been the influence of communications capabilities. In a computerized environment *communications* refers specifically to the movement of data from one location to another. Most people, however, view communications in a relatively limited manner—movement of data over telephone line from one computer to another. In reality, the term *communications* is much more complex, involving movement of data from one memory location to another within a computer system, between internal memory and peripheral devices, between computers in a local area network, over very long distances, or any combination of these elements.

A review of recent developments in telecomputing in the health fields illustrates the potential impact on professional practice. The technology has been used for diagnostic and decision support (Radwin, 1986; Weinstein, Bloom, & Rozek, 1987); networking for sharing information (Carrasco et al., 1986) and to facilitate research (LaPorte et al., 1988); training (Connel & Smyer, 1986); access to large databases (Homan, 1986; Howard & Jankowski, 1986); and in the provision of services (Evans et al., 1986; Schneider & Tooley, 1986). There are many other potential applications as a result of recent developments in telecommunications technology. The purpose of this chapter is to provide an overview of these applications by describing the types of capabilities available to health professionals through telecommunications, and then by providing a technical description of the technology itself.

ON-LINE SERVICES FOR HEALTH PROFESSIONALS

Since the 1960s technologic developments in several areas have been responsible for extending the horizons for telecomputing. Among the most important have been (1) the development of collections of information, either numeric or textual, that have been created by public and private industries, but which are now available from publishers in electronic form; (2) the development of time-sharing computer systems, which allow many users at the same time to use information from a central source; (3) advances in the development of interactive computer software; (4) the increasing capacity and availability of mass storage systems; (5) the improved capabilities and reliability of computer terminals and microcomputers; and (6) the developments in the field of computer communications and telecommunications. With the capabilities provided by these developments, a number of on-line services are available to health professionals including *bulletin-board* and *electronic-mail systems, public-access databases, interactive applications* for the health professions, and what some people refer as *metasystems* (a service that provides many functions and access to many different services).

Bulletin-Board and Electronic-Mail Systems

In a real sense electronic bulletin boards are identical to other more common bulletin boards in educational or community settings. They represent a location where an individual can leave messages or read messages and advertisements that others have left. Instead of physically traveling to a bulletin board, a person dials a phone number and connects a computer or terminal to an electronic bulletin board. Messages are read; information may be copied to the user's computer; and messages, general information, or queries may be posted on the bulletin board.

Bulletin boards may be locally, regionally, or nationally based; they may be run on micro-, mini-, or mainframe computers; and they may be open to all topical areas or restricted to specific content concerns. In a practical sense they represent a public display of information that is open to anyone capable of dialing into it. These systems are generally easy to access and use and provide a wide variety of topical areas and types of information ranging from straight health and medical information, to a forum for exchanging ideas with others who share common interests, to a medium for the review and acquisition of *public domain* or *shareware software,* and in some cases, games, puzzles, and contests.

There are many bulletin-board and electronic-mail systems now available for health professionals, but the first bulletin-board system designed specifically for health educators was created by Dr. Michael Pejsach in the early 1980s. The intent of the Health Education Electronic Forum (HEEF) at that time was to provide a medium within which health educators could communicate freely and receive timely and important information about trends, products, and other matters of interest. Table 3.1 contains a list of some of the more readily available bulletin-board systems for health educators and other health professionals.

An electronic-mail system is similar, but with some very specific differences. Electronic mail refers to the exchange of messages between individuals—either *personal mail* from one person to another, or *group mail* from one person to many others. Unlike bulletin-board systems, electronic-mail systems are designed to ensure that only the specified recipient or recipients of the messages can access the communication. These are not public electronic displays, but a system in which a specific message is placed in a location that is accessible only to the intended audience. The distinct advantages electronic mail has over other forms of mail is its speed and its relative security in transmission.

Both bulletin-board and electronic-mail systems also provide the capacity for *real-time conferencing* in an electronic medium. That is, any number of individuals may dial into a system at a predetermined time and communicate with each other electronically as if they were in the same location. All messages transmitted may be seen by all other members of the conference group, and any may respond electronically. The term *real time* refers to the fact that messages are delivered immediately, without delay, and in their full form as they are being sent.

Public-Access Databases

The availability of *public-access databases* has been spurred by the recognition of the importance of information in today's society. These databases help minimize duplication of effort, rapidly transmit new ideas and data to widespread audiences, and provide supporting documentation for research endeavors. All of these objectives are accomplished in

Table 3.1
Bulletin-Board Systems for Health-Education Professionals

NAME (SYSOP)	TELEPHONE NO.	COMPONENTS
AIDS Information BBS (Ben Gardiner)	415–626–1246	AIDS
Health Forum (SPHTM-HEEF) (Dr. Michael Pejsach)	504–588–5743	Job bank, AIDS training materials for education
Health On Line (Bruce W. Miller)	206–367–8726	Nutrition, self-care for diabetics, alternative therapies
Health Professional BBS (Dr. George Sparrow)	700–322–0405	Pediatric sports medicine, sports medicine
Infomedics (Dr. Chiayu Chen)	703–276–9180	Computers in Medicine, MUMPS
Shrink Tank (Dr. Robert Bischoff)	408–257–0323	Alcoholism
The American Psycho/ Information Exchange (Dr. Marc Martin)	212–662–7171	Mental-health topics
The Health Forum (HEEP) (Dr. Michael Pejsach)	704–264–0674	Human sexuality, preventive medicine, nutrition, drug abuse, other topics
The Testing Station (Dr. Marvin Miller)	317–846–8917	Psychiatry
Wellspring (Steve Clancy, MLS)	714–856–7996	AIDS information, computer literacy for users, other topics

a number of ways, and the databases differ in discipline, breadth, periodicity (i.e., the frequency with which they are updated or changed), geography, and other factors. They also differ in the kind of information they contain. The following examples are provided from *Online Databases in the Medical and Life Sciences* (1987, ix–x):

1. Reference databases point users to another source for more complete information, and include
   • bibliographic databases, which contain citations and sometimes abstracts of published literature;
   • referral databases, which contain references and occasionally abstracts of unpublished literature.
2. Source databases contain original source information (e.g., full text materials), such as
   • numeric databases with raw data from surveys;
   • textual-numeric databases with mixed data;
   • databases with the full text of original sources;
   • software that can be legally *downloaded* to other computers.

Tables 3.2 and 3.3 contain a listing of selected on-line public-access databases and their vendors.

Table 3.2

Sources of On-line Information

<table>
<tr><td colspan="2" align="center">MEDLARS</td></tr>
</table>

There are tremendous amounts of information available to health-related professionals. Perhaps the most familiar of these sources of information is *Medlars* (Medical Literature Analysis and Retrieval Systems), but many of us confuse the name *Medlars* with only one of its most familiar databases— *Medline*. However, there are twenty other databases supported by the Medlars.

Avline. Index to audiovisual materials in clinical medicine.

Bioethicsline. Bibliographic database covering ethics and public policy.

Cancerlit. Journal citations related to major cancer topics.

Cancerproj. Project descriptions for clinical and laboratory research currently underway.

Catline. Six hundred thousand titles—almost the entire NLM catalog.

Chemline. Directory of chemical substances.

Clinprot. Summaries of clinical investigations of new cancer therapies.

Dirline. On-line directory of organizations.

Health Planning and Administration. Citations to nonclinical health literature.

Histline. Citations on history of medicine and related sciences.

Medline. Citations to 5 million articles in biomedicine.

Mesh Vocabulary File. On-line dictionary of Medlars subject terms.

Name Authority File. Authority records for names and titles used in healings in Catline and Avline.

PDQ. Current cancer treatments.

Popline. Citations to literature on population and family planning.

RTECS. Toxicity data for more than 70,000 substances.

Serline. Bibliographic information on all biomedical journals in NLM.

Toxline. Bibliographic database on toxicology of chemicals.

<table>
<tr><td align="center">OTHER DATABASES (LISTED ALPHABETICALLY)</td></tr>
</table>

AAMSI Communication Network. American Association of Medical Systems and Informatics bibliographic and referral system. Full-text searches from health and medical journals in biomedicine, computers and software, conferences and meetings, and information systems. (Source).

Ageline. Citations and abstracts of the literature on aging. Contains about 18,500 citations with abstracts from 1978 to the present. AARP, National Gerontology Resource Center (BRS).

Agricola. Citations on nutrition literature. National Agricultural Library (BRS, Dialog).

AIDS. Contains almost 1,000 citations with many abstracts from 1982 to the present from the international literature on AIDS, retroviruses, and T-lymphotrophic viruses. Etiology, transmission, epidemiology, pathology, immunology, serology, and treatment. Abstracts on Hygiene and Communicable Disease, Bureau of Hygiene and Tropical Disease (BHTD, BRS).

AIDS Policy and Law. Full-text database for legislative tracking. Information on legal issues related to AIDS, and governmental and private employment policies, rights of employees, fair employment practices, housing, insurance, litigation, and new case law. (Executive Telecom System, Inc., Human Resource Information Network).

AIDS Update. Almost 900 citations with many abstracts from 1985 to present. Abstracts on Hygiene and Communicable Disease, Bureau of Hygiene and Tropical Disease (BHTD, BRS).

Table 3.2—*Continued*

Alcohol Use/Abuse. Bibliographic citations and abstracts on chemical dependence from 1968 to 1978. University of Minnesota, Drug Information Services. (BRS).

Biosis Previews. Literature on biology, medicine, and other life sciences. BioSciences Information Services (BRS, Dialog).

Birth Defects Information System. Three databases related to birth defects containing full-text information from the literature from 1982 to present. (1) BDIS Information Retrieval: 1,000 full-text articles on birth defects and malformation syndromes. (2) BDIS Diagnostic Assist: database system designed to assist with differential diagnosis. (3) BDIS Unknowns Registry: database of clinical, demographic, and epidemiological information on cases with no clear diagnosis. (BRS).

Cancerlit. All aspects of cancer research and treatment. National Cancer Institute (BRS).

Centers for Disease Control Information Service. Full-text information services on biomedicine contained in several areas: (1) AIDS Information Service: with definitions, statistics, facts, and references on AIDS; (2) CDC INFO Update: with information on current CDC publications, symposia, meetings, and current research; (3) Continuing Education Programs: containing announcement of training and seminars for health and medical professionals; and (4) Morbidity and Morality Weekly Report. (AMA/NET).

Child Abuse and Neglect. Research project and service program descriptions; audiovisual materials; legal references; bibliographic references. Clearinghouse on Child Abuse and Neglect (Dialog).

CICDOC; CISILO. Bibliographic citations to international literature on occupational safety and health. (Toxline).

Combined Health Information Database (CHID). Information on organizations, publications, and programs related to health promotion and education, digestive diseases, arthritis, and diabetes contained in five files: (1) Arthritis: bibliographic citations from 1978 to present on arthritic and other musculoskeletal diseases; (2) Diabetes: bibliographic citations and abstracts from 1973 to present; (3) Digestive diseases: full text and citations to professional and patient education literature dating from 1980 to present; (4) High blood pressure: bibliographic citations and abstracts to literature from 1981 to present; and (5) Health education: with bibliographic citations and abstracts on patient, school community, occupational and professional health education programs dating from 1977 to the present. Centers for Disease Control (BRS).

Comprehensive Core Medical Library. Complete text of major medical journals and monographs. W. B. Saunders (BRS, BRS/Saunders Colleague).

Computerized AIDS Information Network (CAIN). Bibliographic references and full-text information on AIDS. Electronic mail, bulletin board, and conferencing services. (General Videotex Corp., Delphi).

Congressional Activities. Full text of Congressional Activities newsletter, with calendars of upcoming events. Summaries of bills and resolutions, current status, and citations to speeches in Congressional Record. (NewsNet, Inc.).

Congressional Record Abstracts. Citations with abstracts to Congressional Record from 1981 to current time. (BRS, Orbit).

Table 3.2—*Continued*

Consumer Drug Information. Contains current reference to most drugs prescribed in the U.S., with information about use, side effects, and precautions. American Society of Hospital Pharmacists. (BRS, Dialog).

Current Contents Search. Database with almost 170,000 citations to articles in the current issues of scientific journals. Institute for Scientific Information (ISI). (BRS).

Diogenes. Citations for over 25,000 unpublished Food and Drug Administration regulatory documents, including prescription and over-the-counter drugs, and medical devices. Full text of FDA press releases, reports, and newsletters. (BRS).

Dirline. On-line directory of 15,000 mostly health-related organizations that provide health information to consumers and professionals. National Health Information Center (NLM).

Druginfo. Drug and alcohol abuse literature. Drug Information Services, College of Pharmacy, University of Minnesota (BRS).

Educational Resources Information Center (ERIC). Source of literature on education, including health education, physical education, recreation, and dance. ERIC Processing and Reference Facility (ERIC, BRS, Dialog).

Embase. Literature referenced in pharmaceutical sciences. Elsevier Science Publishing Co., (BRS).

Emhealth. Citations and abstracts to worldwide literature on public health from 1974 to present. (DIMDI).

Epidemiology Information System. Contains almost 9,000 citations to the published and unpublished literature on food contaminants and their effects on health from 1960 to date. (To be available).

Family Resources. Citations to bibliographic and audiovisual resources in medicine, psychology, sociology, marriage and divorce, and therapy. National Council on Family Relations (BRS, Dialog).

Hazardline. Full-text information on regulatory and health data on almost 80,000 chemicals (Occupational Health Services, Inc.). (BRS, Tech Data).

Health Planning and Administration. Information on health planning, organization, financing, management, and manpower; health promotion and education. National Library of Medicine (BRS, Dialog).

Healthlawyer. Citations, abstracts, and text of current law digests, journals, newsletters, and conferences. American Hospital Association (BRS).

Healthnet. Health-care information for consumers on drugs, medical tests, and a variety of health-related content areas (e.g., first aid, nutrition, sexuality, AIDS). (CompuServe, Delphi).

Human Sexuality. Full-text database with articles, programs, information on contraception, relationships, sexual dysfunction, homosexuality, and sexually transmitted diseases. (CompuServe).

IRCS Medical Science Database. Full text of articles from thirty-two biomedical research journals. IRCS Medical Science (BRS).

Medical and Psychological Previews. Literature on medicine and psychology. BRS/Saunders (BRS).

Medline. Largest of the Medlars databases from the National Library of Medicine. References to journals on biomedicine, biology, physical sciences, veterinary medicine, and humanities. NLM (BRS, Dialog, Medis).

Mental Health Abstracts/National Institute of Mental Health. Indexes and abstracts from mental-health literature. NIMH (BRS, Dialog.)

Table 3.2—*Continued*

NTIS (National Technical Information Service). Abstracts of research and development reports by federal agencies and their contractors and grantees. DHHS dissemination mechanism. NTIS (BRS).

Nursing and Allied Health. Citations to current literature on nursing and allied health. CINAHL Corporation (BRS).

Nursing and Allied Health. More than 40,000 bibliographic citations from 350 journals in nursing and ten allied health fields. CINAHL. (BRS, Dialog, Tech Data).

Occupational Safety and Health. Articles, monographs, and technical reports on all aspects of occupational safety and health. NIOSH (Dialog).

PDQ (Physician Data Query). Summaries of all major tumor types; directory of cancer specialists; directory of organizations associated with cancer treatment; cancer treatment protocols. National Library of Medicine (BRS).

Pollution Abstracts. More than 100,000 citations and abstracts on the international literature on pollution research from 1970 to the present. Cambridge Scientific Abstracts. (BRS, Dialog).

Popline. Citations from 1970 to present on demography, family-planning services, programs, and policy issues. National Library of Medicine (NLM).

Population Bibliography. Citations to literature from 1966 to 1984 on population research, with particular attention to areas of abortion, demography, family planning, and fertility issues. (Dialog).

Psycalert. Recent literature in psychology. American Psychological Association (Dialog).

Psychinfo. Formerly *Psychology Abstracts*. References, articles, monographs, dissertations, and reports on psychology and behavioral sciences. American Psychological Association (BRS, Dialog).

Sport Database. Citations and abstracts to journal articles and monographs on athletics and recreation, including sports and medicine. Sport Information Resource Center (Canada) (BRS).

The Merck Index Online. Full text of chemical and pharmaceutical data on 30,000 chemicals. Merck and Company, Inc. (BRS, Tech Data).

Toxicology/Epidemiology Research Projects. Descriptions of research projects supported by the U.S. Public Health Service. NIH, Division of Research Grants. (Toxline).

Work/Family Life Database. Citations on issues of family life as related to work. Management Directions (BRS).

Note. Table 3.2 illustrates the extent of public database offerings available to health professionals, yet this is only a small portion of the more than 3,000 that are currently active. One of the better sources of information in this area is *Online Databases in the Medical and Life Sciences* (1987) a publication of Cuandra/Elsevier. Table 3.3 contains a list of the major vendors through which these databases can be accessed.

Table 3.3

Vendors Providing Access to On-line Databases for Health Professionals

VENDOR	TELEPHONE NO.*	DATABASES
BRS 1200 Route 7 Lantham, NY 12100	800–345–4277 800–345–1161	AgeLine, Agricola, Alcohol Use/Abuse, Biosis Previews, Cancerlit, CHID, Consumer Drug Information, Druginfo, Embase, Family Resources, Hazardline, Health Planning and Administration, Medical and Psychological Previews, Medline, Nursing and Allied Health, Pollution Abstracts, Psychalert, Psychinfo
BRS After Dark 1200 Route 7 Lantham, NY 12110	800–345–4277 800–345–1161	Ageline, Agricola, Biosis Previews, CHID, Consumer Drug Information, Family Resources, Health Planning and Administration, Medline, Nursing and Allied Health, Pollution Abstracts, Psychalert, Psychinfo
BRS/Colleague 1200 Route 7 Lantham, NY 12110	800–345–4277 800–345–1161	AIDS, AIDS Update, Alcohol Use/Abuse, CHID, Consumer Drug Information, Druginfo, Family Resources, Health Planning and Administration, Medline, Nursing and Allied Health, Psychalert, Psychinfo
Dialog 3460 Hillview Avenue Palo Alto, CA 94304	800–334–2564	Agricola, Cancerlit, Child Abuse and Neglect, Consumer Drug Information, Family Resources, Health Planning and Administration, Medline, Mental Health Abstracts, Nursing and Allied Health, Psychalert, Psychinfo
National Library of Medicine 8600 Rockville Pike Bethesda, MD 20209	301–496–6193	Medlars, Avline, Bioethicsline, Cancerlit, Dirline, PDQ, Popline, Toxline, CHID, Toxicology/epidemiology, Research Projects
Tech Data 15 Inverness Way E. PO Box 1154 Englewood, CO 80150	800–525–7052	Ageline, Agricola, AIDS, AIDS Update, Alcohol Use/Abuse, Biosis Previews, CHID, Druginfo, Family Resources, Health Planning and Administration, Medline, Nursing and Allied Health, Psychalert, Psychinfo, Sport

*Telephone numbers accurate as of September 1989.

Table 3.4

Interactive Telecommunications Applications for Health Professionals

VENDOR (APPLICATION)	TELEPHONE NO.	DESCRIPTION
Datanetwork of Applied Business Systems, Inc., (Nutrition Analysis System [DATANETWORK])	800–626–2358	Dietary analysis.
Center for Birth Defects Information Services, Inc. (BDIS Diagnostic Assist [BRS])	800–345–4277	Database for assistance with diagnosis of birth-defect syndromes. More than 600 syndromes supported.
Laboratory of Computer Science, Massachusetts General Hospital. (DxPLAIN [AMA/NET])	800–426–2873	Diagnostics decision support on 2,000 diseases.
Quantitative Medical Systems (Nutrition and Diet [QMS])	415–654–9200	Dietary analysis.

Interactive Applications

Interactive applications refers to a group of public-access telecommunications services that provide software for interactive use. It is as if a user has the software on a personal system. In this case a user dials up the system and uses the application through the communications channel.

Most of these interactive applications are designed to be for diagnosis and *decision support,* and therefore are designed for clinical medicine specialties. However, there are some that provide assistance to other health professionals in the area of nutritional analysis. Table 3.4 contains a summary of the major interactive applications. Be sure to examine the table carefully to determine which applications can be used by which health professionals.

Metasystems

A metasystem is one that provides access to many different services. The purpose of a metasystem is to provide a conduit to these multiple services. There are four primary metasystems that provide specific services and applications for health professionals. See table 3.5 for information on these four systems.

A user should realize that the services and applications presented in tables 3.1 through 3.5 are not usually provided free of charge. The charges may include (1) membership costs (optional with some services); (2) line costs (the cost of the telephone call to the services); (3) connect time (a charge for the time connected to the service); and (4) a service charge. Those interested in such services and applications should consult with the vendors on current pricing structures.

Table 3.5
Metasystems for Health Professionals

VENDOR	TELEPHONE NO.	DESCRIPTION

AMA/NET
    1560 Broadway, Suite 900
    Denver, CO 80202
	800–426–2873	Databases, bulletin boards, electronic mail, interactive applications

BRS
    1200 Route 7
    Latham, NY 12110
	800–345–4277	Databases, bulletin boards, electronic mail

CompuServe
    5000 Arlington Centre
       Blvd.
    Columbus, OH 43220
	800–848–8990	Databases, bulletin boards, electronic mail

Dialog
    3460 Hillview Avenue
    Palo Alto, CA 94304
	800–334–2564	Databases, electronic mail

This section of the chapter will describe the technology necessary for all existing applications to be available, and how communications are created, transmitted, and received. The health professional need not have an in-depth understanding of these technical issues, but a review of common terminology is useful.

Simkin and Dependahl (1987) identify five specific data *communication channels* that are common today for communications over long distances: twisted-pair wires, coaxial cable, microwaves, radio waves, and optical fibers. Although there are many different types of transmission channels for data communications, there remain only two distinctive types of signals—*digital* and *analog*. A digital signal is one that uses discrete pulses to represent data. These pulses may, for example, be either electrical or light pulses and are representative of the same two states that a bit may be in—"on" and "off." An analog signal is a continuous wave form that is "analogous" to the data represented. Figure 3.1 is a graphic representation of these two signals.

Transmission Speed

Of the five major transmission channels, only coaxial cables and twisted-pair wire are capable of both digital and analog transmission; microwave, radio wave, and optical fibers transmit only digital signals. Likewise, the speed at which data can be transmitted across these channels varies widely, and it is important to recognize that speed is a critical criterion for selection of options. Speed, however, is determined by several factors, including the *transmission characteristics* of the signal (e.g., serial or parallel transmission), *data transmission rate,* and the *bandwidth* of the channel used.

COMMUNICATIONS IN A COMPUTER ENVIRONMENT

Communication Channels

Figure 3.1. Analog versus digital signals.

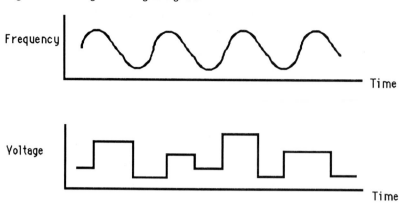

Signal Type	Limitations
Analog	Signal protection is necessary to prevent the introduction of "noise."
	Signal conversion is necessary so computers can use the information (computers can use only digital signals, so data must be converted from digital to analog for transmission, and then back to digital for use).
Digital	Signal protection is necessary to prevent the introduction of "noise."
	Attenuation (loss) of signal strength occurs over long distances.
	High-power requirements are necessary for digital transmission.

One of the more important characteristics that determines the speed and effectiveness of data communications is the nature in which the signal elements are transmitted—*serially* or in *parallel*. Recall that a byte may be partitioned into smaller elements called bits. To represent one character of information (the letter *A*) in binary form requires eight binary digits, for example, 0 0 1 0 0 0 0 1. These eight bits define one character of information. In serial transmission these eight bits are sent over a single wire sequentially, one bit at a time. Parallel transmission of the same data would require eight wires, and all eight bits would be transmitted simultaneously. The distinctions between serial and parallel transmission are graphically illustrated in figure 3.2.

Because of the nature of these signal characteristics, parallel transmission of information is much faster than serial transmission. However, parallel transmission has several distinct disadvantages over serial transmission, including the increased complexity of ensuring that all the bits to be transmitted together are ready at the same time; the problems that might occur if the data on one of the lines is slower or faster than the

Figure 3.2. Distinctions between serial and parallel data transmission.

Serial Transmission

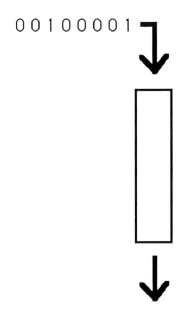

Parallel Transmission

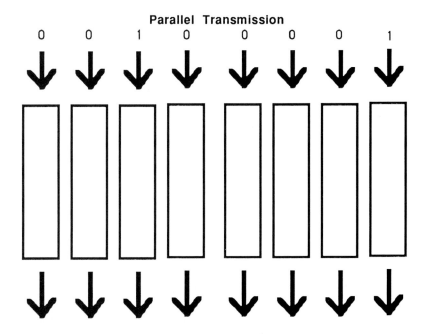

data on another line (e.g., ensuring that all eight bits arrive at their destination together is made more complex by distance); and the increased cost of the extra wires necessary for parallel transmission of data. Because of these problems, parallel transmission is more often used for transmission over short distances, and serial transmission is used for long distances.

Baud rate is the term most often used to describe the rate at which data are transmitted. The term *baud rate* comes from the French communications specialist Jean Maurice Baudot and refers to the number of signals transmitted per second—(twelve hundred baud is equivalent to twelve hundred bits per second). *Bandwidth* is the carrying capacity of the channel being used for transmission. Three types of bandwidth are commonly used: narrowband or baseband channels (e.g., telegraph lines) have a carrying capacity of approximately thirty characters per second; voiceband channels (e.g., telephone lines) can carry as many as one thousand characters of information per second; and broadband channels (e.g., coaxial cables, microwaves, fiber optics) can carry as many as several million characters per second. Modern fiber optics can carry up to fifty thousand channels on a half-inch diameter cable.

Communication Protocols

A *communications protocol* describes the entire process of communications between two points. In this case the term *protocol* refers to a set of agreements that ensure that both computers are talking the same language with the same rules. In order for information to be successfully transmitted, both points (stations) must be prepared to handle data in the same way. However, the process of transmitting data goes beyond transmission speed, channel of communication, and parallel or serial transmission. The communications protocol also includes conventions regarding the nature in which the data are to be communicated. These protocols are necessary to ensure that the data, once successfully received, can be understood.

One mechanism to ensure correct interpretation of data is to select between *synchronous* and *asynchronous* transmission of data. Simkin (1987, p. 666) defines synchronous data transmission as "the transmission of data in a long, continuous data stream and the use of synchronized timing clocks to send, and later decipher, this data." He goes on to define asynchronous data transmission as using "one or more 'start bits' and 'stop bits' for each character to indicate the beginning and ending of a character, instead of a synchronized timing pattern" (p. 653).

The primary advantage to synchronous transmission is its speed—there is no need to add start and stop bits so that the receiver knows the beginning and end of each character of data being transmitted. Synchronous transmission also allows transmission to many recipients simultaneously. However, synchronous transmission depends upon the accuracy of the timing signals, and the equipment is more costly than asynchronous communications equipment.

Asynchronous communications protocols have their advantages as well and are the most commonly used protocols today. There is no need for timing clocks, the equipment is less costly, and the transmission of each character of information is relatively independent of all others due to the start and stop bits that are part of the message. These bits, however, add to the length of the message and therefore increase transmission time.

The terms *simplex, half-duplex and full-duplex* transmission refer to protocols regarding the physical transmission of information between points. *Simplex* refers to one-way communications only, and duplex to two-way communications. It is worth examining more completely how these protocols differ.

With simplex transmission of data, information can go only in one direction—from a transmitter to a receiving station. An example of simplex transmission is the transmission of signals from a radio station to a radio: there is currently no mechanism that allows the car or home radio to communicate back to the transmitter at the station. Duplex transmission occurs when both stations are capable of receiving and transmitting information. There are two different protocols for duplex transmission—half duplex and full duplex. With half-duplex transmission one station must complete its transmission before being able to receive any information. With full-duplex transmission information may be exchanged in both directions simultaneously. An example will serve to clarify the distinction. A person speaking over a walkie-talkie will not be able to receive any information at the same time. However, two people talking on a telephone can talk at the same time (even though this is probably not the best method for understanding one another). All of these terms and their definitions are summarized in exhibit 3.1.

As stated earlier, data communications occur internally within the computer, between the computer and peripheral devices (e.g., printers), and between computers themselves. The latter kind of communication occurs in two primary ways, either in *networks* or by *telecommunications*. A network is an organized pathway linking several computer systems and may be either a *local-area network (LAN)* or a *wide-area network (WAN)*.

A LAN is characterized by relatively close proximity between *nodes* (computers, terminals, or peripherals) on the system. The distance is often no more than a few hundred feet. A WAN may involve many hundreds or thousands of miles of communication channels between nodes.

Networks and *distributed processing* are growing in importance in today's computing environment, and there are many reasons why this is so. Simkin and Dependahl (1987) suggest at least six primary reasons for the growing number of networks in professional settings: (1) they facilitate communication between key personnel in any environment by

Networks to Facilitate Communications

EXHIBIT 3.1

SUMMARY OF COMMUNICATION TERMS

Many people consider communications the most difficult aspect of computing to understand. It may be useful here to review the most commonly used terms.

A *communications channel* is the medium over which information is transmitted. There are five primary channels in common use today: coaxial cable, twisted-pair wires, microwaves, radio waves, and fiber-optic cables. The *signal* itself can be transmitted in one of two ways, either as a continuous (*analog*) signal or in discrete (*digital*) elements. The *speed* at which information can be communicated is affected by three factors: the *baud rate* (number of signals in the channel per second), the *bandwidth* (the carrying capacity of the channel), and whether the data elements are sent *serially* or in *parallel* (one bit at a time in a continuous stream, or one byte at a time over parallel wires).

There are certain agreements or *conventions* necessary to ensure interpretability of the information and understanding between sender and receiver. These conventions include *protocols* such as *synchronous* and *asynchronous* communications, conducted in one direction only (*simplex*), or in two directions (*half duplex* or *full duplex*).

use of such applications as electronic mail; (2) they improve communication speed and accuracy through instantaneous transmission of messages exactly as they are created; (3) they allow for the sharing of expensive peripheral equipment (e.g., hard-disk drives, CD-ROM drives, laser printers, plotters, and scanners) among several workstations; (4) they permit sharing of files with other authorized users on a network; (5) they permit sharing of software among users of a network when site licenses are purchased for file servers; and (6) they enable computers from a variety of vendors to communicate. Exhibit 3.2 describes site licenses and file servers.

There are many different configurations, on network structure, for LANs, and each has its advantages and disadvantages. Figure 3.3 illustrates the most common network topologies found in LANs.

A *switch network* is generally one of the simplest and least costly configurations. Its primary purpose is generally to allow multiple computers to share peripheral devices such as printers. In a switch network cables are extended from each computer into a single switch box, and one or more cables may extend from the switch box to one or more peripheral devices. By simply setting the switches on the box, any computer in the network may access any of the peripheral devices on the network. While functional for sharing peripheral devices, this type of network does not allow information sharing to occur between computers on the network (nodes). All of the remaining configurations allow for both resource (peripheral devices and software) and information (data)

EXHIBIT 3.2

SITE LICENSES AND FILE SERVERS

The current copyright laws prevent the unauthorized copying of software for more than one user at a time. Therefore, if an office or agency has six computers in a variety of locations, and the users at each of the computers want to use a particular piece of software, the laws require that a separate copy of the software be purchased for each station that will be using the application concurrently with others. This can be very costly. There are, however, two legal ways to reduce the cost and not limit the software utilization—the purchase of a site license, or a network version of the software.

A *site license* allows an agency or individual to make authorized copies of the application up to a specified number, and the cost of a site license is usually far less than the cost of purchasing the same number of individual packages. For example, a statistical-analysis package may cost $500 per copy. If an agency has six computers, purchasing a single copy for each station would cost $3,000. However, a site license may be available for $1,000, plus $200 for each additional copy. In this case, the total cost for the application software would be $2,200— a savings of $800. A site license is analogous to a volume discount found in other merchandise, and like volume discounts, the greater the number of units agreed upon, the greater the savings.

A characteristic of many networks is the availability of a *file server*. A file server is a central workstation, usually with a high-capacity hard-disk drive, which holds software and data files that can be accessed by all authorized users on the network. In this case the individual users at other workstations do not require a copy of the specific application, but can get access to it from the file server. It is illegal, however, to put a single-user version of any copyrighted application package on a file server for use by more than one person at a time. An agency, however, may purchase a *network version* of the application. As with a site license, the network version allows the agency to have more than one person using the software simultaneously. In addition, a network version will cost more money than a single-user version of any software.

Although a network version of an application may allow more than one user to access the application simultaneously, this does not mean that they may access the same files through that application simultaneously. This requires an additional level of sophistication that permits *multiuser* access to files. With multiuser access several different people on a network may simultaneously view and change the same data file, an arrangement that differs from two people using the same statistical package simultaneously.

Figure 3.3. Basic network configurations.

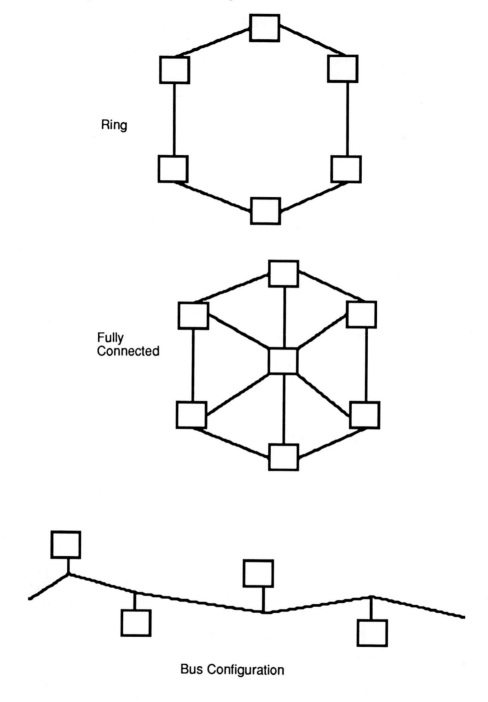

Ring

Fully
Connected

Bus Configuration

Communications

Figure 3.3. Basic network configurations (continued).

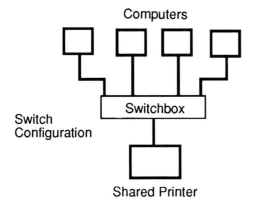

Computers

Switch
Configuration

Switchbox

Shared Printer

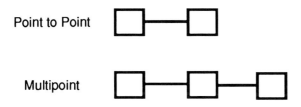

Point to Point

Multipoint

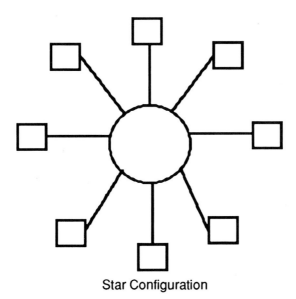

Star Configuration

sharing among the nodes. Each has advantages and disadvantages that must be considered in deciding on a configuration.

A *point-to-point,* or *multipoint,* network is a serial connection of computers. This kind of network allows for the sharing of information from station to station, with each station connected to no more than two other stations. The biggest drawback of a point-to-point or multipoint network is that a breakdown at any point in the serial chain will disable the network by isolating some nodes from others. To minimize this problem and to enhance the reliability of these networks, a *ring network* configuration is often the next option. If there is a break in the network at any node in the ring, communications can still be passed to each station by the unbroken connections. It is important to recognize, however, that neither point-to-point nor ring networks have a central node or *file server.* The absence of a file server prevents the sharing of software and centralized security or information sharing. Therefore, the communication that does occur across nodes in these two configurations is somewhat limited.

A *star network* is the first to provide a central node, called a file server or host computer. In this configuration several peripheral nodes (computers) are each connected to a file server. In the simplest star configuration, each node is connected only to the file server, but there are configurations based on the star typology in which each node is also connected to every other node. This is a *fully connected* star configuration. These fully connected configurations are often the most expensive type of LANs. However, the presence of a file server allows for centralized access to software, file backup, data security, and password protection for access to different network resources.

The final primary network configuration is called a *bus network.* In a bus network a single bidirectional cable serves as a pipeline between all nodes. This cable is capable of carrying synchronous messages between any of the nodes on the network. The bus network may have a central file server, but it requires costly equipment to configure in this manner.

In setting up a network there are a number of different choices available. A network may be set up by hardwiring a custom configuration, by using one of the many commercially available LAN configurations, or by using a telephone-based system (either a private branch exchange [PBX] or central office system [centrex]). In choosing among these options, it is worthwhile to note that custom-designing a network is very costly and probably unnecessary for most applications, considering the many choices of commercial networks (e.g., Ethernet, ARCnet, IBM Token Ring, Appletalk). The telephone-based system allows an agency to avoid rewiring between offices by using the existing telephone equipment already installed. Exhibit 3.3 provides an illustration of how network technology was put to use in the Department of Health Education at the University of Maryland.

Regardless of the network configuration selected, Simkin and Dependahl (1987, p. 270) identify several common problems of all LANs: (1) The cost may vary dramatically depending upon which configuration is chosen. (2) The use of any network always requires training for all the users. (3) The more complicated the network becomes, the greater the task of upkeep and management—and many networks require an individual specifically identified to maintain a network. (4) Once users experience the benefits of a smoothly operating network, they and the organization will become dependent upon its resources and capabilities; such dependency can be hazardous if the LAN crashes or fails. (5) Information/data security becomes a concern whenever multiple users have any access to the data of others. To minimize security problems requires specific attention to such issues as *file backup*, data *encryption*, and *password security*.

The term *telecommunication* refers to the sharing of information between computers by telephone. Telecommunications requires both hardware and software. This section will briefly describe the characteristics of both.

As stated earlier, today's computers deal almost exclusively with digital signals. Telephone lines transmit audio carrier frequency signals such as the human voice. In order to use the capabilities of the telephone system to communicate over long distances, the digital signals of the computer must be converted to audible frequencies for transmission and converted back to digital signals at the other end of the transmission for interpretation by the receiving computer. The device that does this is called a *modem*. A modem is capable of modulating (converting digital signals to audible carrier frequencies) and demodulating (converting audible carrier frequencies to digital signals), hence the term *mo-dem*.

Modems may be found in many configurations with a wide variety of capabilities. The most common are internal modems, external modems, and *acoustic couplers* (see figure 3.4). Internal modems often fit into internal spaces inside the computer; these spaces are called slots, and the platform that holds all the internal components is called the *motherboard* of the computer. External modems plug into serial ports, which are devices through which serial signals enter the computer. Acoustic couplers also plug into serial ports. The primary difference between acoustic couplers and the first two modems is the fact that a telephone headset must be placed into an acoustic coupler, thus requiring that all signals pass through the microphone and speaker elements of the headset. This reduces the reliability of transmission. Both internal and external modems are called direct-connect modems because there is no need to transmit signals through microphones and speakers.

By now it should be clear that both sending and receiving computers must have access to a great many pieces of information in order for effective communication to occur. Both computers have to be aware of the protocols being used for transmission and interpretation and must have

EXHIBIT 3.3

SETTING UP AN OFFICE NETWORK

As a large department of health education, we were recently faced with the need to network our office. This networking was deemed necessary for several reasons, including the importance of sharing information; the cost efficiency of sharing software; the need to increase telecommunications access; and the need to cut down on the mounting costs of diskettes. As in most universities the campus has a wide array of computers, with IBM and Macintosh computers the most prevalent. Our office had entered the computer world a few years earlier with Apple IIs. These were selected at the time because of the large amount of software in health promotion available for Apple IIs, and for the relatively low price if purchased through the Apple University Consortium.

In determining how best to network, we considered software needs, compatibility with the university Ethernet system, cost, speed, and flexibility for future expansion. We decided to use an Appletalk network (by Apple Computers) since we had mainly Apple hardware and the new Appletalk system allowed for Macintosh and Apple IIGS computers to network. Even Apple IIe's and IBMs could be added with some extra work. Incidentally, several other departments have excellent IBM networks, and we are all able to communicate effectively. We needed to phase in our system due to budget limitations. We found this extra time most helpful in giving us the opportunity to train secretaries and a core of faculty. We began by networking our core offices (secretaries and administrators), connecting five Apple IIGS computers and two Macintosh computers via an Appletalk network, and simply sharing our first laser printer.

The next step several months later was to add a dedicated file server (a Macintosh II with 80 megabyte hard disk), which gave full network capability, and we began sharing software and files. (In September 1989 we upgraded the file server to 160 megabytes.) We also began adding Macintosh computers as resources allowed. In faculty offices we have tried to add dot-matrix printers as well so that faculty can have draft-quality printouts when they cannot have access to the centralized laser printers. This option also lowers the demand on the laser printers. To access the network someone must have the correct password, and even then the person has access only to those files designated for personal use. Additional security is provided for any files of a very sensitive nature, such as personnel files or budgets, by an encryption program that is virtually impossible to enter without the password.

The final step was to add a connection to the campus Ethernet system. We accomplished this by installing a single gateway (a kinetics fast-path gateway) that gives all our Macintosh stations access to the university system. The gateway was installed at a much lower cost than the cost of a special gateway card for each individual computer. We can all conduct library searches, send messages to other faculty on campus or around the world, and communicate with our several mainframe computers. Administrators with passwords can access student records, personnel records, and even campus budgets. Currently we have fifteen Macintosh and five Apple IIGS computers, four laser printers, and twelve dot-matrix printers. Our next step was to add a high-speed tape backup system for the file server, a one-hour power backup, a high-quality surge protector system, and a CD-ROM player. In the future we have the flexibility to add whatever else comes along that makes sense for us. The system has worked very well. Its most challenging aspect, however, has been securing the resources and providing adequate training.

Note. Contributed by Dr. Glen G. Gilbert, Professor, Department of Health Education, University of Maryland.

Figure 3.4. Three types of modems.

Three types of modems: (a) internal modems built on communications "cards" that install inside a microcomputer or terminal, (b) external modems that connect to a microcomputer or terminal via a standard telephone jack, and (c) acoustic coupler modems that use telephone handsets.

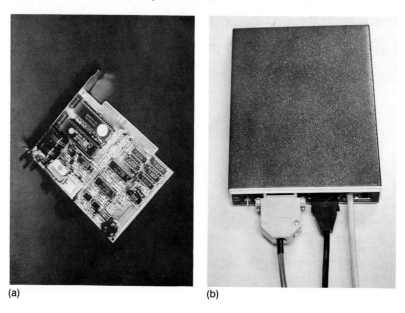

(a) (b)

(c)

instructions on how to deal with all aspects of the transmission as well as receipt of information. The set of instructions that accomplishes this task for the computer is called *communications software.* There are many such packages available either commercially or through freeware or shareware. However, the process cannot occur, even if the hardware is in place, unless the proper software is also available. Communications software is an application designed to mechanize all of the components of telecommunications, including containing information about various communication protocols, *uploading* files (sending files to another computer) and *downloading* files (receiving files from other computers).

SUMMARY

Telecommunications provides the capacity to extend the capabilities of computers in the practice of health education. Rapid sharing of information over long distances, availability of public-access database utilities, interactive teleconferencing, bulletin boards and electronic-mail systems, all provide some potential benefit to the practicing health educator. Perhaps the biggest problem with these capabilities lies specifically in the health educator's lack of training.

DISCUSSION QUESTIONS

1. With the extensive use of telecommunications capabilities available to health professionals today, what is the biggest need in terms of training health educators to use those capabilities?
2. Among the different types of services available to health professionals (e.g., bulletin boards, electronic mail, public-access databases), how can each be applied specifically to health education?
3. What are the advantages of teleconferencing? What are the disadvantages?

RECOMMENDED READINGS

Boutwell, B., & Sandefur, R. R. (1987). Biomedical communication: The next chapter. *Journal of Biocommunications. 14* (2), 4–6.
Cuandra/Elsevier. (1987). *Online databases in the medical and life sciences.* New York: Cuandra/Elsevier.
Grundner, T. M., & Garrett, R. E. (1986). Interactive medical telecomputing: An alternative approach to community health education. *The New England Journal of Medicine. 314* (15), 982–985.
Homan, J. M. (1986). End-user information utilities in the health sciences. *Bulletin of the Medical Library Association, 74* (1), 31–35.

4

INSTRUCTIONAL USES OF MICROCOMPUTERS IN HEALTH EDUCATION

By the completion of this chapter, the student will be able to

- differentiate between drill and practice, tutorials, problem solving, simulation, and game applications used for instructional purposes;
- recognize the characteristics of instructional materials that are important for their evaluation;
- distinguish between the different types of instructional applications;
- describe how computers can be used as instructional devices for training, evaluation of knowledge and skills, and in the delivery of health-education programs and services;
- recognize how widespread the instructional use of computers is in health education;
- distinguish between informatics and computer literacy;
- describe the range of potential objectives for training health educators in the use of computers;
- describe the major steps involved in acquiring and evaluating health-promotion software.

Computer literacy: An understanding and recognition of the capabilities and limitations of computer technology, including hardware and software. For health educators computer literacy also implies a recognition of the potential applications of this technology to the practice of health education and the training of health educators.

Computer-assisted instruction (CA):   The utilization of computer technology to provide instruction, assist in the instructional process, or manage data necessary to improve the instructional process. Related terms include computer-assisted learning (CAL), computer-based instruction (CBI), and computer-managed instruction (CMI).

Drill and practice: A form of computer-assisted instruction. In drill-and-practice programs, learners are given the opportunity to answer questions about material presented. The process is continued until a learner displays mastery of the material.

Games: A special form of simulation program used for recreation and learning. Games take many forms, but most often involve competition between learners or between a learner and the computer.

Informatics: A field of study that examines the use of information in a discipline.

Problem solving: A form of instructional software in which the learner uses the computer as a tool to solve complex problems.

Simulation: A model that represents real-world situations or problems. Computerized simulations are often used for training professionals (e.g., flight simulators) or testing skills (e.g., driving simulators). Computerized simulations of health-related scenarios (e.g., spread of pollution in the environment) train health educators to solve problems or to study how events can be altered by changing important elements of the problem.

Tutorials: A form of CAI, tutorials are used to present new information to a learner.

**Overview of
Instructional
Strategies and
Principles**

Since the early 1950s computers have held much promise for promoting and improving instructional capabilities of learners. The traditional taxonomy of *computer-assisted instructional (CAI)* applications includes the following five formats.

1. *Drill-and-practice applications.* These applications operate much like electronic flash cards: a problem is presented, a response is requested, feedback is given, a score is tallied, and the computer may provide summary diagnostics to a learner. In health education, drill and practice may be used to assist with the reinforcement of material learned in such areas as terminology.

2. *Tutorials.* These programs use branching based on student reponse. Depending upon a learner's responses to a particular section, the program may move to a different section. In this way not all learners are exposed to the same material. Such applications include all the necessary instruction and they usually allow the learner to ask for help, examples, rules, and review. As Saba and McCormick (1986, p. 363) suggest, a tutorial is "an extension of drill and practice but allows more feedback, since the student can move forward to new material or backward (remedial) depending on the response." An example of a health-education tutorial might be a program that teaches a learner the concepts of excess risk from epidemiology. Such a program would use the graphics capabilities and animation capacities of microcomputers to demonstrate the relationship between exposure to a risk factor and the subsequent probability of developing a disease.

3. *Problem solving:* In this kind of program the computer is used as a high-speed calculator. Problem solving is a tutorial in the sense that it helps learners see how to solve problems, but it maximizes the capabilities of computers by allowing students to work on discipline-specific problems. A problem-solving program might take the previous example on excess risk one step further. By providing mathematical problems and allowing a learner to calculate risk of disease based on varying exposure levels, it can help a student to improve understanding of the concepts.

4. *Simulation.* These applications copy existing systems and then let learners make decisions on system parameters in order to observe the resulting outcomes. A student or professional using simulations can experiment on very difficult problems and tasks with no threat to the system or to the student. In health education a simulation program may be used to test a variety of ways to minimize the problems associated with the spread of a disease in a community. In this case a learner might vary the number of people immunized against a disease and examine the effect on the subsequent number of cases of the disease.

Health educators may work with clients in any setting, such as a lab or classroom as shown in this photo.

5. *Games.* Games are a special form of simulation in which the computer becomes entertainer, data bank, desk calculator, and referee. Because they are such a widely used variation of simulations, and because they have some important characteristics that distinguish them from other simulations, they are regarded here as a fifth type of application. Whereas professional simulations attempt to clearly model, copy, or emulate real systems to be manipulated, games make more use of drama, fantasy, and competition. In games learners make decisions and then must react to the consequences of those decisions. For example, an animated game might involve a miniature submarine, which is injected into the bloodstream of a patient with cancer. The learner in this game must then pilot the submarine successfully to the site of the cancer and remove it before the patient dies. In games the challenge of winning points, or operating against a clock, often provides added enjoyment, but it is important to understand that the logic used in the design of games is very much like all other simulations.

These formats provide the framework for most applications in education. There are, however, a few characteristics that serve to discriminate between the best and worst applications. The best programs are those that pay close attention to learning theory and that include:

- Immediate response to learner queries and answers. If a learner is confused about a concept, additional information may be requested and subsequently provided to the learner.

- Responses that are determined by the learning sequences. As a learner moves through a program, the instructional sequence should be specific to the learner's needs. This is accomplished by assessing patterns of responses to questions posed by the computer and providing learning experiences geared to the learner. In this way the computer acts in the same way as programmed instruction.
- Learner self-pacing, allowing movement through a program at a comfortable pace. This pace should be determined by learner needs, experience, and ability.
- Record keeping on learner progress. This is an essential element if the instructional sequence is individualized.
- Random access to information. A learner should be able to pose any question relevant to the program and obtain an answer on demand at any time.
- Coordination with other media. Video and sound capabilities provided by other equipment may improve the instructional quality of a program. In this case a computer program may turn on a video disk player when appropriate so that a student can see a video sequence on the material presented. Most computers cannot provide this kind of video directly, but they can be hooked up to video players and screens, thereby controlling them for improved program quality.

The lessons learned by teachers who have spent years developing instructional materials are important because these same principles apply to the development and/or evaluation of computerized instructional materials. Eisele (1978) suggests that the most important matters we can consider as teachers include the following:

- appropriate learning outcomes for a group and individuals within that group;
- content or subject matter related to these outcomes;
- instructional activities that will introduce the desired behavior to the student, provide opportunities for acquiring the behavior, and give the learner opportunities to practice the behavior;
- the most appropriate media for transmitting the data to be learned;
- evaluation procedures and devices;
- appropriate and individualized content, activities, media, and evaluation procedures for each learner.

If these principles are effectively attended to, the following benefits and desirable teaching strategies are likely to follow:

- holding the attention of the learner throughout the instructional sequence;

- informing the learner of the benefits and goals that can be expected from the program;
- calling attention to relationships with already-familiar material in order to make the instructional sequence more worthwhile;
- using only material that is directly related to the learning task;
- offering guidance for learning at any point in the program and at the request of the learner;
- appraising performance and providing useful feedback to the learner;
- presenting material in such a way as to ensure that a learner sees its relevance to other issues, problems, or events;
- providing enough practice or feedback to ensure that the learner will retain the information.

Table 4.1 summarizes some important points about the instructional applications of computers. As the continuum moves toward capabilities that are unique to computers, the applications become more effective.

INSTRUCTIONAL APPLICATIONS OF COMPUTERS

As an instructional medium, computers can be used as informational, motivational, self-assessment, or monitoring devices. A large number of specific programs fit into these categories, including health-risk appraisals, dietary analyses, specific instructional content programs (using drill and practice or tutorial strategies), simulations, and games. Health-risk appraisals and dietary analyses are considered in chapter 5, "Health Assessments."

Among the many instructional areas in which these programs may be applied, three primary ones stand out: (1) the training, both preservice and in-service, of health educators and related professionals in information and skill areas; (2) the evaluation of knowledge and skills, including both testing and monitoring of competencies; and (3) the delivery of health-education programs and services to clients in clinical, classroom, community, and worksite settings. All of the instructional strategies (i.e., drill and practice, tutorial, problem solving, simulation, and games) can be applied to each of these areas.

Training Health Professionals

The literature in this area is heavily weighted toward those health professions that are clinically oriented. Moreover, there are two very different types of training used in the preparation of health professionals: the first aims at making health professionals computer literate, the second aims at using computers to train health professionals in their own field. The former is based on the assumption that no practicing health professional today can provide high-quality service to a client population without using the power provided by modern computer technology. Gross and Ellis (1987) report that "the proliferation of microcomputers and the introduction of fourth generation applications software have dramatically changed the computing needs and expectations of health

Table 4.1

Instructional Uses of Computers—A Continuum

CONTINUUM	PROGRAM CHARACTERISTICS
Greater Potential of Computer	Student-designed automation
	Student-developed simulations of real systems
	Open-ended problem solving
	Student-programmed automata
	Student-developed instruction
Increased Student Control	Exploration of simulated systems or environments
	Interactive information retrieval
	Generative computer-assisted instruction
	Instruction-management systems
	Calculation
Lesser Potential of Computer, Decreased Student Control	Tutorials
	Testing and record keeping
	Drill and practice

Note. Adapted from "How Should Computers Be Used in Learning?" by S. Milner and A. M. Wildberger, 1974, *Journal of Computer Based Instruction, 1,* pp. 7–12.

professionals. . . . More importantly, today's health professionals have to be able to critically assess their personal and professional computer needs and provide valuable guidance to those making system acquisition decisions" (p. 347). The latter approach, using the power of the technology as an effective instructional medium, is based on often-repeated research results which suggest that computers are an enjoyable, highly effective medium for individualizing instruction at all educational levels. Piggins et al. (1987) describe their conclusions following a pilot test at Harvard Medical School: "Based on the experience of the pilot project, the medical school administration, faculty, and students all agree that information technology is a vital education and information management tool. It is seen as a key resource in assisting the student in the mastery of the scientific basis of medicine and in the development of problem-solving skills (p. 445). These results appear to be common in today's academic centers for the training of all health professionals. However, there have been some major impediments to the spread of instructional use of computers in the health professions, and in health education in particular. Coggan, Hoppe, and Hadac (1984) summarize several ongoing problems with the educational use of computers:

1. Poor understanding of the educational capabilities of the technology and how to achieve its potential.

2. Lack of knowledge about the complexities of the educational system itself and how to integrate a new technology in such a way that is not threatening.

3. Weaknesses in the research data on efficacy and effectiveness with respect to attitude change.

Table 4.2

The Extent of Use of Microcomputers in Graduate Health Education Training Programs (N = 120)

INSTRUCTOR'S CLASSROOM USE OF COMPUTERS	PERCENT
Offered a course in microcomputer applications	20.0
Planned to offer a course in the near future	5.8
Required student to take course in other departments	25.8
Used computers in other health-education classes	38.3

Note. Adapted from *The Diffusion of a Curriculum Innovation in Higher Education: A Course in Microcomputer Applications for Health Educators* by E. A. Randolfi, 1986, unpublished doctoral dissertation, University of Oregon.

4. Technical problems with the medium itself, including poor reliability of earlier equipment and difficulty in programming sophisticated applications.

5. Production and distribution problems, including lack of faculty interest and incentives, and poor-quality applications.

6. High cost of hardware and software.

To these difficulties Piemme (1988) adds limitations on transferability of courseware and the fact that many CAI materials are the products of "Cottage Industries," resulting in much duplication of effort, as there is no easy way to trace all that is being done. Piemme disagrees somewhat with Coggan et al. by stating that there are many studies of the effectiveness of CAI, and that it has repeatedly been shown to be effective in its reduction of time for instruction and its beneficial effects on professional practice (Piemme, 1988, p. 369). Today, in most health professions, the computer is regarded as a standard and necessary instructional medium.

In an attempt to gauge the extent of use among professionals involved in the training of health educators, Randolfi (1986) conducted a national study of programs. He found a growing number of academic programs in health education following the same lead with the same conclusions common to the other health professions. Table 4.2 summarizes the results of one component of his survey which attempted to discover how many universities were using computers in their graduate training of health educators. There are, in fact, many ways in which computers can be used to train health professionals, and exhibit 4.1 provides an illustration of some of those ways.

Table 4.3 contains a partial list of some software useful in the training of health educators and related professionals. A review of this table reveals the wide variety of content in such software. Most of the software runs primarily on IBM-PCs and compatibles, Apple II series computers, and Apple Macintosh computers. When reviewing this table and others that list software, the reader should remember:

• There are several catalogs published periodically with complete and current information about such software.

EXHIBIT 4.1

INTEGRATING COMPUTER USE WITH THE HEALTH-EDUCATION CURRICULUM

We believe it is important to integrate computer use with several of our courses. This encourages the use of content-specific software and forces students to apply what they have learned in other classes. In our health-education methods and materials course, we teach word processing and require all assignments to be completed on a word processor.

One assignment in particular involves the integration of health and computer software. After introducing students to several word-processing packages (Print Shop™ [Broderbund Software], and Crossword Magic™ [L & S Computerware/Mindscape]), students are asked to construct a newsletter on an assigned topic for a specific population. Examples include a drug-prevention newsletter for a community coalition against drugs, a hospital health-education department conducting a patient-education program on cardiovascular risk reduction, and a public-school teacher communicating to parents about an upcoming sex-education unit.

Students are also asked to develop a two-page newsletter, including major heading, headlines, stories, and a crossword puzzle on the specific topic assigned. Most of these newsletters turn out first-class, and doing the assignment greatly enhances the students' computer skills as well as health-education skills.

Note. Contributed by Dr. Glen G. Gilbert, Chairperson, Department of Health Education, University of Maryland

Table 4.3

Selected List of Training Software for Health Professionals

TITLE	VENDOR	SYSTEM
AIDS for the Health Care Worker	MEDI-SIM, Inc.	IBM-PC, Apple II
Blueprint for Decision Making	MCE Inc.	Apple II
CAI Nursing Research	MOSBYSYSTEMS	Apple II, IBM-PC
Chronic Illness and Disability CAI	MOSBYSYSTEMS	Apple II, IBM-PC
Communicable Diseases in Children	MEDI-SIM, Inc.	Apple II, IBM-PC
Computer Literacy for Nurses	MEDI-SIM, Inc.	Apple II, IBM-PC
in the Control of Hypertension	MEDI-SIM, Inc.	Apple II, IBM-PC
Infant Nutrition: Newborn to Two Years	MEDI-SIM, Inc.	Apple II, IBM-PC
MacAnatomy	MacMedic Publications, Inc.	Macintosh
Maternal and Fetal Nutrition CAI	MOSBYSYSTEMS	Apple II, IBM-PC
Mental Health Concepts and Community Nursing	MEDI-Sim	Apple II, IBM-PC
Myocardial Infarction	MEDI-SIM, Inc.	Apple II, IBM-PC
Nursing Research CAI	MOSBYSYSTEMS	IBM-PC, Apple II
Principles of Pharmacology	Biosource Software	Apple II
Psychiatric Assessment CAI	MOSBYSYSTEMS	Apple II, IBM-PC
Shock	MEDI-SIM, Inc.	Apple II, IBM-PC

- There is no replacement for the careful evaluation of software for your specific needs (see section on evaluation of software).
- Both software and the field of health education change rapidly. To ensure up-to-date information, a health educator must continually reassess needs and the availability of resources.
- The appearance of software in these lists does not represent a recommendation based on quality.
- A complete list of vendors may be found in the appendix.

These applications in instructional settings primarily use the drill-and-practice paradigms, along with simulation capabilities, database potential, and computational ability of computers. Ordinarily, the most sophisticated applications are those combined with training and practice for licensure examinations. For example, there are several major programs available to help nurses practice for their licensure examinations, including

Evaluation of Knowledge and Skills

- NURSESTAR (available from C. V. Mosby, St. Louis), a program containing almost four hundred questions that follow the standard licensure format linking knowledge items to case studies;
- NUSRSIMS (available from J. B. Lippincott, Philadelphia,) which provides a series of clinical simulations in pediatrics, psychiatry, maternal/child, and medical/surgical areas. These simulations are designed to test the decision-making capabilities of nurses both in training and in service.

Many similar applications can be found in other health professions where licensure is available. In health education, public-school teachers have been certified for many years, but only in rare cases does certification require a licensure-type examination, and no major CAI testing systems have been found to help prepare health teachers for this form of licensure. However, all of this may change in the near future. Since 1978 the Task Force on the Professional Preparation and Practice of Health Educators has been helping to move the health-education profession toward another individual certification—Certified Health Education Specialists (CHES). The task force is now through with the preparation for such a certification process, and standardized testing will soon be available for obtaining this credential. This is a competency-based credential and should follow the lead of those in other professions. A microcomputer-based application to help health educators prepare for that examination will undoubtedly be available soon.

The delivery of health-education programs to clients involves many settings, including classroom, clinical, community, and worksite settings. Each of these settings carries with it a special set of challenges.

Delivery of Health Education to Disparate Settings

The *classroom* deals primarily with populations that are assumed to be generally healthy and not inherently motivated to assume full responsibility for their future health status. Time is constrained both in terms of total contact hours and the length of time allowed for classroom sessions. A health educator is often constrained by a disproportionate student/professional ratio, and school systems are among those least likely to provide high-budget dollars toward high technology for a "secondary subject" such as health education.

Clinical settings are primarily dominated by either those who are unhealthy or those who perceive themselves to be unhealthy. In these settings patients are anxious to see the health professional—the doctor or the nurse—and recognize that many peripheral activities will not be covered even by the most progressive insurance policies. Here patient health education is often regarded as one of those peripheral activities not covered by third-party reimbursement. Because of this, practitioners are less likely to commit resources to health education, and patients are less likely to respond very favorably.

In *community settings* public and community health professionals deal with very diverse populations. Many of the most important target populations are indigent, poor, or transient. Outreach programs are often a mainstay. When dealing with poor or transient populations in varied settings, technology often takes a backseat to personal contact as the primary health-education strategy.

In *worksite settings* technology is often available to assist with the business of making products, providing services, and earning profits. High levels of productivity are essential, and workers are often constrained by their perceptions of the motives of their employers. Moreover, it is difficult to get employers to release workers for health-promotion programs.

Although each of these settings presents a special series of problems to the health educator, they are not unique problems associated with technology. All health-education, patient-education, public and community health-education, and worksite health-promotion programs face these same constraints. Many are becoming easier to deal with as records of success become available. Increasing evidence of the efficacy and effectiveness of computer applications are also likely to enhance their use. Table 4.4 contains a sample list of CAI software available for the delivery of health-education programs in many of these settings. Although a great deal of software exists, there are still problems of quality that health educators in particular must face. Exhibit 4.2 discusses the origin of some of these problems.

SIMULATIONS

Simulations, and a special subset of simulations called games, have been so important in today's use of computers in health-related settings that they deserve special attention. In all cases the logic in developing games is very much the same as for all other simulations. Simulations are programs that simulate or copy existing systems, events, or happenings and

Table 4.4
Selected List of CAI Software

TITLE	VENDOR	SYSTEM
Healthlines	Wm. C. Brown Publishers	Apple II
Heart and Exercise	CompTech Sys. Design	Apple II
Human Genetic Disorders	HRM Software	Apple II
Improving Your Self Concept	MCE Inc.	Apple II
Nutri-Bytes	Public Interest Software	Apple II, IBM-PC
Nutrition Express	Public Interest Software	Apple II
Stress and the Young Adult	MCE Inc.	Apple II
Substance Abuse CAI	Substance Abuse Ed, Inc.	Apple II, IBM-PC
The Human Brain	Biosource Software	Apple II

EXHIBIT 4.2

WHY SO LITTLE HEALTH-PROMOTION SOFTWARE

I was rather taken aback recently to hear a colleague comment on how he had given copies of a copy-protected dietary software program to all his students. When I asked if he had permission to do so, he responded that his students could not afford it. When I noted that software companies cannot afford to publish for free, he took offense.

This brief incident summarizes one of the major reasons why there is so little high-quality health-promotion software. The market at present is still limited when compared to other markets such as business or reading education. Companies cannot stay in operation without sales. Already several high-quality programs in health promotion are no longer available because the company is out of business or larger companies do not find a big enough profit margin to continue handling such items. As health educators, we need to set a positive role model in this regard.

Note. Contributed by Dr. Glen G. Gilbert, Chairperson, Department of Health Education, University of Maryland.

then ask the user to make decisions that will alter the system. Simulation is thus a technique rather than a kind of logic.

These are some of the primary advantages of simulations and games:

1. They permit controlled experimentation with the opportunity to consider many factors, manipulate many individual units, consider alternate policies, and permit little or no disturbance of the actual system.

2. They provide effective training tools when sophisticated skills are needed.

3. They provide operational insight into systems.

4. They dispel myths about the operation of systems.

5. They make programming and practice more effective.

These advantages occur at some cost:

1. The development of sophisticated models is especially costly.

2. Simulations and games often require fast, high-capacity computers.

3. These kinds of programs can take long periods of time to develop and test.

Simulation is a technique that provides an effective means of testing, evaluating, and manipulating a proposed system without any direct effect on the real system. Several hours, days, weeks, or even years of operation can be simulated in a matter of minutes on a microcomputer. In most cases simulation is not a precise analog of the actual system, but rather reflects a symbolic representation of that system. It can, however, provide experiences and measurement that cannot be obtained in any other way.

EVALUATION OF COMPUTER APPLICATIONS IN HEALTH EDUCATION

The literature is extensive in the area of instructional applications in health-education work. Well-designed CAI reduces time on task (Piemme, 1988; Eberts, 1986), and patients feel comfortable interacting with computers while perceiving positive benefits from the interaction (Donovan et al., 1983). There is an extensive history of many applications covering a wide array of health conditions, including cancer (Cook, 1982), hypertension (Donovan, 1983), postmyocardial infarction (Lyons, Krasnowski, & Greenstein, 1982), health promotion (Naditch, 1983), prenatal education (Yates, 1982), venereal disease (Van Cura et al., 1975), alcoholism (Kadden & Wetstone, 1982), nutrition (Dennison, 1982), diabetes (Mazzola, Rowe, & Rowe, 1983; Wheeler, Wheeler, Ours, & Snider, 1983), mental health (Slack & Slack, 1977), and early childhood health education (Anderson, Needle, & Masow, 1986). Just as extensive is the literature on settings, including schools (Anderson et al., 1986), clinics (Ellis, Raines, & Hakanson, 1981; Somand, 1981), communities (epidemiologic studies: LaVenture et al., 1982; community health nursing: O'Grady, 1984; preschool screening: Robertson, Mc-Donnell, & Scott, 1976), and worksites (Naditch, 1983).

INFORMATICS VS COMPUTER LITERACY FOR HEALTH EDUCATORS

The emerging field of *informatics* is so new that its members cannot clearly decide on a definition. In a study conducted by Greenes & Seigel (1987, p. 414), he found that three definitions stood out among others:

1. The application of computer and information science to medicine and health services.

2. The field concerned with the properties of medical information (i.e., data, information, knowledge) and its processing.

3. A term that encompasses information science, information engineering, and information technology used for medical practice, medical education, and medical research.

At the Twelfth Annual Meeting of the Symposium on Computer Applications in Medical Care, Romano and Heller (1988) presented a curriculum model for graduate specialization in nursing informatics. In it they describe the kind of study that a specialist in nursing informatics would follow: identification of the properties, structure, use, and flow of clinical and management information from the patient to the health-care provider, and subsequently throughout the health-care organization; assessment of real and potential problems related to the communication, accessibility, availability, and use of information for clinical and administrative decision making; analysis of the cause and scope of information-type problems and the determination of priorities for investigation; the delineation of alternative methods of information handling and of system-design option; the orchestration of change; and evaluation of the cost/risks in relation to the benefits or effectiveness of information technologies. Exhibit 4.3 contains a review of the objectives of a nursing informatics program.

As these objectives and goals indicate, informatics, though important, represents a highly specialized area of study. Computer literacy for health educators is much less demanding and a more critical need for all health educators. Practicing health educators need not become computer specialists, but they do need to know how to apply the technology for professional benefits. The objectives found in table 4.5 provide a more realistic set of expectations for an introductory course in computer literacy for health educators. These objectives provide an introduction to the many potential applications of computers in health-education and related settings and should result in a familiarity that encourages experimentation and use. Emphasis should be placed on the use of applications rather than on programming. While there may be some controversy about these two very different approaches, Randolfi's (1986) study indicated that the use of existing applications rather than programming is preferred by most health educators.

The area of health promotion is a relatively new field, and the delivery system is multifaceted. The quantity and quality of software varies tremendously. Many programs have been written by persons with inadequate background in health or health education. The result is clearly a case of caveat emptor—let the buyer beware. The following guidelines, though not exhaustive, should provide some basic information to help one become an informed evaluator and consumer of health-promotion software.

1. Assess your needs. Before purchasing software, carefully examine your personal software needs. Make a list of your intended uses of the software before you visit a store or place an order. Don't be too

EVALUATING HEALTH-PROMOTION SOFTWARE

EXHIBIT 4.3

EDUCATIONAL SPECIALIZATION IN NURSING INFORMATICS

Those completing a program in nursing informatics will be able to

1. analyze nursing-information requirements for clinical- and management-information systems;
2. analyze information needs and technological issues related to productivity and quality-assurance programs in nursing;
3. develop strategies to manage technological and organizational change and innovation;
4. apply management and nursing theories and information science to the planning, development, implementation, and administration of nursing-information systems;
5. evaluate the effectiveness of nursing-information systems in patient-care delivery;
6. define methodologies related to technology and engineering planning for information systems in health care and nursing;
7. apply concepts of budget, staffing, and financial management to the design of management-information systems;
8. apply concepts of nursing theory and research to the design of health-care clinical-information systems;
9. develop and implement user-training programs to support the utilization of clinical- and management-information systems;
10. analyze the contribution of information technology to nursing education, administration, clinical practice, and research;
11. examine the political, social, ethical, and influential forces in health care as they relate to the use of information technology and management;
12. evaluate hardware, software, and vendor support for information technologies that underpin clinical and management decisions in nursing;
13. examine database-management principles in relation to nursing-information system file structures;
14. apply concepts of programming logic to the analysis of a simple computer program.

Note. From "Curriculum Model for Graduate Specialization in Nursing Informatics" by C. A. Romano and B. R. Heller, 1988, in *Proceedings of the Twelfth Annual Symposium on Computer Applications in Medical Care*, pp. 343–349, New York: Institute of Electrical and Electronic Engineers.

Table 4.5

Sample Goals and Objectives for an Introductory Computer-Literacy Course for Health Educators

COURSE DESCRIPTION	GENERAL COURSE OBJECTIVES	SPECIFIC COURSE GOALS
Microcomputer Applications in Health Education is a course designed for students with little or no previous experience with microcomputers. The course will be applications oriented, with an introduction to the potential uses of microcomputers in the field of health education and related fields.	By the completion of this course, students will have 1. an understanding of the capabilities and limitations of microcomputers; 2. an understanding of the instructional, database, text-processing, and administrative applications of microcomputers in health education; 3. an understanding of how to evaluate and select hardware and software for personal and professional applications; 4. hands-on experience with microcomputers.	1. Describe the general capabilities and limitations of microcomputers and microcomputer systems. 2. Identify ways in which microcomputers can be used in health-related settings as (a) motivational devices; (b) teaching tools; and (c) tools for the reinforcement of learning. 3. Describe the ways in which microcomputers can be used in health-related settings as an administrative tool for information processing, word processing, database management, and data processing. 4. Describe the ways in which microcomputers can be used in health-related settings as a clinical tool for computer-assisted clinical decision making; clinical laboratory subsystems; physiologic monitoring systems; pattern recognition; and as an aid to the handicapped. 5. Describe the ways in which microcomputers can be used in health-related settings as a research tool to acquire data; manage data; manipulate data; and analyze data. 6. Describe characteristics that differentiate several popular microcomputer systems and that make them desirable for specific applications.

easily impressed with the advertised features of today's software; always keep in mind that if it does not fit your specific needs, it is not worth buying.

2. Examine documentation and author's credentials. The mystique surrounding the computer has given rise to some peculiar practices. Whereas it would be unacceptable for any journal or text author to make claims without proper documentation, many of the presently available health programs offer health-risk appraisals and other predictions or information without adequately explaining formulas or references. Unfortunately, there seems to be something about the magical box in the computer that makes this practice acceptable to the uninformed. Every health program should provide information on the team or individual that developed the software. It should include their credentials and explain the development process. If this information is not included, contact the company and ask for it. The program should also detail assumptions and sources. The educational objectives of the program should be clearly presented and the appropriate audience indicated. Be wary of programs that claim they are appropriate for everyone.

3. Ask for recommendations. Only a small number of health-promotion software programs have been critically reviewed by health professionals. Reviews can obviously be very helpful; contact with someone who is using the software is also an excellent source of information. Although there is currently no single best source for this kind of information, *Health Education* and other journals do occasionally run software reviews.

4. Try the software. Perhaps the best way to determine if the software is appropriate for your use is to try it. Good software stores will not hesitate to let you sit down and use a program before you buy it. Many companies will allow you to preview a copy of a program, though some do not allow mailed previews because of widespread software "piracy" (see chapter 8 for a discussion on piracy). It is also an uncommon practice to send demonstration copies of inexpensive programs. Some programs are very difficult to use, and the only way to be certain is to give them a try. Do not be overly impressed with packaging or fancy manuals. Some manuals are written by individuals unfamiliar with the program, and others are written by authors who assume you know as much about programming as they do. Well-written manuals are the exception.

5. Consider cost. Cost is an obvious limitation, but you should remember that in many cases it has little relationship to the quality of the product. Programs for under one hundred dollars are sometimes superior to programs that sell for over one thousand dollars.

6. Examine support and training promises provided with the software. Expensive software should provide both training and a "hotline" number for assistance. Less-expensive software should include a telephone number for assistance and a quality instruction manual.

EXHIBIT 4.4

QUICK HEALTH-PROMOTION
SOFTWARE REVIEW

1. Have you conducted an appropriate needs assessment and determined that this program meets your needs?

2. Is there evidence of a good health-education basis for the software? (Author's credentials in health, appropriate advisory help, etc.)

3. Is the manual easy to follow, and have you been able to find answers for two or three questions without difficulty?

4. Have you personally tried the software, or do you have recommendations from more than two people whom you trust and who have similar needs?

5. Is the cost reasonable for what you will receive?

6. If the program costs one hundred dollars or more, is there a helpline, and have you called it to see what kind of help is available?

7. Does the program use the capabilities of the computer, or would it be just as effective as a book or other medium?

8. Has the program been pilot tested with an audience comparable to your intended audience, with good results?

9. Will the program run on your system, or does it warrant purchase of special hardware?

10. Are you reasonably certain that this is the best program you can find to accomplish this task? (It is very upsetting to find another, better, program at lower cost a few weeks after making an important purchase.)

If you cannot answer yes to all questions, it is time to reevaluate your selection. Do not purchase until you can answer yes to all questions.

Note. Contributed by Dr. Glen G. Gilbert, Chairperson, Department of Health Education, University of Maryland.

---

7. Consider compatibility issues. As you know, not all software will work on all hardware. This is a serious limitation of health-promotion software. Currently more health-promotion software is available for the Apple II series, and IBM and Macintosh are acquiring more. It is imperative that the software you choose works with your equipment. Most experts suggest selecting software before choosing hardware.

The software review in exhibit 4.4 provides specific questions that will help you meet these seven criteria of software evaluation.

Exhibit 4.5 contains a detailed checklist for evaluating instructional software.

EXHIBIT 4.5

CHECKLIST FOR EVALUATING
INSTRUCTIONAL SOFTWARE

Program Content

☐ • The program content is accurate.

☐ • The program has education potential.

☐ • The program is free of stereotypes.

☐ • The intended target audience is identified clearly.

Program Objectives

☐ • Instructional objectives are clearly stated in the program.

☐ • Instructional objectives are presented in documentation.

☐ • The material is presented in a manner suggesting that the objectives are achievable.

☐ • If the program is lengthy, it is divided into logical subunits.

Program Instructions

☐ • The instructions for operating the program are effectively presented in documentation.

☐ • The instructions are available to the learner on screen during operation of the program.

☐ • The instructions are clearly stated and unambiguous.

☐ • A learner can bypass instructions if desired.

Program Operation

☐ • The program is easy to use if intended for novices.

☐ • The operation of the program is not distracting from the instructional sequence.

☐ • There are no lengthy delays in the operation of the program.

☐ • The program may be easily "crashed."

☐ • The program is free from programming errors.

☐ • The program can handle learner input constantly throughout.

☐ • The program can handle inappropriate input effectively.

☐ • The instructional screens are uncluttered and easy to read.

☐ • The program allows a learner to proceed in a self-paced manner.

☐ • The learner is able to move easily to different sections of the program.

- ☐ • The learner is able to exit the program as desired.
- ☐ • The language level and reading level are appropriate for the target audience.

Instructional Uses

- ☐ • The program begins with an educational assessment.
- ☐ • Graphics and sound are used appropriately and effectively to enhance learning.
- ☐ • Sound may be turned off by the learner.
- ☐ • Graphics and sound serve an educational function.
- ☐ • Visuals are well designed and technically sound.
- ☐ • Rewards are appropriately used.
- ☐ • "Hints" and assistance are offered as needed.
- ☐ • Multiple attempts to answer questions or solve problems are permitted.
- ☐ • Response to incorrect or inappropriate answers is handled in a nonthreatening manner.
- ☐ • Only one idea is presented at a time.
- ☐ • The instructional capabilities of the computer are used appropriately.
- ☐ • Learner input may be corrected or changed easily.
- ☐ • Instructional sequences are logically ordered.
- ☐ • Student progress is monitored.
- ☐ • Educational prescriptions are provided.

Documentation

- ☐ • A teacher-and-student guide is provided with the program.
- ☐ • Thorough descriptions of program operation are provided.
- ☐ • Sample screen displays and printouts are demonstrated.
- ☐ • References on related material are provided.
- ☐ • The documentation is clearly written.
- ☐ • The documentation is well organized.

Adapted from "Guidelines for Developing Health Education Software" by D. Horne and R. S. Gold, 1983, *Health Education, 14* (3), pp. 85–86.

SUMMARY

This chapter has provided an overview of the broad range of health-education instructional applications available on microcomputers, including drill and practice, tutorial, problem solving, situations, and games. The greater the student/client involvement in the program, and the more active the learner, the greater the potential for instructional benefit. Instructional applications in health education can serve many purposes, including the training of health educators, the teaching and evaluation of knowledge and skills, and the delivery of health-education programs and services to many locations and settings.

Although computers have been available for many years, the extent of their use in health education is somewhat limited. This scarcity of software instruction in the field is often the result of inadequate preparation of health educators and the lack of high-quality programs. Guidelines have been provided in this chapter to assist in the evaluation and acquisition of software, including conducting a needs assessment, evaluating the content of a program, checking credentials of the authors and the adequacy of the documentation, obtaining recommendations from others who have used the programs, and evaluating cost.

DISCUSSION QUESTIONS

1. Why do you think a great many more applications exist for the training of allied health professionals other than health educators?

2. What training applications do you think should be developed for health education?

3. Which instructional setting holds the most promise for the application of technology? the least?

4. Which instructional area holds the most promise for the application of technology? the least?

RECOMMENDED READINGS

Deardorff, W. W. (1986). Computerized health education: A comparison with traditional formats. *Health Education Quarterly, 13* (1), 61–72.

Ellis, L. B. M., Raines, J. R., & Hakanson, N. (1981). Health education using microcomputers. I. Initial acceptability. *Preventive Medicine, 10* (1), 77–84.

Ellis, L. B. M., Raines, J. R., & Hakanson, N. (1982). Health education using microcomputers. II: One year in the clinic. *Preventive Medicine, 11* (2) 212–224.

Gustafson, D. H., Bosworth, K., Chewning, B., et al. (1987). Computer-based health promotion: Combining technological advances with problem-solving. *Annual Review of Public Health, 8,* 387–415.

5

HEALTH ASSESSMENTS

By the completion of this chapter, the student will be able to

- describe the potential uses of health appraisals;
- summarize the history of the use of health-risk appraisals;
- list the potential benefits and problems with the use of the full range of health appraisals, including health-risk appraisals, dietary analyses, fitness assessments, and stress appraisals;
- describe the variety of ways in which these applications can be utilized;
- identify the limitations of such appraisals conducted by computer.

K E Y   W O R D S   &   P H R A S E S

Anthropometric measures: Measures of either size or girth of different parts of the body, or the capacity of different body systems.

Body composition: Measures of the physical stature of the human body, particularly percentage of body fat.

Computerized health assessments: The application of computerized strategies to assess different levels of health or risk to health.

Dietary analyses: Assessments of dietary behavior, including nutritional composition of someone's diet, or assessment of personal recommended daily allowances of different nutrients.

Exercise prescriptions: A sophisticated mechanism for providing a recommendation for exercise following an appropriate assessment of an individual's needs and exercise capacity.

Fitness appraisals: Assessment of different aspects of individual fitness (e.g., cardiorespiratory fitness, body composition).

Health-risk appraisals: Assessment of an individual's overall health risk based on life-style choices, genetic predisposition, health behaviors, and other measures.

Stress assessments: Measurement of sources and stress on an individual and/or coping skills.

INTRODUCTION

Computerized health assessments used by health educators can be considered analogous to screening techniques. This chapter will examine several different types of computerized assessment techniques; however, it will be useful to begin with a review of the definition of screening (see exhibit 5.1) and to follow that with a brief overview of issues related to assessments of health status.

Health professionals use many different strategies in assessing health status. Among them are observation, health histories, *anthropometric* measurements, and diagnostic tests. These all contribute in a slightly different way to the assessment of health status. Although this chapter is concerned with the application of computerized health assessments, it is important for the health professional to recognize both the potential and limitations of these strategies. The principal assessments examined in this chapter include *health-risk appraisals, dietary analyses, fitness appraisals,* and *stress-assessment software.* In examining each of these general areas, both the potentials and the problems will be reviewed.

HEALTH-RISK APPRAISALS

You may recall that Green (1978) has defined health education as "any combination of learning opportunities designed to facilitate voluntary adaptation of behavior which will improve or maintain health." To that end Fielding (1982, p. 338) reports that health-risk appraisal (HRA) is potentially useful because it can

- serve to gauge the risk of a defined population for a number of preventable diseases;
- serve as a sensitive indicator of community health complementing morbidity and mortality statistics;
- be put to work to recognize and quantify insurance-relevant health risks under the individual's control and help set life-insurance rates based on these risk levels;
- provide a permanent document with personalized information that can be taken home, consulted at will, discussed with family, and used to track progress (or lack of it) in ameliorating health risks over time;
- provide a feasible way for risk-reduction programs to give feedback on "silent" risk indicators such as blood pressure, cholesterol, or seat-belt use;
- provide reinforcement, which should in turn support continuation of the desirable behavior.

Wagner, Beery, Schoenbach, and Graham (1982, p. 347) suggest a number of characteristics that make HRAs particularly attractive to health educators:

- They provide a rationale and teaching aid to focus discussions of health and behavior.

Health Assessments

EXHIBIT 5.1

THEORETICAL DEFINITIONS OF SCREENING

Screening is defined as the presumptive identification of unrecognized disease or defect by the application of tests, examinations, or other procedures which can be applied rapidly to sort out apparently well persons who probably have a disease from those who probably do not. A screening test is not intended to be diagnostic. Persons with positive or suspicious findings must be referred to their physicians for diagnosis and necessary treatment.

—Commission on Chronic Illness, 1957

A screening test is used to separate from a large group of apparently well persons those who have a high probability of having the disease under study, so that they may be given a diagnostic work-up and, if diseased, brought to treatment. Screening is applied to groups, and is in reference to one disease. Screening tests have one criterion, and there is one cut-off point beyond which patients are classified as positive (diseased). Screening tests are interpreted by this single objective criterion, rather than by a subjective judgment or evaluation of a number of symptoms, signs, and laboratory findings, as in diagnosis.

Screening test results are arbitrary and final. Diagnosis is applied to single patients who are sick. All diseases are considered. Diagnosis is not final, but modified in light of new evidence. Diagnosis is the sum of all evidence. Screening and diagnosis are not competing, but are different procedures, and different criteria apply to each.

—Study Guide to Epidemiology and Statistics, 1979, p. 59

- They can rely on self-administered questionnaires, simple physiologic measurements, and computer-assisted calculations, making their application to large groups feasible, efficient, and relatively inexpensive.

- They have all the trappings of modern science with reference to studies, precise numbers, and computer-printed reports and are, therefore, consistent with the established values of many segments of American society.

- They are consonant with current thinking and publicity about the role of life-style in disease etiology.

- Their data-gathering devices, computer software, and other aspects can be marketed as a package.

Some Background on Health-Risk Appraisals

Health-risk appraisal is a term used to represent a family of techniques and applications that provide the basis for an estimate of an individual's risk of death. These estimates are often used to make recommendations for behavioral changes designed to reduce those risks. Health-risk appraisals allow individuals to assess their risks, to understand how those risks affect their health and well-being, and to take positive action regarding their health and well-being. Beery et al. (1986) suggest that the development of HRAs "reflects the convergence of several trends, each of which contributes to the current interest in the appraisal and reduction of health risks (p. 2)." Most pertinent among these according to this study are

- the continuing orientation of the health professional toward preventive medicine;
- the current focus on chronic diseases as a public-health priority, now that infectious diseases are increasingly brought under control;
- the existence of major prospective studies of disease risk;
- the continuing growth of family medicine;
- a shift away from medical education that is primarily disease oriented;
- growing interest in health promotion;
- the increasing use of computers in medical care.

Fielding (1982) reminds us that the original intention of Lewis Robbins, the father and indefatigable champion of health risk appraisal, was to develop instruments that physicians could put to practical use in counseling patients. Ironically, use among physicians has risen slowly. . . . Restricting the use of health risk appraisals to physicians, however, is neither feasible nor desirable. A physician telling a patient that he or she must stop smoking to reduce health risk may have less effect than a psychologist or other professional with appropriate training who can also teach him or her how to reinforce the decision to quit, how to control stress likely to result from trying to quit, and how to improve the odds of long-term abstinence. (p. 338)

Although originally seen primarily as a motivational tool to stimulate behavioral change (Lauzon, 1977), HRA has been used for many purposes according to Beery et al. (1986, p. 37), including:

- to stimulate interest and participation in health-promotion and disease-prevention programs;
- to communicate general information on the relationship between health and the concepts of relative risk;
- to communicate specific information on risk behaviors and high-risk individuals;
- to induce behavioral change;
- to structure interaction between counselor and client;
- to train physicians and reorient medical practice toward prevention;
- to screen asymptomatic persons for medical problems;
- to identify high-risk persons most in need of screening tests;

- to develop a data-base for epidemiologic research and health planning;
- to provide an index of health risk and health-related behaviors.

Because of the potentially broad applications of these techniques, HRA has become more familiar to health educators and widely used by them in a variety of settings.

Applications

As early as 1984 the U.S. Office of Disease Prevention/Health Promotion, through the National Health Information Clearinghouse, identified more than sixty commercially available HRAs—many available for microcomputers. They ranged in style and capacity from a ten-question self-scored instrument to a twenty-five page assessment that was sent to a vendor for analysis. Among those available as stand-alone computerized applications were quality-of-life assessments, assessments of the probability of contracting a chronic disease, and the generalized applications most common to HRA technology.

The number of applications available are too numerous to review in detail in this chapter, and the nature of the applications are so different that there really is no standard to present as representative of the entire group. However, table 5.1 contains an overview of the kinds of information that may be available from most health-risk appraisals. An examination of this table reveals that an HRA can be used to assess the age-, gender-, and race-specific long-term risks to health. Based on this assessment, the program can branch to a series of predictive questions designed to gather more information about the individual and generate even more specific estimates of risk. Most programs will end by making recommendations for changes in behavior which would result in a reduction of the individual's risk. This ability to calculate risk, and to demonstrate potential changes in risk if behavior is modified, provides the greatest motivation for the client.

Some Problems and Warnings

A number of reviews are available detailing the potential benefits and problems associated with the use of HRAs for these purposes (Beery et al., 1981; Beery et al., 1986; Dunton & Perkins, 1985; Imrey, 1985). Moreover, in 1981 the Society of Prospective Medicine published guidelines for health-risk-appraisal systems. Among the essentials proposed were

- a written statement of the objectives and limitations of the program;
- evidence of a scientific base;
- appropriate risk-reduction resources made available to participants;
- sound organization of risk-appraisal/reduction programs by a competent staff in accordance with stated objectives;

Health Assessments   131

Table 5.1
Ten Leading Causes of Death by Age, Gender, and Race

AGE _____ GENDER _____

RACE _____ NAME _____

LEADING CAUSES OF DEATH	INITIAL RISK	FINAL RISK
_____	_____	_____
_____	_____	_____
_____	_____	_____
_____	_____	_____
_____	_____	_____
_____	_____	_____
_____	_____	_____
_____	_____	_____
_____	_____	_____
_____	_____	_____

- clear appraisal results made available with recommendations to consult an appropriate health provider when needed;
- assured confidentiality of all data;
- periodic evaluation of the program in relation to objectives.

Although these recommendations are reasonable standards, and they address many of the concerns raised about HRAs, my own concern is that not enough people are being trained to understand these principles. The Association for the Advancement of Health Education has identified more than 350 institutions of higher education in which degrees in health education are offered at the baccalaureate, master's, and doctoral levels. Moreover, there are approximately 30 schools or programs of public health, and several hundred medical schools training primary-care practitioners. How many of these approximately 600 institutions are teaching people how to use HRAs? We do not know.

I will conclude this section with some recommendations made by Beery et al. (1986, p. 61), which directly address some of the concerns raised about HRAs:

1. An HRA should be used in a one-on-one, or small-group, educational or counseling setting.

2. An HRA may be presented to clients as a convenient and interesting way to personalize statistics relating health behavior to disease risk.

3. Interpretation of HRA feedback appears to be essential and should be done by someone trained in the meaning of HRA results and in broader issues relevant to health promotion and disease prevention. Giving appraisal results over the telephone or by mail is inadvisable.

4. The degree of emphasis a counselor puts on a particular behavior should reflect the adequacy of the database as well as the documented importance for risk or mortality and morbidity.

5. Measurement of physiological variables that may lead to medical referral, such as blood pressure, needs to be carried out with sufficient precision to avoid false positives and attendant costs.

6. The most appropriate client groups for current HRA approaches are educated adults older than age twenty and younger than age sixty.

The reader is also encouraged to examine table 5.2, which contains a list of selected health-risk appraisal software for microcomputers. Exhibit 5.2 is a telling illustration of the possible problems involved in faulty interpretation of health appraisals.

DIETARY ANALYSIS

With the availability of high-speed computers, we have reached a point at which many hundreds of thousands of computations can be completed at a very rapid pace. This ability is particularly useful when we must perform tedious calculations that nobody enjoys doing by hand, but whose results can be very useful to the practice of health education. An example of this kind of computationally intensive activity is the analysis of dietary intake.

Anyone who has done a dietary analysis by hand for even a small set of foods has learned just how tedious this activity can be. When the number of foods increases or when the number of days over which we are doing the analysis increases, or when the number of nutrients that we are interested in increases, the difficulties multiply. All of these activities, however, can be made easier by managing these computations and analyses by computer.

Dietary analyses are useful for a number of purposes. Many dietary-analysis tasks can be simplified with a wide variety of existing dietary-analysis packages for microcomputers. Those packages most commonly used by health educators include Nutritionist III™ by N-Squared Computing, The DINE System™ by DineSystems, Incorporated, and The Food Processor™ by ESHA, Incorporated. Although each of these packages is widely available and comparable in their capabilities, I will concentrate here specifically upon the DINE System. The opening screen of the DINE System is pictured in figure 5.1. However, before I begin with specific analysis potential, I will establish some necessary baseline information.

Table 5.2

Selected List of Health-Appraisal Software

TITLE	VENDOR	SYSTEM
AAHPERD Norms Disk Program	Ted Baumgartner	1
Analysis of College Age Health Related Fitness	AAHPERD	1
Calmpute	HesWare	1
Cardiac Risk and Stress	Human Factors Software	1
Health Age	Wellsource, Inc.	1,2
Health Age and Longevity	Wellsource, Inc.	1,2
Health Analysis Program: Personal Version	MEDMICRO	2
Health Analysis Program: Professional Version	MEDMICRO	2
Health Awareness Games	HRM Software	1,3
Health Maintenance, Volume II	MECC Distribution Center	1
Health Related Physical Fitness Student Profile	CompTech Systems Design	1
Health Risk Appraisal	University of Minnesota Media Distribution	1,2
Healthcheck	American Wellness Systems, Inc.	2
Healthstyle	Wellsource, Inc.	2
Heart Chec—Coronary Risk	Wellsource, Inc.	2
Heart Check	Medical Software Consortium	2
Heart Check Plus	Medical Software Consortium	2
HEARTCHEC	Wellsource for Health and Fitness	2
LIFE (Lifestyle Inventory and Fitness Evaluation)	Medical Software Consortium	2
Life Change Events Package	MEDMICRO	2
LIFE Interest Survey	Wellsource, Inc.	2
LIFE Pre/Post Testing	Wellsource, Inc.	2
LIFE Scanner	Wellsource, Inc.	2
Lifescan	National Wellness Institute	2
Lifescore M	Center for Corporate Health Promotion	2
Lifetime Health Monitoring Plan	NursePerfect Software	2
Lung Function	Wellsource, Inc.	1,2
Personal Health Profile	CompTech Systems Design	1,2
Problem Solving, Stress and Conflict	CBS Software	1
Risk Assessment and Exercise Prescription	K. Ruppert and B. Fernhall	2
RISKO—Heart Health	Wellsource, Inc.	1,2
Smoker's Profile	Wellsource, Inc.	2
Stress Assess	National Wellness Institute	2
Stress Profile 2.0	Wellsource, Inc.	2
Testwell	National Wellness Institute	2
Why Smoke?	Wellsource, Inc.	2

Note. 1 = Apple II; 2 = IBM-PC and compatibles; 3 = TRS-80.

EXHIBIT 5.2

HHA/HRA: MISINTERPRETATION WAITING TO HAPPEN

As is often the case, the general public has a hard time interpreting sophisticated health information. The following anecdote illustrates how someone can take the correct information and misapply it. Bob S. is a forty-year-old male in generally good health. He agrees to fill out an HRA instrument to get a handle on how he is doing. After filling out the appraisal, he gets his results in the mail and finds that his life expectancy is eight-four years, which pleases him. In a subsequent section of the report, he reads that there are some actions he can take to extend his life expectancy—and one of them is to submit to regular screenings for certain high-mortality diseases. The one that strikes his eye is an annual proctologic examination. If he has one done each year, it will increase his life expectancy by six months. Bob is an intelligent person, and it doesn't take long for him to figure out that he will have to have forty-four proctologic examinations in order to increase his life expectancy by six months at age eighty-four. He decides it is not worth the pain and aggravation and therefore will not have any such diagnostic examinations.

1. Was Bob's assessment accurate?
2. Where did Bob's logic fail him?
3. How often do health professionals as well as the general public make similar mistakes in judgment?

Figure 5.1. The DINE system.

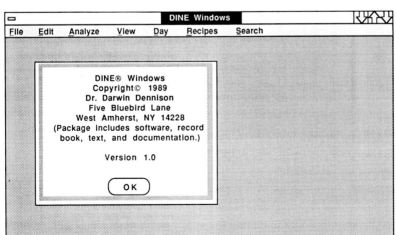

Assessment of Recommended Daily Dietary Allowances

Although it is not the purpose of this book to replicate information found in nutrition textbooks or courses, some such information is necessary to understand the ways in which nutrient-analysis packages are used in health education.

Many different criteria exist for assessing the value of a person's diet, including the Recommended Daily Dietary Allowances (RDAs), the USRDAs, and the U.S. Dietary Goals. I will distinguish between these here because of the important complementary role they each play.

- The *Recommended Daily Dietary Allowances* are made available from the Food and Nutrition Board, National Research Council of the American Academy of Sciences. The NRC periodically reviews data on the nutritional needs of Americans and sets standards based on a number of individual characteristics such as age, gender (and for women gestational and lactation status), height, weight, and activity level; the RDAs are specific to these characteristics. For example, the RDA for iron varies with different ages and between men and women. The purpose of the RDAs is to provide some guidelines for the intake of several nutrients that would ensure the continued health of the majority of the population, keeping in mind, of course, that within each group individual variation exists, and that not everyone of the same age, gender, height, weight, and activity level requires the same amounts of each nutrient. The RDAs, however, remain our best guess for a required handful of nutrients: protein, calcium, phosphorus, iron, vitamin A, thiamine, riboflavin, niacin, and ascorbic acid.

- The *USRDA's* are the recommendations of the Food and Drug Administration and are meant as general, all-inclusive guidelines. These recommendations are not broken down for different segments of the population. The USRDA for each of the nine nutrients just mentioned is actually the highest level of RDA. When you read a nutrition label, for percentages of the recommended allowances, what you see are the USRDA percentages. In practice, the USRDA is calculated to ensure that everyone in the population has adequate nutrient intake, but in many cases the USRDA is higher than what may actually be required for any single individual.

- The *U.S. Dietary Goals* originated with testimony taken in the United States Senate in 1977. At that time the Senate Select Committee on Nutrition and Human Needs issued the Dietary Goals for the United States. These dietary goals were formulated in an attempt to reduce the incidence of the major chronic diseases that are responsible for enormous morbidity and mortality in the United States—cardiovascular disease, cancer, hypertension, stroke, diabetes, and cirrhosis of the liver. Seven goals were recommended to provide guidance for dietary change. Exhibit 5.3 contains a summary of these goals.

EXHIBIT 5.3

DIETARY GOALS OF THE UNITED STATES

1. To avoid becoming overweight, consume only as much energy (calories) as is expended; if overweight, decrease energy intake and increase energy expenditure.
2. Increase the consumption of complex carbohydrates and "naturally occurring" sugars from about 28 percent of energy intake to about 48 percent of energy intake.
3. Reduce the consumption of refined and processed sugars by about 45 percent to account for about 10 percent of total energy intake.
4. Reduce overall fat consumption from approximately 40 percent to about 30 percent of energy intake.
5. Reduce saturated-fat consumption to account for about 10 percent of the total energy intake; and balance that with polyunsaturated and monounsaturated fats, which should account for about 10 percent of energy intake each.
6. Reduce cholesterol consumption to about three hundred milligrams a day.
7. Limit the intake of sodium by reducing the intake of salt to about five grams a day.

These three sets of standards are intended to be used for different purposes. The dietary goals are nutritional guidelines for the general population, the USRDAs provide a mechanism for monitoring some important nutritional elements useful for comparing similar foods, and the RDAs are important for very detailed individual dietary analysis. One must clearly understand these differences in order to use dietary-analysis software properly.

**Why Conduct a DINE®
Nutrient Analysis?**

Today's food choices consist of more processed foods than ever before. We are eating an increasing number of meals outside the home. When we do eat at home, we often eat carry-home meals, or we have meals delivered. The food marketplace has become internationalized and diverse with ethnic foods, gourmet foods, and specialty foods. Many of us do not know the nutrient composition of these foods.

The current nutritional environment is much more complex than it was even ten years ago. Two foods may look and taste similar and yet have very different ingredients; one of them is the nutritionally better choice. Food companies may tout a product for one good nutrient (e.g., dietary fiber) and then include a bad one (saturated fat). It is very difficult to know how many calories you are consuming, or if you are getting enough fiber, too much sodium, or too much saturated fat and cholesterol in the foods you eat.

Figure 5.2. Nutrition-improvement schema.

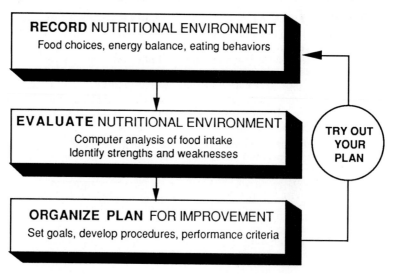

A computerized nutrient-analysis software program may be the only way you will know for sure the nutrient composition of your foods. Using such software to plan your meals will insure compliance with guidelines and provide you with the assurance of meeting the criteria for healthful food choices.

Nutrient analysis is an emerging multidisciplinary methodology involving the nutritional, behavioral, and computer sciences. The methodology consists of three steps (see figure 5.2). The first step involves recording your activity, food, and personal information. The second step involves evaluating the foods you are eating to identify the strengths and weaknesses in your diet. This step uses the microcomputer to analyze your diet and compare it to criteria established by national organizations. The third step involves organizing a plan to improve your food choices. During this step you will set goals, develop a daily and weekly eating plan, and organize a management system to evaluate your success. If these steps are followed adequately, nutrient analysis provides a functional framework to improve your nutritional behavior.

STEP 1

Recording Your Nutritional Environment

This step involves completing a food and activity record. Select one 24-hour period, from when you awaken to when you go to bed, to complete your record. Keep the record with you so that you can record your meals immediately after eating or completing the activity. This will improve the accuracy of the record.

Measure your portions whenever possible; otherwise, estimate portion sizes using common household units (cups, tablespoons, etc.). If in doubt of an exact measurement, overestimate. Most people tend to underestimate their food choices.

List breakfast, lunch, dinner, snack foods, and beverages. Indicate the brand name of your food choices, or the restaurant where eaten, if known. Indicate how the food was cooked, that is, fried, baked, broiled, microwaved, steamed, and so on.

On your activity record list only those activities that make you breathe hard and sweat, or that tire you out.

STEP 2

Computerized DINE Analysis of Your Nutritional Environment

The crux of the second step is entering your data into the microcomputer. The DINE System provides a very easy, menu-driven, point-and-click procedure to enter your personal information and your food choices and activities. After these data have been entered, you select, analyze, and print.

The screens as depicted in figures 5.3 and 5.4 show how your personal information and food choices are entered.

- Enter personal information (see figure 5.3).
- Enter food choices and activities (see figure 5.4).
- After your personal information, food, and activity choices have been entered into the computer, simply select "Analyze and Print."

A special feature of the DINE System is the clear, easy-to-use, and understandable printouts. The first of the three printouts is the DINE analysis, which summarizes on one page your nutrient profile based upon the entered personal, food, and activity information. The second page of the printout is the "Additional Values." This part provides detail regarding recommended percentages and ratios of nutrients in your diet. The third page is the verification of the foods with corresponding nutrient values. Examples of the printouts appear in figures 5.5 through 5.7.

Figure 5.3. Entering personal information.

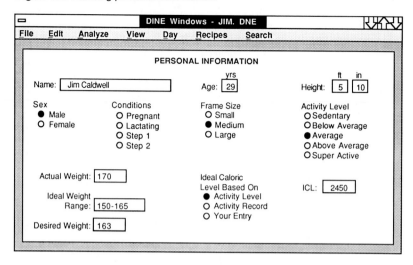

Figure 5.4. Entering food choices.

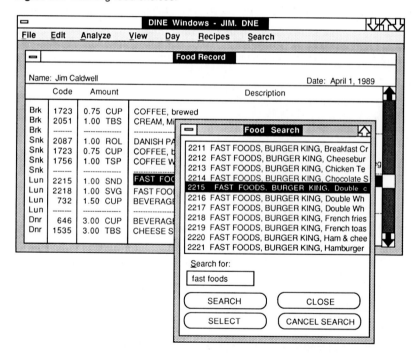

Figure 5.5. DINE printout: analysis.

			Your Diet	Ideal Diet			DINE Score
Jim Caldwell Apr 1, 1989	DINE Systems, Inc. Five Bluebird Lane West Amherst, NY 14228 (716) 688-2492						Day(s) 1
	TOTAL CALORIES		2773	2280	to	2520	0
LARGE NUTRIENTS	Protein	(Cal)	376	240	to	360	0
	Saturated Fat	(Cal)	377	240	or	less	0
	Monounsat Fat	(Cal)	433	240	or	less	0
	Polyunsat Fat	(Cal)	187	240	or	less	+.5
	Complex Carb	(Cal)	769	1080	to	1920	0
	Dietary Fiber	(gm)	12	20	to	35	-.5
	Sugar	(Cal)	435	240	or	less	0
SMALL NUTRIENTS	Cholesterol	(mg)	311	300	or	less	0
	Sodium	(mg)	3756	1100	to	3300	0
	Potassium	(mg)	2332	1875	to	5625	+.5
	Vitamin A	(RE)	388	1000	or	more	0
	Vitamin C	(mg)	48	60	or	more	0
	Iron	(mg)	15	10	or	more	+.5
	Calcium	(mg)	565	800	or	more	0
	Phosphorus	(mg)	1531	800	or	more	+.25

DINE Score: 1.25

VERY POOR

Figure 5.6. DINE printout: additional values.

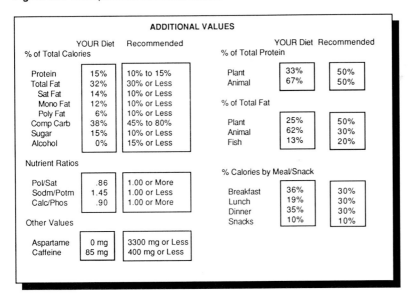

ADDITIONAL VALUES

% of Total Calories	YOUR Diet	Recommended
Protein	15%	10% to 15%
Total Fat	32%	30% or Less
Sat Fat	14%	10% or Less
Mono Fat	12%	10% or Less
Poly Fat	6%	10% or Less
Comp Carb	38%	45% to 80%
Sugar	15%	10% or Less
Alcohol	0%	15% or Less

Nutrient Ratios

	YOUR Diet	Recommended
Pol/Sat	.86	1.00 or More
Sodm/Potm	1.45	1.00 or Less
Calc/Phos	.90	1.00 or More

Other Values

Aspartame	0 mg	3300 mg or Less
Caffeine	85 mg	400 mg or Less

% of Total Protein	YOUR Diet	Recommended
Plant	33%	50%
Animal	67%	50%

% of Total Fat	YOUR Diet	Recommended
Plant	25%	50%
Animal	62%	30%
Fish	13%	20%

% Calories by Meal/Snack	YOUR Diet	Recommended
Breakfast	36%	30%
Lunch	19%	30%
Dinner	35%	30%
Snacks	10%	10%

Figure 5.7. DINE printout: verification.

DAY 1												Large Nutrients	
	Code	Description	Amt	Unt	Cal	Prot (Cal)	Satf (Cal)	Mono (Cal)	Poly (Cal)	Carb (Cal)	Fibr (gm)	Sugr (Cal)	
B	1723	Brewed coffee	0.75	CUP	4	0	0	0	0	3	0.0	0	
	2051	Half and half	1.00	TBS	20	2	9	4	1	3	0.0	0	
S	2087	Frt dnsh pastry	1.00	ROL	235	16	35	47	26	35	0.8	76	
	1723	Brewed coffee	0.75	CUP	4	0	0	0	0	3	0.0	0	
	1756	Pwdr cof whtnr	1.00	TSP	11	1	6	T	T	4	0.0	0	
L	2215	Double chsbrg	1.00	SND	436	120	87	105	17	101	0.1	16	
	2218	B King fr fries	1.00	SVG	227	12	63	45	9	84	2.2	12	
	732	Coca-cola	1.50	CUP	154	0	0	0	0	0	0.0	154	
D	646	Beer	3.00	CUP	292	6	0	0	0	108	0.0	0	
	1535	Cheez-whiz sprd	3.00	TBS	120	24	54	26	3	12	0.0	0	
	1994	Ritz crackers	9.00	CRK	158	9	20	27	20	54	0.5	27	
	1585	Batr frd chikn	1.00	PCE	364	146	44	69	39	49	T	0	
	4380	Msh pot/mlk/mrg	0.75	CUP	167	8	12	26	17	105	2.7	0	
	432	Cnd snap beans	0.50	CUP	13	3	0	0	0	10	1.5	0	
	4716	Parkrhouse roll	2.00	ROL	150	16	6	12	6	98	0.8	8	
	3594	Stk marg/soybn	1.00	TBS	101	0	21	48	27	0	0.0	0	
	44	Swtnd aplsauce	0.50	CUP	97	1	1	0	1	48	1.8	44	
S	4216	Mcrwv pcrn butr	4.00	CUP	110	12	9	24	21	40	2.4	0	
	3358	Crnbry-grp cktl	0.75	CUP	110	0	0	0	0	12	0.0	98	

DAY 1									Small Nutrients		
	Code	Description	Chol (mg)	Sodm (mg)	Potm (mg)	VitA (RE)	VitC (mg)	Iron (mg)	Clcm (mg)	Phos (mg)	Asp (mg)	Caf (mg)
B	1723	Brewed coffee	0	4	96	0	0	0.7	3	2	0	103
	2051	Half and half	6	6	19	16	0	0.0	16	14	0	0
S	2087	Frt dnsh pastry	56	233	57	11	T	1.3	17	80	0	0
	1723	Brewed coffee	0	4	96	0	0	0.7	3	2	0	103
	1756	Pwdr cof whtnr	0	4	16	T	0	0.0	T	8	0	0
L	2215	Double chsbrg	85	685	376	70	3	3.9	107	257	0	0
	2218	B King fr fries	14	160	484	T	4	1.0	T	114	0	0
	732	Coca-cola	0	8	T	0	0	0.0	0	54	0	46
D	646	Beer	0	38	18	0	0	0.2	36	44	0	0
	1535	Cheez-whiz sprd	23	735	104	60	T	T	225	483	0	0
	1994	Ritz crackers	5	270	34	T	T	0.9	45	14	0	0
	1585	Batr frd chikn	119	385	282	28	0	1.8	28	258	0	0
	4380	Msh pot/mlk/mrg	3	464	455	36	9	0.5	41	74	0	0
	432	Cnd snap beans	0	170	74	24	3	0.6	18	13	0	0
	4716	Parkrhouse roll	0	254	46	T	T	1.0	18	42	0	0
	3594	Stk marg/soybn	0	132	6	141	T	0.0	3	3	0	0
	44	Swtnd aplsauce	0	4	78	2	2	1.4	5	9	0	0
S	4216	Mcrwv pcrn butr	0	200	46	T	T	0.7	T	59	0	0
	3358	Crnbry-grp cktl	0	0	45	T	27	T	T	1	0	0

STEP 3

Organize a Plan for Diet and Activity Improvement

Improving your food choices involves reviewing your DINE printout and developing a plan. Or if you are already familiar with your analysis, you may use on-screen procedures to plan an adequate diet based upon your individual needs and food preferences.

The DINE Score provides a comparison between your diet and an ideal diet based upon nationally accepted guidelines. The objective is to select foods that will give you a DINE Score of 8 or more. If you received a zero (0) or a minus (−) in a category, you must review your verification to find out which foods and/or portion sizes created the difficulty.

Note that in figure 5.5 Jim did not receive a plus (+) in protein. He consumed foods that contained much more protein than was recommended and thus received a zero, indicating noncompliance. He also ate much more animal protein than plant protein. Note the percentage differential in the additional values section (figure 5.6) for source of protein. High-protein foods, generally from animal sources, are often high in fat content.

From the verification (figure 5.7) observe that Jim had a double cheeseburger for lunch and batter-fried chicken for dinner. These foods pushed both his protein and saturated fat over the limit. The plan for an improved diet would be to reduce the portion size of the food, limit the number of times you have the food per week, or have the food only occasionally. In Jim's situation, he could try two hamburgers in lieu of the double cheeseburger or have the chicken broiled or baked. Figure 5.8 contains additional information regarding Jim's analysis.

Here the DINE features on-screen searches for foods that are high or low in selected nutrients. Jim may also wish to consult *The DINE System: How to Improve Your Nutrition and Health,* a text that contains examples of diets, recipes, and snacks at various caloric levels that are within national guidelines. Use these procedures to plan your diet, and you will be eating foods with nutrient levels high enough to achieve a DINE Score of 8 or more—excellent!

Figure 5.8. Nutrient search.

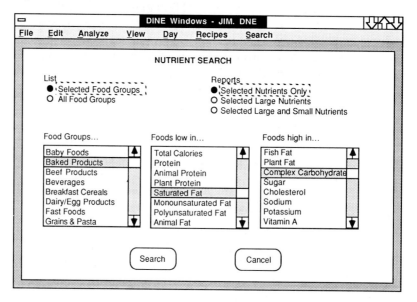

Validity and Reliability of DINE

Over the past eight years the developers of DINE have been working to improve the accuracy of nutrient-analysis methodology. Because of external variance, any analysis system will have variability in measurements. For example, there is a natural variation of caloric intake from day-to-day, and the measurement, though variable, may be very accurate. The accuracy of nutrient analysis is related to reducing the variability of components within the analysis system.

Five factors affect the accuracy of nutrient analysis: the variation of reported day-to-day food intake (intraindividual variance); the variance related to generic food compositions; the natural variance of nutrient values in foods; the variability of laboratory techniques in determining the nutrient values in foods; and the variance between nutrient-composition information and labeling provided by food companies.

Simplified activity and food-recording procedures have helped to reduce intraindividual variance. Other methods that have proved helpful in this regard include DINE's on-screen verification of food items, the user's ability to change food entries on-screen, and the use of an on-screen record that resembles the food-record form. Food data may also be entered by common food name, rather than code, for ease of use. The common-name data entry allows an individual to search for a restaurant name or brand name that further increases the accuracy of data input.

DINE's 5,600+ food database, consisting of both generic and brand-name foods, allows for the inclusion of 80 percent or more of specific food choices. When substitute foods are used for more than 20 percent of the actual food choices, there is a decrease in intraindividual validity.

Small databases or databases with a significant number of missing values contribute to decreased validity. The DINE database, using estimation and interpolation of nutrients, has no missing values, thereby increasing accuracy and reducing variance. Foods that represent ethnic, social, and geographic selections have also been included in the database to reduce *inter*individual variance. This is important when comparisons are made between populations, or when there is heterogeneity in the population under study.

Health educators should understand the limitations of dietary analysis when conducting such assessments. With no clear understanding of these limitations, health professionals can often make inappropriate judgments. The following is a brief examination of some of the most common limitations of computerized dietary analyses.

1. *The methods used for collecting food intake information, including issues regarding their reliability and validity.* There are many methods for collecting information about food intake. Some involve keeping a running record as choices are made; others depend upon memory. Each of these has its limitations. Properly identifying serving sizes also creates some complications in the process of conducting dietary analyses.

2. *The distinction between food selection and food consumption.* At some time in almost all our lives, we have found ourselves in a serving line with food being offered cafeteria style. There are few people who have not put more food on their plate than was eaten. Health educators need to recognize the importance of recording the quantity of food actually consumed, not what was originally selected. Often, when we ask people to recall what they've eaten, they remember only the amount that was first put on their plate or tray, not the amount they ate.

3. *The influence that cooking has on the retention of nutrients in foods.* It is clear that the process of cooking changes the nutrient density of foods (i.e., the amount of nutrients, other than calories, per serving). Although these changes may seem of minor importance, they become important over long periods of time.

4. *The adequacy and appropriateness of the nutrient database.* All dietary analyses need to begin with an adequate and appropriate database of foods and their associated nutrient values. If the database is inadequate, or if the food choices are inappropriate for the population of interest, then the subsequent analyses will be of limited value. An inadequate database is one that has incomplete, incorrect, or dated information.

5. *The reliability of the data-entry process.* Most people have at one time or another made mistakes in the transcription of numbers or other data, and the same can happen when we transfer a client's food-intake data to a computer.

6. *The reliability and validity of the software's computational algorithms.* An algorithm is a combination of the strategies and formulas that a computer program uses to solve a problem. It may not be readily evident if an algorithm is incorrect.

7. *The adequacy and appropriateness of the analysis.* Even when algorithms are mathematically sound, they may be applied inappropriately.

8. *The adequacy of the interpretation of the results by the health professional and the communication of those results to the client.* It is critical for the health professional to understand the nature of the analysis needs, the limitations of the strategies applied, and the adequacy of the database used in the analysis. If these limitations are not clearly understood, interpretation will be clouded. In order to deal with some of these problems, the health educator should seek the benefit of advice or guidelines from nutrition experts, particularly quality of software. In addition, substantive reviews for software should be examined before making purchasing decisions. Exhibit 5.4 contains an example of how these programs may be used by health educators.

Problems and Warnings Related to Dietary Assessment

As with other substantive health assessments, dietary assessments can be conducted under many different circumstances. Potter and Perry (1987) suggest that nutritional assessments should be part of every health-professional/client relationship because of the basic biological needs that all humans have for food and the important role it plays in health and illness. They go on to suggest, however, that a complete assessment includes "observation, a [nursing] history focusing on diet, anthropometric measurements, diagnostics tests, and consideration of factors that influence the client's dietary patterns" (p. 700). These are all essential elements because any comprehensive health-promotion program involving dietary patterns must consider all factors influencing the situation. Potter and Perry go on to list seven specific factors that influence dietary patterns, including (1) health status, (2) culture and religion, (3) socioeconomic status, (4) personal preference, (5) psychological factors, (6) alcohol and drugs, and (7) misinformation and food fads.

Dietary analysis is a powerful tool when the problems associated with its use are understood, and the tedium related to its computation is removed. Computerized dietary-analysis packages are now readily available for any of the major microcomputer systems, and many have extensive capabilities. However, the effective health educator will recognize that dietary analysis has its limitations, and that there are many other components to a comprehensive program. Table 5.3 contains a partial list of selected dietary-analysis software currently available for microcomputers.

EXHIBIT 5.4

ILLUSTRATION OF APPLICATION OF DIETARY ANALYSIS

The Wellspirit Health Promotion Program attempts to provide adequate counseling for minimizing problems associated with high-risk cholesterol levels. Once a cholesterol is established at baseline, a thorough nutritional analysis may be conducted to examine eating choices that put an individual at high risk. When the food patterns that contribute most to high cholesterol are identified by the analysis, the health educator may work with the client to develop better skills in choosing foods as part of the diet. Follow-up can include not only another serum cholesterol screen but a new dietary analysis as well. This will allow for a more thorough and potentially effective program strategy.

Table 5.3

Selected List of Dietary-Analysis Software

TITLE	VENDOR	SYSTEM
Diet Analysis	Albion Software	1
Dietician	AlSoft	3
DINE System	DINESystems, Inc.	1,2
Food Processor	EHSA Software, Inc.	1,2,3
Macnutriplan	Micromedx	3
Nutricalc	CAMDE Corporation	3
Nutricalc Plus	CAMDE Corporation	3
Nutrition Analysis	Wellsource, Inc.	2
Nutrition Profile	Wellsource, Inc.	1,2
Nutrition Wizard	Center for Science in the Public Interest	2
Nutritional Assessment of the Pregnant Woman	MEDI-SIM, Inc.	1,2
Nutritionist II	N-Squared Computing	2,3
Nutritionist III	Turnkey Electronics	2,3
The Balancing Act I	Soft Bite, Inc.	1,2
The Short Report: Micro	Nutritional Services Division of Health Development, Inc.	1,2

1 = Apple II, 2 = IBM-PC and compatibles, 3 = Apple Macintosh.

FITNESS APPRAISALS

Lepanto and Jenkins (1984) define fitness as "a state which characterizes the degree to which a person is able to function efficiently," often described in three dimensions: (1) cardiorespiratory endurance; (2) flexibility, coordination, and relaxation; and (3) muscular strength and endurance. These terms are defined in Mullen, Gold, Belcastro, and McDermott (1986, p. 148) as follows:

- *Cardiorespiratory endurance* is the body's ability to sustain strenuous activities for long periods of time and depends upon the circulatory and respiratory systems to provide the necessary oxygen.
- *Flexibility* is the ability of a specific joint to move throughout its entire range of motion.
- *Muscular strength* is the maximum amount of force that a muscle is able to exert in a single effort.

As in other health domains, there are a number of fitness-assessment areas in which microcomputer technology may be applied, including fitness instruction, the measurement of fitness or exercise capacity, exercise prescription, and surveillance and monitoring of individual and/or group fitness plans and activities. The first area, fitness instruction, is comparable to other instructional areas examined in chapter 4 and will not be addressed here. The others are specifically addressed in the next three sections.

Measurement of Fitness and Exercise Capacity

Measurement of fitness and exercise capacity is a multidimensional effort, and in many cases proxy measures are used in these assessments. A proxy measure is an indirect measure or indicator of a concept rather than a measurement of the concept itself. Proxy measures are taken when an accurate and direct measure of the concept is not possible. For example, rather than measuring fitness directly, we may measure other factors associated with fitness, such as cardiorespiratory fitness (aerobic capacity), athletic ability flexibility, strength, agility, and body composition. Each of these elements of fitness has a number of measures designed for their direct assessment. Of these, the two most frequently represented by microcomputer applications are cardiorespiratory-endurance measures and body-composition measures.

One of the most accurate ways to measure cardiorespiratory fitness today is the assessment of oxygen uptake or exercise EKGs (also known as a stress test). During these tests trained professionals monitor heart rate, blood pressure, and other indicators of cardiovascular stress in response to strenuous exercise. In the absence of computer technology, these tests would be both less accurate and more dangerous. There are many measures that must be monitored to minimize the likelihood of a cardiovascular accident, such as a heart attack, during testing.

Most microcomputer applications in this area, however, tend to be based on proxy measures of fitness that are highly correlated with the results of exercise EKGs. These tests often require the expenditure of

Fitness testing, such as an exercise EKG has been improved by the availability of computer systems to interpret complicated information as it is produced.

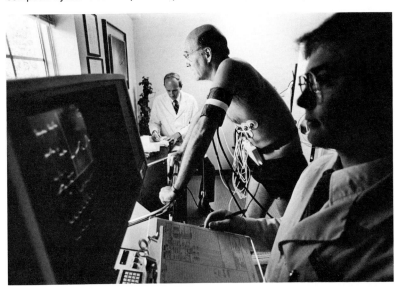

energy during a specified exercise, and then accumulation of easily obtainable measures such as distance covered, time required for completion, heart rate, blood pressure, or respiration. On occasion recovery time (the time it takes to return to a baseline level from a peak of energy expenditure) for one of these measures is monitored as well. Some combination of these data are entered into a microcomputer program, and the results of computational algorithms are compared with norms for age, gender, height, and weight to provide an estimate of fitness levels. There are many of these programs, some based on Cooper's work in aerobics, the President's council on Physical Fitness and Sports' Youth Related Fitness Test, or the Health Related Fitness Test of the American Alliance for Health, Physical Education, Recreation, and Dance (AAHPERD). Table 5.4 contains a partial list of selected fitness-assessment software.

Body composition refers to the physical stature of the human body, and in particular to measures such as percentage of body fat. There are, of course, many ways to estimate percentage of body fat, ranging in precision and reliability from very high to very low. Among the most common strategies are

- hydrostatic (underwater) weighing, based on water-displacement principles;
- skinfold measures, based on a physical measurement of the thickness of several pinches of skin;
- electrical impedance procedures, based on the relationship between percent body fat and the speed with which electrical impulses travel through the body;

Table 5.4

Selected List of Fitness-Assessment Software

TITLE	VENDOR	SYSTEM
One-and-a-Half-Mile Run	Human Factors Software	1,3
Twelve-Minute Run	Human Factors Software	1,3
Aerobic Evaluation	Human Factors Software	1
Bicycle Ergometer Test	Human Factors Software	1,3
Cardiovascular Fitness—Step Test	Wellsource, Inc.	2
Cardiovascular Fitness—Treadmill	Wellsource, Inc.	2
Fitlog	Wellsource, Inc.	2
Fitness Analysis	L. Keyes and M. Simons	2
Fitness Assessment and Exercise Guidelines	Programs for Health and Fitness	1,2
Fitness for Life	Persimmon Software	1
Fitness Inventory and Exercise Trainer	C. A. Milesis	2
Fitness Profile	Wellsource, Inc.	2
Fitness Testing	W. Couldry	1
HEALTHLINES: Fitness	Wm. C. Brown	1
High School Fitness Profile	Wellsource, Inc.	1
Improve Your 10-K Time	Human Factors Software	1,3
Metabolic Costs	W. Couldry	1
Oxygen Uptake	Human Factors Software	1
Physical Fitness Assessment and Exercise	CompYOUtr-cize Inc.	1,4
Physical Fitness Evaluation 1.0	Wholebody Health Management	1,2
President's Council Physical Fitness Program	Hartley Courseware	1
Protocol-Fitness	Health and Fitness Systems	2
Rehabilitation Fitness Evaluation 1.0	Wholebody Health Management	1
Risk Assessment and Exercise Prescription	K. Ruppert and B. Fernhall	2
The Running Program	Computerized Health Appraisals	2
Universal Fitness Report	Persimmon Software	2

1 = Apple II, 2 = IBM-PC and compatibles, 3 = Apple Macintosh, 4 = Tandy Computers.

- body-girth measures and height/weight algorithms, based on comparison of several physical measures with norms for age, gender, and other variables.

This list runs roughly from the most to the least precise and reliable. Table 5.5 contains a number of body-composition applications currently available to those interested in these assessments. It is important to point out that those applications used for analyzing data collected by the more reliable methods (e.g., hydrostatic weighing, skinfold measures) are more precise than those based strictly on algorithms for comparing girth, and other anthropometric measures, against norms. These different approaches may yield a wide degree of variability between estimates.

Table 5.5

Selected List of Body-Composition-Assessment Software

TITLE	VENDOR	SYSTEM
Body Composition—Hydrostatic Weighing	Wellsource, Inc.	2
Body Composition—Skinfold	Wellsource, Inc.	2
Body Composition Analysis	Digitealth	1
Body Composition for Females	Human Factors Software	1
Body Composition for Males	Human Factors Software	1
Body Profile	Human Factors Software	1,3
Computer Assisted Somatic Evaluation	C. A. Milesis	2
HEALTHLINES: Fitness	Wm. C. Brown	1
Skinfold Measurements	M. Goldman	1
Skinfolds	Persimmon Software	1
Underwater Weighing	Human Factors Software	1,3

1 = Apple II, 2 = IBM-PC and compatibles, 3 = Apple Macintosh.

Fitness and Exercise Prescriptions

A number of the applications listed in tables 5.4 and 5.5 provide *exercise prescriptions* as well as assessments. These prescriptions range from the very specific, such as how to reduce event times (e.g., ten-kilometer road races—see *Improve Your 10-K Time,* or *The Running Program*); to prescriptions designed to improve cardiorespiratory fitness (e.g., *Fitness Assessment and Exercise Guidelines* or *Risk Assessment and Exercise Prescription*); to those that deal with very complex disease-risk-reduction programs (e.g., *Rehabilitation Fitness Evaluation 1.0*). Each are based on different conceptual frameworks, use different logic, and rely on different batteries of measures and computational algorithms. Anyone looking for fitness-assessment/exercise-prescription software should be aware of the different approaches in each case. Such software must be understood conceptually (i.e., the logic and method behind the assessment), as well as operationally (i.e., how to make the program run and read its output).

Surveillance and Monitoring

The terms *surveillance* and *monitoring* here go beyond the computational needs for estimates of fitness or body composition and refer to the ability to maintain longitudinal data on individuals and groups, to analyze changes in the data over time, and to produce a variety of reports from these databases. These programs are hybrids between assessment software and general-purpose database applications (see chapter 6 for a more complete explanation of database software). Exhibit 5.5 contains a case-study example of how the variety of fitness measures may be incorporated into an effective strategy for health education and health promotion.

EXHIBIT 5.5

CASE EXAMPLE—FITNESS ASSESSMENT

In an attempt to help some of their clients lose weight and decrease their cardiovascular risk, the staff at the Wellspirit Health Promotion Program (WSHPP) have decided to look for software to assist with fitness assessment and evaluation. After a review a program called FITSOLVE™ is found, published by Wm. C. Brown. This program is intended to be instruction and was created to accompany other activities in health, physical-education, or wellness programs. It is designed to follow fitness testing but can also be used as part of individual wellness exhibition days.

FITSOLVE™ consists of the following components: (1) a screening for potential programs associated with the specific problems of an individual; (2) height, weight, blood-pressure, and body-fat measures (skinfold or circumference measures); (3) tests of cardiovascular fitness; (4) abdominal, arm-strength, and muscle-endurance tests; (5) measures of hamstring and lower-back flexibility. The initial screening consists of a coronary-risk profile, and the client then enters data for the other elements.

The documentation provided with FITSOLVE™ contains detailed instructions for how to conduct each of the tests and measures. Once the data are entered into the computer for each client, the program provides a thorough report and interpretation of results. A health educator may then use these results to work with a client and to improve the likelihood that an appropriate physical activity program can be added to the overall wellness strategies.

Warning: The documentation for FITSOLVE includes the following warning (p. 2):

Although fitness testing of the type used in the FITSOLVE program carries very little risk, there is a risk nevertheless. Before using these or any other exercise tests, it is advisable to consult the American College of Sports Medicine Guidelines for Exercise Testing and Prescription.

Note. From *FITSOLVE: Software to Accompany the Teaching of Health-Related Fitness Concepts* by J. R. Whitehead, 1988, Dubuque, IA: Wm. C. Brown.

Problems and Warnings

In all cases the same problems and warnings associated with health-risk appraisals and dietary assessments also apply to fitness assessments. The health professional needs to understand the objectives of the applications, their capabilities and limitations, and the importance of providing clients with adequate analysis and interpretational guidance for results. Mullen et al. (1986, p. 151) suggest that four principles be emphasized when considering guidance and interpretation:

- *Overload.* In order for individuals to benefit from exercise programs, there should be increasing levels of activity and energy expenditure. This objective can be accomplished by increasing the frequency, intensity, and duration of exercise.

- *Specificity.* Different exercises provide benefits to different muscle groups and body systems. An exercise prescription should be specifically designed to meet the needs of an individual.
- *Individual variation.* Each person benefits from exercise differently than others. Any prescription should take a person's unique characteristics into consideration.
- *Reversibility.* Because a loss of fitness capacity will result from inactivity, one must maintain a program to continue benefiting from it.

Any program that provides individual assessments and prescriptions should demonstrate a recognition of these principles.

As a final word on fitness assessments, I will reiterate several important points. Fitness assessments are just as important, and just as easily misunderstood and misinterpreted, as other assessments. Even if health professionals have been trained to use HRAs, fitness assessments require additional training. It is generally inadvisable to conduct fitness appraisals without such training, because measures of body composition are difficult to interpret and subject to wide variation depending on method and professional technique; there may be far greater immediate risk to the client than in other kinds of assessments.

Most are familiar with Selye's definition of stress as the "nonspecific response of the body to any demand made upon it," and the implication that these demands may come in any form. Mullen et al. (1986, p. 49) suggest that appropriate management of stress involves three major elements: (1) regular assessment, or the process of recognizing sources of stress and the magnitude of the demands they are making; (2) intervention, or the use of habits, practices, or skills to reduce the magnitude of the stress response; and (3) reinforcement, or the payoff in improved health and well-being.

Many methods have been developed to accomplish these objectives, including both professional and self-help approaches to coping with stress. The literature indicates many avenues for the latter type of approach, including books (Greening & Hobson, 1979), diet control and exercise (Charlesworth & Nathan, 1982), audiotapes (Gersham & Clouser, 1974), and relaxation techniques (Quick & Quick, 1984). Smith (1987) suggests that "the recent introduction of the microcomputer has allowed for the possibility of computer programs designed to help people with emotional problems, including stress. . . . These computer programs provide options and choices to the user as to personal thought, feelings, and behaviors which help to determine specific sources of stress and allow for the development of customized stress coping strategies" (p. 38). Reitman (1984) and Selmi (1983) report that programs designed to help

STRESS MANAGEMENT AND COPING

people deal with stress can in some ways substitute for direct personal contact. Software programs do exist that are designed to deal with the first two major elements of stress management and coping: regular assessment and interventions.

Computers in Psychology/ Psychiatry

A brief review of the literature indicates that many of the most widely used applications in mental health, psychology, and psychiatry have been in the area of computerized testing (see table 5.6 for a summary of such literature). There have been applications designed to take psychiatric histories, to conduct clinical interviews and assessments, and to identify specific behavioral problems such as suicidal tendencies, alcohol abuse, anxiety, and phobias. Several different research projects have indicated that patient response to these computerized assessments is positive, and that there is a better chance for accurate response when the information is sensitive (e.g., information regarding sexual behavior, drug use).

Other computerized applications have enhanced the storage of data on patients, the identification of patient problems, the generation of psychiatric diagnoses, and the administration of psychometric tests. Examples of such testing applications include Raven's Standard Progressive Matrices, Wisconsin Card Sort test, the Shipley-Hartford IQ Test, the Minnesota Multiphasic Personality Inventory (MMPI), the Millon Clinical Multiaxial Inventory (MCMI), the Eysenck Personality Inventory, the Beck Depression Inventory, and various attempts to measure Type A behavior patterns.

Effectiveness of a Self-Help Strategy for Stress

In 1985 Smith conducted a doctoral dissertation to determine if a computerized self-help stress-coping program was effective in reducing stress in adult males. The program, titled *Coping with Stress, Version 1.0,* uses cognitive learning theory as the basis for its content and recommendations. It was developed by Reitman (1984), and it consists of eleven sessions ranging from thirty to forty minutes in duration. The purpose of the program is to provide some insight into the irrational thoughts and ideas that produce stressful responses to stimuli. Exhibit 5.6 includes the titles of the eleven sessions.

Subjects were randomly assigned to experimental and control groups. Smith (1985) found no significant difference in the areas of occupational environmental stress and trait anxiety (e.g., long-term anxiety, often based on personality characteristics) between those exposed to the programs and those not exposed. He did, however, find a reduction in personal strain and state anxiety (e.g., short-term anxiety, usually related to a specific situation or event) and some increase in personal resourcefulness for coping with stressful situations. He concluded that short-term gains in certain areas (e.g., state anxiety, personal strain) could be demonstrated from such programs, but cautioned that assessment of long-term benefits would still need to be established.

Table 5.6
**Summary of Literature on the Use of Computers
in Psychiatry/Psychology**

SUBJECT	AUTHOR(S)/YEAR
Administration of psychometric tests	Editorial, 1983
Alcohol abuse	Lucas et al., 1977
	Skinner & Allen, 1983
Anxiety	Gottschack & Bechtel, 1982
Beck Depression Inventory	Williams, Johnson, & Bliss, 1975
Clinical interviews and assessments	Klinger et al., 1977
	Likenhoker & McCarron, 1974
Data on patients and identification of patient problems	Hale & DeL'aune, 1983
	Hammond & Munnecke, 1984
Eysenck Personality Inventory	Katz & Dalby, 1981
Generation of psychiatric diagnoses	Griest et al., 1983; Robbins et al., 1981
Millon Clinical Multiaxial Inventory (MCMI)	Green, 1983
Minnesota Multiphasic Personality Inventory (MMPI)	Stillman et al., 1969
	Williams, Johnson, & Bliss, 1975
	Green, 1983
Phobias	Carr & Ghosh, 1983a, 1983b
	Biglan, Villwock, & Wick, 1979
	Branham & Katahn, 1974
	Evans, & Kellman, 1973
	Lang, 1969
Psychiatric histories	Carr, Ghosh, & Ancill, 1983
Raven's Standard Progressive Matrices	Calvert & Waterfall, 1982
	Rock & Nolen, 1982
	Watts, Baddeley, & Williams, 1982
Sexual behavior, drug use	Williams, Johnson, & Bliss, 1975
	Lucas et al., 1977
	Carr & Ghosh, 1983a, 1983b
	Thompson, 1983
Shipley-Hartford IQ Test	Williams, Johnson, & Bliss, 1975
Suicidal tendencies	Griest et al., 1973a; Griest, Klein, and Van Cura, 1973
	Gustafson, Tianen, & Griest, 1981
Type A behavior patterns	Howland & Siegman, 1982
Wisconsin Card Sort test	Beaumont, 1981

Although potentially useful for assessment and some training (e.g., bio-feedback), there are few systematic evaluations of stress-related software. Each of the programs has limitations, and the license disclaimer found on many software products often disavows any proved health-related benefits from using these programs. There is nevertheless a great deal of potential, as indicated in the work by Smith. A number of programs are now commercially available; table 5.7 contains a brief list of some of the more widely used of these programs.

Problems and Warnings

EXHIBIT 5.6

COPING WITH STRESS—AN ELEVEN-PART PROGRAM

Reitman developed an eleven-lesson program that includes the following components: (1). feeling stress, (2). myths, misconceptions, and misunderstandings, (3). stress and your self-image, (4). stress and others, (5). stress and your body, (6). transition to part 2, (7). the main causes of stress, (8). actual stress, (9). anticipated stress, (10). assumed stress, (11). coping with stress.

Note. From *Coping with Stress, 1984*, Woodland Hills, CA: Psycomp.

Table 5.7

Selected List of Stress-Related Software

TITLE	VENDOR	SYSTEM
Calmpute	HesWare	1
Conquering Stress	KJ Software	2
Feeling Better	Dynacomp	1
Lessons on Stress	Wanda Monthey	1
Life Dynamic Transformation	Avant-Garde Creations	1
PC-Relax	Tru-Image	2
Relax	Mindset	2
Relax: The Stress Reduction System	Synapse Software	1,2
Stress and the Young Adult	MCE Inc.	1
Stress Management	Control Health Software	1
Stress Profile	Comp. Health Appraisals	1,2
Stress/Positive Thinking	Control Health Software	5,6

1 = Apple II, 2 = IBM-PC and compatibles, 3 = Apple Macintosh, 4 = Tandy, 5 = Commodore, 6 = Atari.

THE POTENTIAL FOR USING ASSESSMENT SOFTWARE AS INSTRUCTIONAL APPLICATIONS

Although these applications are developed principally to conduct assessments, they may also serve as instructional software. They can be used, for instance, to illustrate the relationships between behavior, body composition, and overall health risk. More specifically, hypothetical data for a subject might be entered into a series of assessments. It would then be possible to use the output from these programs to illustrate how different items affect overall risk. Individual responses could be modified to demonstrate the resulting change in the assessment, and a variety of such changes could be applied to compare their potential impact on health. Used in this way, health assessments actually become very similar to simulation software and therefore can serve a dual purpose—instruction and individual assessment/prescription.

Health assessments come in many forms and are readily available to the health professional and consumer. To use these applications appropriately, health professionals should understand both their conceptual and operational elements and should provide clients with adequate preparation, guidance, and interpretation to help them understand the results.

This chapter has provided an overview of the potential uses of health appraisals in health education, including health-risk appraisals, dietary assessments, fitness assessments, and stress assessments. Also included in the discussions was specific information about the applicability and problems associated with such appraisals. Specifically emphasized was the warning that these appraisals should not be used by persons who are untrained, nor should they be used with groups of clients unless a trained health educator assists with their interpretation.

SUMMARY

1. What kind of training and experience should health educators have in order to use computerized health appraisals correctly?
2. What are the major limitations of these applications?
3. What do you think are the major liability issues associated with the use of computerized health appraisals?
4. What do you think are the major liability issues associated with *not* using computerized health appraisals?

DISCUSSION QUESTIONS

Byrd-Bredbenner, C., Pelican, S. (1984). Software: How do you choose? *Journal of Nutrition Education, 16,* (2), 77–79.

Foxman, B., Edington, D. W. (1987). The accuracy of health risk appraisal in predicting mortality. *American Journal of Public Health, 77* (8), 971–975.

Mattes, R. D., & Gabriel, S. J. (1988). A comparison of results from two microcomputer nutrient analysis software packages and a mainframe. . . . *Journal of Nutrition Education, 20* (2), 70–76.

Penfield, M. P., Costello C. A. (1988). Microcomputer programs for diet analysis: A comparative evaluation. *Journal of the American Dietetic Association, 88* (2), 209–211.

Scott, H. D., & Cabral, R. M. (1988). Predicting hazardous lifestyles among adolescents based on health-risk assessment data. *American Journal of Health Promotion, 2,* (4), 23–28.

Skinner, H. A., Palmer, W., Sanchez-Craig, M., et al. (1987). Reliability of a lifestyle assessment using microcomputers. *Canadian Journal of Public Health, 78* (5), 325–329.

RECOMMENDED READINGS

6

ADVANCED TOPICS IN MICROCOMPUTING

By the completion of this chapter, the student will be able to

- summarize the potential in health education of artificial intelligence and expert systems;
- describe the variety of research and statistical applications of microcomputers.

Analog-to-digital conversion: The conversion of continuous signals (e.g., temperature) into discrete signals (a series of numbers) so the data can be used by a computer.

Artificial intelligence: A broad name for a family of computer applications that mimic human intelligence and/or behavior.

Critical Path Methods (CPM): A strategy for assessing implementation of a project. The critical path is the sequence of events that must occur on time for the project to be completed as planned.

Data acquisition: The use of computers to accumulate or acquire raw data.

Data presentation: The use of a variety of strategies to present information in the most concise and easily understood manner.

Decision assistance: A computer system that provides a user with information that is useful in making difficult administrative, practice, or other programmatic decisions. A related term is *decision-support systems* (DSS).

Expert systems: A subset of artificial intelligence, expert systems are designed to mimic the behavior and problem-solving ability of experts in a field.

Gantt Charting: A family of strategies and procedures for tracking the flow of operation of large projects or programs.

Neural networks: Computer chips connected in such a way as to simulate the human brain.

Program Evaluation Review Techniques (PERT): A tool for planning and monitoring large projects.

Project-management software: A name given to a variety of computer applications that assist in the planning, management, monitoring, surveillance, or evaluation of large projects. Among the components found in such software is Gantt Charting, PERT, and CPM techniques.

Statistical analysis: The use of a computer to conduct a variety of descriptive or analytic procedures on a set of data.

Note: This chapter prepared by Robert S. Gold, Ph.D., Dr.P.H. (University of Maryland), Simon Priest, Ph.D., and William Montelpare, Ph.D., (Brock University, St. Catherines, Ontario, Canada, L2S 3A1).

If statistics are the tools of researchers, then computers are the tools of statisticians.

—Anonymous

INTRODUCTION

The use of microcomputers in the field of health education is growing dramatically, making it increasingly necessary for students pursuing a career in the field to familiarize themselves with the contributions of microcomputers to field research. This chapter identifies some advanced applications that use the microcomputer either as a research tool or in artificial intelligence. Because this is a basic text, no effort will be made to do more than introduce the reader to these possibilities.

The original use of computers in research was solely for the *statistical analysis* of data, as a look inside the more well-known research textbooks will reveal. These books, and countless others, index the computer strictly as a machine for analyzing data. With the recent advent, and subsequent acceptance, of mainframe computer programs such as SPSS (Statistical Package for the Social Sciences) and SAS (Statistical Analysis System), statistical analysis has indeed resulted in the extensive use of computer time.

However, this is not the only use for computers in research. They enjoy widespread usage beyond data analysis. Recently evolving applications in *data acquisition* and *data presentation* (see chapter 2 on graphics) are some of the many popular examples of how computers can aid the researcher. In order for health educators to better understand the wide array of computer-enhanced research possibilities, this chapter will briefly review several different topics.

RESEARCH DESIGN AND MANAGEMENT

The microcomputer can be a useful tool for the planning and execution of research projects. Several common software programs have broad applications for the managing of such projects. These include database managers, electronic worksheets or spreadsheets, scheduling programs, and communications software. Chapters 2 and 3 provided a detailed review of some of these functions.

As described in chapter 3, communication capabilities place a whole new world of information at the health researcher's fingertips. By connecting the microcomputer via modem to common telephone lines, a researcher can access other computers around the globe, thus gaining admission to shared databases. It is also possible to call another microcomputer user and transfer information, such as files, facsimiles, or mail. As described in chapter 2, computers are commonly used to connect to bibliographic retrieval services or health libraries (Brodman, 1985). For example, a researcher looking for information on the application of different health-behavior models might search (perhaps by modern connection) the database of published materials on Medline using key words like "health-behavior model" or "social-learning theory." After receiving a printout of all the known literature on this topic, the researcher could then request specific articles from other researchers, which could be sent in the form of facsimile copies to the researcher's own microcomputer.

A group of software applications known as *project-management software* continues to be underutilized by most health-education professionals. Project management involves a number of interrelated skills that ensure timely completion of complex tasks. Several different microcomputer-software packages currently offer many capabilities to assist with these tasks.

The most common project-management techniques found in use today include Gantt Charting, Program Evaluation Review Techniques (PERT), and Critical Path Methods (CPM).

Gantt Charting was developed by Henry L. Gantt, a pioneer in scientific project management in the early twentieth century. Gantt Charting will look familiar to those who have seen project timetables with tasks identified according to initiation and completion times. The brief example in figure 6.1 suggests that the two primary components of Gantt Charting are (a) breaking down a project into discrete tasks and listing them, and (b) plotting these tasks against a timeline.

Program Evaluation Review Techniques were developed for the Navy Special Project Offices in 1958 to help (1) minimize production delays, interruptions, and conflicts on large projects; (2) coordinate and synchronize various parts of complex projects; and (3) expedite completion of projects. PERT is a management technique that shows how activities and events interrelate from the beginning to the end of large projects. The two major tasks of PERT involve (1) events, sometimes referred to as specific accomplishments, but also referred to as points or milestones marking the beginning or end of an activity, and (2) activities, which represent work that is required to complete a specific event. PERT can serve as a tool for planning and monitoring large projects and requires three principal steps: (1) identification of all component activities; (2) estimation of completion time for each activity; and (3) plotting milestones or events. Figure 6.2 contains a sample PERT chart.

Critical Path Methods were developed in 1957 to assist with scheduling continuing maintenance of chemical plants. A critical path is one whose shortest completion time defines the earliest possible project-completion time. Delays in the critical path always cause overall project delays. Delays that occur off the critical path may not have an impact on final project completion.

Many professionals involved in grants and contracts use project-management techniques, and there are a wide variety of procedures that can be used to help manage these activities. However, almost any set of activities, no matter how large or how small, can benefit from the application of management strategies. Anytime professional trips are made, programs are planned, or services delivered, project-management strategies can be applied.

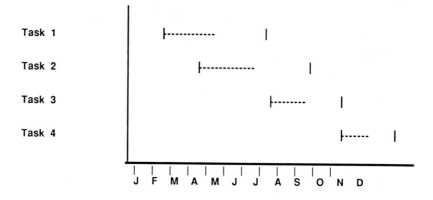

Figure 6.1. Format for a Gantt chart.

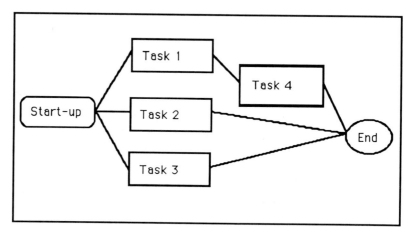

Figure 6.2. Format for a PERT chart.

ARTIFICIAL INTELLIGENCE AND STATISTICAL DECISIONS

Artificial intelligence techniques hold a great deal of promise in the area of research in health education. That potential comes in several areas, including the use of *expert systems* to assist in the planning and conduct of sophisticated statistical analysis, the computation of sample sizes, the allocation of subjects to random assignments, and the planning of complex research designs. Illustrations of each of these capabilities follows.

Selection of Statistical Tests

One of the most important areas of current research in expert systems is their application to statistical analysis. Statistical analysis benefits from such development in several ways, including in *decision assistance,* or assistance with the selection of appropriate analytic strategies, and in help with sophisticated statistical decision making involved in complex analyses.

One of the biggest difficulties that health educators face in the planning of studies is the computation of appropriate sample sizes. Such computations are necessary if a research design is to ensure the chance of finding significant differences that really exist. The key is to find a sample size large enough to do the job, yet economical at the same time. A sample size far larger than what is needed adds unnecessary expense to a study. Although many formulas and tables of power curves are readily available in survey and other research textbooks, a number of specific pieces of software have been designed to provide assistance when deciding on sample size.

Most health professionals who have had adequate research training are familiar with the related but somewhat different problems of selecting a random sample from a population, and randomly assigning subjects to study groups. Even the most elementary courses in research and statistics provide some introduction to the use of random-number tables for both these tasks. Although these tables are useful for small samples, their use for larger samples becomes both tedious and error prone. To deal with these problems, a number of applications have been developed to assist the health researcher.

Once a project has been thoroughly planned, and procedures have been tested, the conduct of the study becomes the critical issue. Just as there are concerns with the reliability and validity of measures, there are quality-assurance concerns in the research process itself. In this case the researcher is concerned about faithfully following the research design. Microcomputer software currently exists to assist with this phase of the research process as well. Here the primary concerns revolve around data acquisition, data analysis, and reporting the results.

Data Acquisition

The microcomputer may be used to acquire data automatically. This kind of data acquisition has typically been accomplished by the use of electronic hookups. Stroke volumes, core temperatures, brain waves, and other functions may be recorded from cardiac catheters, rectal probes, and ECG skin electrodes with the data directly entered into a microcomputer. Such sensors accept continuous data (e.g., temperature, pressure) which will be converted to the appropriate format for use by the computer. The mechanism involved in this process is called *analog-to-digital conversion* (i.e., A/D).

Another research approach, for which microcomputers are increasingly being used, is telephone surveying. Through similar interactive packages, the microcomputer is programmed to dial a number at random. In some systems, when the potential respondent answers the phone, the microcomputer records responses signaled by the number that is pressed on a touch-tone dial (Shangraw, 1986). The microcomputer also coordinates the survey questions. On the basis of specific responses, certain predetermined questions may not be asked, or others may be added to the survey.

Data Analysis

Data may be quantitative or qualitative and each kind is analyzed differently. Complex statistical packages, previously available only on the mainframe as SPSS and SAS, are now becoming available for microcomputers. With the increasingly faster execution speeds and greater memory capacities of microcomputers, complex statistical procedures are just as easily performed on microcomputers as on the mainframes. The use of a microcomputer is also less costly and more convenient for many researchers.

A wide variety of statistical software is available for microcomputers in today's market. In choosing a statistical program, health researchers should consider several characteristics, including compatibility with hardware and software systems, cost, speed, accuracy, documentation, ease of use, and sophistication of analysis. Health researchers should be absolutely clear on their analysis needs before selecting a program. Table 6.1 contains a list of statistical routines currently available in microcomputer applications, reflecting the surprising breadth of routines that a health researcher can access in today's microcomputer environment.

Reporting the Results

Once acquired and analyzed, the presentation of data and the reporting of findings are most important to the health researcher. Problems cannot be solved without the communication of results. In the domain of presentations the microcomputer is a capable ally for the health educator. Several common software programs can help in a variety of ways to present data in an appealing manner. These include graphic packages, word processors, desktop publishers, charting packages, and desktop presenters, all of which were thoroughly described in chapter 2. Table 6.2 contains a summary of some of the more readily available statistical packages for microcomputers.

DECISION ASSISTANCE

With the increasing technological capabilities of microcomputers comes the realization that until now advances in hardware have far outdistanced advances in software. Although thirty-two-bit architecture is now common in microprocessors, executing instructions several million times per second, with more than 1 million bytes of main memory and optical disks capable of storing more than 600 million characters of information, the dominant applications in use today are still word processing, spreadsheets, and database software. In order to move beyond the limited benefits of these applications, it will be necessary to access the technologies

Table 6.1

Statistical Routines Currently Available in Microcomputer Applications

STATISTICAL PROCEDURE	ROUTINE	
Analysis of variance	ANCOVA	Latin-square
	Factorial	Nested designs
	Planned comparisons	Post-hoc comparisons
	Repeated measures	Split-plot
	Unbalanced	
Cluster analysis	Multiway tables	Chi-square tests
Contingency tables	Other tests	
Correlation	Fisher's transform	Partial correlations
	Pearson correlations	Spearman rank-order
Data handling	Case selection	Computed variables
	Free-field formatting	Lag variables
	Merging data files	Missing-value options
	Import/export files	Sort cases
	Spreadsheet editor	Transformation
	Transposition of data	Variable labels
Graphics	Box-whisper plots	Casement plots
	Chernoff faces	Contour plots
	Histograms	3-D histograms
	Line graphs	Log/semilog plots
	Pie charts	Probability plots
	Cumulative probability plots	Scatter plots
	Stem-and-leaf plots	X-Y-Z plots
Log-linear models	MANOVA	MANCOVA
Multidimensional scaling	Factor analysis	Hotelling's T
Multivariate analyses	Cononical correlation	Discriminant analysis
	Principal components	Rep. measures MANOVAs
Nonparametric tests	Fisher's exact test	Friedman ANOVA
	Mann-Whitney U	Kendall's Tau
	Kolmogorov-Smirnov	Wilcoxon
Regression	Logistic	Multiple
	Nonlinear	Residual analysis
	Ridge	Stepwise
Survival analysis	Box-Jenkins Arima	Cross-correlation
Time-series analysis	Auto-correlation	Auto-spectral analysis
	Cross-spectral analysis	Data smoothing
	Fast fourier transform	
T-tests	Independent	Paired

Table 6.2

Selected Research, Statistical, and Epidemiological Analysis Packages

TITLE	VENDOR	SYSTEM
BMDP/PC	BMDP Statistical Software, Inc.	IBM-PC
CAI Nursing Research	Mosbysystems	Apple II
Clinical Research System I, II, and III.	R. H. Searle	IBM-PC
Crunch Statistical Package: Version 3.1	Crunch Software	IBM-PC
CSS Statistical System	Statsoft Software	IBM-PC
Epistat	T. Gustafson	IBM-PC
Nursing Research CAI	Mosbysystems	IBM-PC
Solo: Version 101	BMDP Statistical Software, Inc.	IBM-PC
SPSS/PC Plus: Version 2.0—Base Package	SPSS Inc.	IBM-PC
SPSS/PC Plus: Version 2.0—Data Entry	SPSSInc.	IBM-PC
SPSS/PC Plus: Version 2.0—Graphics	SPSS Inc.	IBM-PC
SPSS/PC Plus: Version 2.0—Mapping	SPSS Inc.	IBM-PC
SPSS/PC Plus: Version 2.0—Trends	SPSS Inc.	IBM-PC
SPSS/PC: Version 2.0—Advanced Statistics	SPSS Inc.	IBM-PC
SPSS/PC: Version 2.0—Tables	SPSS Inc.	IBM-PC
StatView 512+	BrainPower, Inc.	Apple Macintosh
Systat	Systat, Inc.	IBM-PC Apple Macintosh

associated with artificial intelligence. One of these areas of application, expert systems, holds considerable potential for health educators. This technology is instrumental in assisting with the complex decision making often faced by the health professional.

Expert systems have proved useful in situations when human-resource information is scarce, lost, or has a widespread, unmet need (Jewell, Abraham, and Fitzpatrick, 1987). These systems are structured, in a process similar to that demonstrated by an organized team of experts, to offer information and guidance to health professionals regarding decision-making strategies. Once the human experts and the clients determine the problem, collect the related cognitive information, and outline effective strategies, a knowledge base can be created for the system. Production rules or guidelines can then be inserted so that the computer can analyze the knowledge base it has and make conclusions or recommendations to the user. The availability of such systems to health educators can help accomplish the complex synthesis of knowledge from recognized experts with the computer's capacity to store, organize, and deliver theoretical information upon command.

Over the past twenty years, most of the expert systems developed in the health fields have been in clinical settings but have been devoted to many different types of medicine. The following are some of the most important developments in this area:

- AI/COAG (Kingsland, Gaston, Vanker, & Lindberg, 1982) in the area of coagulation/hematology;
- AI/RHEUM (Lindberg et al., 1980; Kingsland & Lindberg, 1983) in the area of rheumatology;
- SPE (Weiss et al., 1981) designed to interpret serum protein electrophoresis data;
- INTERNIST/CADUCEUS (Miller, Pople & Meyers, 1982; Pople, 1982), a very extensive project designed to encompass the entire domain of internal medicine;
- PIP (Pauker, Gorry, Kassirer, & Schwante, 1976), for diagnosis in the area of kidney diseases;
- Digitalis Advisor (Gorry, Siverman, & Pauker, 1978), to oversee medical management of digitalis therapy;
- ABEL (Patil, Szolovits & Schwante, 1981), for work in the area of electrolyte disorders;
- VM (Fagan, Kunz, Feigenbaum, & Osborn, 1979), in the area of ventilatory management of a person in respiratory therapy;
- ONCOCIN (Shortliffe et al., 1981), for assistance in the area of implementation of oncology protocols;
- ATTENDING (Miller, 1984), a system designed to critique a physician's plan for anesthesia management.

We are drowning in information but starved for knowledge.
—**John Naisbitt, *Megatrends*, 1984**

OVERVIEW OF ARTIFICIAL INTELLIGENCE

The field of artificial intelligence maintains an aura of mystery and surrealism. Over the years filmmakers have filled the screens, and our imaginations, with computers whose abilities range from starting a nuclear war to falling in love with a human being. Although advancement in artificial intelligence is rapid, technology is far from producing a society of humanlike robots.

Defining artificial intelligence is not an easy task, due primarily to the evolving nature of the field of study and the broadness of the knowledge base. The following definition by Barr and Feigenbaum (1981), cited in Jackson (1986, p. 2), provides representative consensus in the field: "Artificial intelligence (AI) is the part of computer science concerned with designing intelligent computer systems, that is, systems that exhibit the characteristics we associate with intelligence in human behavior—understanding language, learning, reasoning, solving problems, and so on."

In other words, the function of AI is to provide computer programs that simulate human behavior and reasoning (Jackson 1986). Artificial intelligence draws from technological advances in computer science, linguistics, psychology, philosophy, and engineering to achieve the goal of creating intelligent systems. It is this broad disciplinary basis that provides artificial intelligence its power, but in addition conversely provides the field with a series of potential problems due to the complexity of the task of simulating human behavior.

Currently the goal of artificial intelligence is to replicate "the functionality of the human mind" (Parsaye & Chignell, 1988, p. 9). Many proponents of artificial intelligence suggest that the field has now advanced beyond functional replication of the brain to an ability to replicate the internal structure of the brain. The most sophisticated example of efforts to understand and replicate the structure of the brain are demonstrated in computer models of *neural networks* (Parsaye & Chignell, 1988; Ackley, Hinton & Sejnowski, 1985). Brain simulation through neural networks has advanced rapidly over the past five years and provides the most promising link to the representation of the learning process (Hinton & Anderson, 1981; Feldman & Ballard, 1982; Rumelhart & McClelland, 1986). Chances are that neural networks will explain the critical link between information and knowledge, which will enhance comprehensive efforts in health education (Gold & Kelly, 1988).

IMPLICATIONS AND TRENDS FOR HEALTH EDUCATORS

As stated earlier, the most popular and widely used expert systems in health are found in the clinical setting. Although these expert systems are increasing in use and popularity by the medical profession, most do not have specific application to health-education settings.

Recent efforts have been made to expand expert-system applications in the area of prevention, but none completely utilize the full potential of expert-system capabilities. Expert-systems technology in health education can provide valuable assistance in the area of training and technical assistance by teaching individuals how to plan effective programs, select and apply appropriate statistical tests, or organize community efforts for participation in an intervention. Depending on the topic of interest, expert systems can be developed for use by the general population regarding health-promotion and disease-prevention efforts, as well. It is believed that repeated exposure to expert-system technology can teach decision-making and problem-solving skills, which can be transferred to other health situations. Decision-making skills are considered an integral component in health-education programs and critical in the long-term change of people's health values and behaviors.

Software that draws upon the remarkable power of the computer as well as the benefits of artificial intelligence is currently underutilized and underdeveloped in health education. Knowledge of the potential capabilities as well as the limitations of microcomputer software is necessary to improve its utilization by health educators in research, planning, and decision assistance.

The field of artificial intelligence provides health educators with the unique opportunity to link the present programs, such as health-risk appraisals and dietary analyses, to the future. Examples of potential systems might include simulated programs that visually demonstrate the metabolic processes of a specific client when a daily diet chart is inputted. Another possibility is an expert system that assists in the comprehensive planning process and complex decisons that must occur in program planning and evaluation. The special quality of these systems, however, will always be the presence and accessibility of human expertise at one's fingertips.

SUMMARY

1. How should health educators be trained to recognize the potential for the application of technology to the research process?

2. What are the potential advantages and disadvantages of the use of expert systems in the planning and conduct of health-education research?

3. How would you distinguish between the traditional health-hazard/risk-appraisal approaches to life-style assessment and the application of expert-system technology to life-style assessment?

4. Describe potential applications in the field of health education suitable for expert-systems development.

DISCUSSION QUESTIONS

Birkett, N. J. (1988). Computer-aided personal interviewing: A new technique for data collection in epidemiological survey. *American Journal of Epidemiology, 127*(3), 684–690.

Elmer-DeWitt, P.(1988, March 28). Fast and smart. *Time*, p. 54–58.

Frenzel, L. E. (1987). *Understanding expert systems.* Indianapolis: Howard W. Sams and Company.

Gold, R. S. (1983). Computing health: Choosing statistical software for microcomputers. *Health Education, 14*(7), 33–35.

Hart, A. 1986. *Knowledge acquisition for expert systems.* New York: McGraw-Hill.

Hill, M. (1986). Why a statistical package on a micro? *Psychopharmacology Bulletin 22*(1), 65–72.

Jacobsen, B. S., Tulman, L., Lowery, B. J., & Garson, C. (1988). Experiencing the research process by using statistical software on microcomputers. *Nursing Research.* (University of Minnesota), *37,*(1), 56–59.

Kelly, M. A. & Gold, R. S. (1988). Expert systems in health education. *Health Education, 19*(6), 32–33.

Linden, E. (1988, March 28). Putting knowledge to work. *Time*, pp. 60–63.

RECOMMENDED READINGS

7

LEGAL AND
ETHICAL ISSUES

By the completion of this chapter, the student will be able to

- describe the potential legal, ethical, and moral dilemmas facing a health educator using computers in professional practice;
- understand the concepts of liability, negligence, and defective program and practice;
- distinguish between anonymity and confidentiality of information;
- describe the methods available to protect data from unauthorized access and modification;
- explain the issues pertaining to the regulation of health-related software;
- recognize the potential of computer crime;
- explain the major issues related to computer viruses;
- identify the primary ethical concerns of the use of computers in health education.

Anonymity: A situation in which the identity of a person providing information is unknown.

Computer crime: The use of computers to access, modify, or change data unlawfully.

Computer viruses: A section of program code that attaches itself to a computer's operating systems and does subsequent damage to the information stored in the computer.

Confidentiality: Assurance that data collected from persons will not be reported in any manner that allows the individual to be identified by others.

Data backup: The process of making copies of electronic information to protect against loss.

Hacker: A person who is very knowledgeable about the technical characteristics and operation of computer systems.

Liability: Legal responsibility for producing goods or services as promised and in a manner that is not harmful to the recipient.

Negligence: Failure to comply with a set of professional standards or rules that govern professional behavior. As a legal concept, a professional may be held liable for not adhering to such standards of practice.

Password: A word or code used to identify an authorized user of a computer system, programs, or data files. When the password provided by a user is incorrect, access is denied.

Privacy: Refers to the legal right to control information about oneself.

Unauthorized access: Occurs when any security measures are breached or overridden in order to secure access to data.

INTRODUCTION AND OVERVIEW

A look back to the early 1960s, and to the introduction of computerized technology to record keeping in health-related fields, would reveal that financial and laboratory records were most frequently maintained in this way. Over the course of almost thirty years, many changes have occurred in both the technology and the attitudes of health professionals toward using that technology. In addition to storing, managing, and retrieving information, computers are used today to assist with professional decision making and to teach; furthermore, communications technology permits the linkage of databases never before connected. It is clear that technology has solved many problems, not only of record maintenance but of utilization as well. Prospective payment systems, diagnosis-related groups, and registries are all made possible today through the changes in technology described in this book. However, with the benefits come costs, and the purpose of this chapter is to examine some of the nonfinancial costs. This subject naturally gives rise to legal and ethical issues.

Even if health educators do not maintain medical records, there is a great deal of information that they collect from people in their programs, and much of it is personal and some very sensitive. However, the maintenance of records is not the only area of legal or ethical concern when the use of computers in a professional setting is concerned. Health-risk appraisals and other health assessments provide information and suggestions for changes in behavior; and instructional software developed for the wide variety of target populations that health educators serve provide information about health and behavior that can be misused, misinterpreted, or misunderstood. Clearly, then, the legal concepts associated with *liability, negligence,* and *malfunction,* and the legal/ethical concepts associated with individual human rights, apply to the use of computers in health-education settings. Ironically, Watson and Bernstein (1988) raise the issue of liability when *not* using computers, given the traditional rules of "reasonable prudence" and "standards of care." If it can be shown that computers are widely used in a profession, and improve the capacity of practicing professionals to do their job, then those professionals not using computers may be liable for negligence.

LIABILITY FOR PERSONAL INJURY CAUSED BY DEFECTIVE PROGRAMS

Brannigan and Dayhoff (1981) state that "during the past ten years, the use of computer programs in medicine has become increasingly prevalent. As these programs proliferate, however, their potential to injure patients also increases. Although the question of liability for personal injuries caused by defective medical computer programs has not been addressed by the courts, it is inevitable that this question will arise in a judicial form" (p. 123). As computers in professional settings become increasingly common, the issue raised by Brannigan and Dayhoff (1981) grows critical to health-education professionals, even more so as the sophistication of health-related software increases. Health assessments, whether health-risk, dietary, fitness, or stress, invariably provide information to health-education clients about their personal behaviors and risks, and many also make recommendations for changes in behavior. Because of the increasing use of these programs by health professionals without adequate training, combined with the difficulty in interpreting health information, the likelihood of a health educator facing a plaintiff claiming injury in court is inevitable.

If a health educator uses software, and a person becomes injured as a result of changes in behavior resulting from that use, the courts are faced with important legal problems. This field of law is still relatively young and still developing—and while there have been a few cases, there is currently no definitive case law upon which to stand. The principal legal question arises from the issue of whether health-related computer programs represent products or services. If computer programs are legally judged to be products, then "manufacturers, distributors, and purveyors of programs are likely to be held to a strict products liability standard" (Brannigan & Dayhoff, 1981). If they are deemed to represent a professional service to health-education clients, then the developer and health professional will be held liable only if negligence can be demonstrated.

A related but slightly different legal issue is as follows: If there is a program error, does that error represent a *design* or a *production defect?* The courts will also have to decide which of the creators and/or users of the program should be held liable for a plaintiff's injury. It may be useful to add that computer programs used by health educators generally fall into one of three categories: (1) programs that the client interacts with directly; (2) programs upon which the health educator relies entirely for educational diagnoses or prescriptions; and (3) programs upon which the health educator relies in part for educational diagnoses or prescriptions. Because of the differences in the nature of these programs and how health educators use them, courts will have a wide variety of theories of liability to consider when assessing case outcomes, including negligence, breach of contract, breach of express or implied warranty, or products liability (Brannigan & Dayhoff, 1981, p. 127). Although the nature of each of these bodies of law is beyond the scope of this book, it is safe to say that health educators should not be casual users of computer software in their practice. That one is uninformed is not an adequate defense. The selection of software for use in professional practice, and the way in which that software is used, require careful attention to these issues.

REGULATION OF HEALTH-RELATED SOFTWARE

Because of the recent advances in health-related software, and the prospects of injury resulting from its use, the Food and Drug Administration is currently examining its options for regulating the manufacture, sale, and use of software as a medical device under the auspices of the Food, Drug and Cosmetic Act (FDCA). Such regulation was first authorized by Congress under the FDCA of 1938. The original legislation has been reviewed and modified by amendment several times since then, with the most pertinent changes occurring in 1976 when Congress decided that the term *device* meant both worthless items resulting from quackery as well as legitimate articles. Article 201(h) of those amendments states that a device is "an instrument, apparatus, implement, machine, contrivance, implant, in vitro reagent, or other similar or related article, including any component, part, or accessory, which is . . . intended for use in the diagnosis of disease or other conditions, or in the cure, mitigation, treatment, or prevention of disease, in man or other animals." Although most authorities assume this definition relates to medical and clinical applications, it is important to recognize that health educators work in the areas of primary and secondary prevention. With the impending credentialing of health educators, implying specified competencies in these areas, the practice of health education probably falls within the scope of the FDCA device regulations. Again, it is beyond the scope of this book to examine the legal definitions of "instrument, apparatus," etc., but it is not unreasonable to assume that the use of computer software within the context of health-education practice might be covered by the term "contrivance" (Brannigan, 1987, p. 348).

Whether regulation of health-related software is properly regulated under the medical-devices statutes will continue to be a difficult question to answer. However, it is safe to assume that there will be some form of regulation imposed on this type of software with its increasing use. The task for the health educator is to become involved in the identification of the vehicle for such regulation, because product regulation under the FDCA statutes can have many negative outcomes. Brannigan (1987, pp. 353–354) suggests at least five: (1) Such regulation tends to stifle program development and limits activity in this area to those developers most adept at dealing with the legal concerns raised. (2) Product regulation results in centralized production by only a few firms. (3) Product regulation limits professional flexibility in adapting software to individual needs. (4) Liability protection (e.g., insurance) is costly to professionals and increasingly difficult to obtain. (5) Each application would have to be assessed for its applicability under the product-liability statutes. Although far from being settled at this time, these are issues with which the health educator should be familiar.

PRIVACY AND CONFIDENTIALITY: A CONCEPTUAL OVERVIEW

Romano (1987) suggests that a conceptual overview of the issues related to *privacy* is difficult to construct because of the relationship between privacy issues and others such as freedom, autonomy, solitude, and secrecy. But she goes on to define privacy as "control over exposure of self or information about oneself and freedom from intrusion" [and suggests that the issue is] "related to the human vulnerability to harm as well as to the human need to retain a sense of control over one's personal life" (p. 99). Privacy is, in essence, the right to decide how much personal information to share with others, and includes the potential for protecting that information from misuse by others on unrestricted disclosure.

Although improperly used as a synonym for privacy, *confidentiality* is quite different. Confidentiality begins with the assumption that someone is providing personal information to another, and is specifically concerned with the nature of the relationship between the provider and the recipient of information. Confidentiality refers to the issue of redisclosure by the recipient of personal information. As Romano (1987) states, "Privacy is normally controlled by the person to whom one confides or relinquishes privacy. Confidentiality, then, is logically dependent on a loss of privacy. Privacy is viewed as a person's right. Confidentiality is seen as the health professional's duty—the duty to safeguard the secrecy of information collected, stored, transmitted, and retrieved in a health care information system" (p. 100).

Legislative and policy initiatives regarding privacy and confidentiality are quite incomplete and sometimes contradictory from a legal and ethical standpoint. Contrary to popular opinion, even though the Constitution itself contains references to privacy in six of the first fourteen amendments, there appears to be no constitutional right to its protection (Winslade, 1982; Hiller & Beyda, 1981). There are, however, federal, state, and local statutes, regulations, and legal decisions that carry the force of law. Table 7.1 contains a review of major federal legislation about which health educators should be knowledgeable.

Legislation and Policy Regarding Privacy of Information

Under the terms of the Federal Privacy Act of 1974, a Privacy Protection Study Commission was established to recommend appropriate legislative and regulatory mechanisms to ensure protection of privacy. Following a two-year study period, the commission suggested the following principles be used as guidelines (Hsiao, Kerr, & Modnick, 1979):

- *Openness.* A private individual shall have the right to know what records are created and how they are used by agencies.
- *Access.* A private individual shall have the right to access, see, and copy personal information collected.
- *Correctness.* A private individual shall have the right to correct and/or amend personal information collected by agencies.
- *Limits.* There should be limits on the types of information an agency can collect and how that information will be used.

Simkin and Dependahl (1987) suggest that the Federal Privacy Act has been the most important of the major pieces of federal legislation identified. However, they go on to say that "at present there is no federal statute requiring businesses or other organizations to guard private data files. This means, for example, that there is no law requiring a doctor or lawyer to safeguard personal information about you beyond what might be required by a personal code of conduct or professional ethics. The conclusion is that, at local levels, personal data is data at risk" (p. 309).

Table 7.1

Legislative Attention to Privacy of Information

DATE	ACT	IMPLICATIONS
1970	Fair Credit Reporting Act (PL 91–508)	Requires that an individual be informed as to why credit application is denied and gives the right to challenge the information in a credit rating.
1970	Freedom of Information Act	Provides the public with the right to obtain information from federal agencies. Medical records are exempt from FOI requests.
1974	Federal Privacy Act (PL 93–579)	Restricts the disclosure of individual personal information. This act does not apply to state, local, or private sectors.
1985	Electronic Communications Privacy Act	Extends personal-privacy protection to personal and corporate communications and to electronic communications systems.
1986	Computer Fraud and Abuse Act	Makes malicious trespass into private computer systems for any of the following purposes a felony: (a) obtaining top-secret military information, personal or private credit information; (b) committing fraud; (c) altering or destroying federal information.

Data Security

Although a full coverage of legal issues related to protection of privacy is beyond the scope of this book, Watson (1981) suggests that the law deals with protection within the context of several mechanisms, including tort litigation (invasion of privacy, infliction of emotional distress, libel, slander, abuse of trust), and violation of federal or state privacy acts. Four points are of particular significance for health educators involved in the creation, management, or use of databases with health-related data:

1. Health educators should be aware of the general policies governing their activities under the U.S. Department of Health and Human Services regulations on the protection of human subjects (USDHHS, 1984).

2. Only one Supreme Court decision has dealt specifically with the issue of privacy of health records in database systems (*Whalen v. Roe,* 1977), and in that case the court permitted such systems to continue to exist because of the existence of regulations on the protection of privacy. The following section of the decision from *Whalen v. Roe* (reported in Brannigan & Dayhoff, 1986, p. 51) provides the thrust of the Court's logic:

A final word about issues we have not decided. We are not unaware of the threat to privacy implicit in the accumulation of vast amounts of

EXHIBIT 7.1

ARE STANDARDS OF PRACTICE ENOUGH?

In 1946 the court found an entire industry, the tugboat industry, negligent because the tugs were not equipped with radios (the case of the TJ Hooper). The fact that all tugs did not have radios was no protection for an individual boat and captain. This case was extended to the health professions in *Helling v. Carey* (1974) in which the court decided that a glaucoma test should have been provided to a twenty-year-old woman, even though no evidence could be shown that the test fell within the professional standards of the time.

Note. Helling v. Carey, 83 Wash. 2d 514, 519 P.2d. 981 (1974). *In re* TJ Hooper, 60 f.2d 737 (2nd cir. 1932).

personal information in computerized data banks or other massive government files. . . . The right to collect and use such data is typically accompanied by a concomitant statutory or regulatory duty to avoid unwarranted disclosure. . . . We therefore need not, and do not, decide any question which might be presented by the unwarranted disclosure of accumulated private data—whether intentional or unintentional—or by a system which did not include comparable security provision.

3. Generally accepted professional standards may not be enough protection for health educators against tort liability. In other words, there are adequate precedents to suggest that even if all health educators follow the same practices in maintaining security of data as might be considered professionally adequate, an entire profession may be held negligent. Exhibit 7.1 contains a more complete explanation of this issue.

4. Most of the protection in the Federal Privacy Act for professionals in practice involves the need to prove deliberate misuse of computerized data. In other words, if a health educator can show that misuse was not deliberate, then negligence is not an issue. However, it now appears probable that deliberate misuse may be construed unless health educators provide adequate security against unauthorized access to those data.

These four points are worth emphasizing for their unique importance to health educators using computers in their practice. In the first instance, health educators should be aware that there are specific federal regulations concerning the collection of data on human subjects. Most health educators are familiar with these regulations regarding protection of human subjects within the context of informed consent. However, these guidelines also relate to the issues of privacy and confidentiality of data. Second, the Supreme Court decided that protection for practicing health professionals (educators) comes from adequate attention to, and implementation of, existing standards of protection. Third, there are adequate precedents which indicate that practicing health educators are not necessarily protected from liability just because they employ the same standards and protections of the general community of practitioners. Fourth, it appears that protection of data must include by definition security from unauthorized access. In other words, a health educator may be held liable for unauthorized use of data if adequate security for the database has not been provided. This possibility forces the practitioner to become aware not only of the mechanisms that can be applied to ensure data security, but also of the potential danger of computer crime.

Unauthorized access, modification, destruction or theft of information can occur through many means, but when it is done maliciously and/or deliberately, it is a crime in all fifty states. Perhaps the clearest case of this occurring in the health fields is a case known as the *Milwaukee 414s*. The city of Milwaukee is in the 414 zip-code area of Wisconsin. In July 1983 an FBI investigation uncovered a group of young teenagers in Milwaukee who considered themselves hackers. In the 1970s the term *hacker* originally meant someone who was very skilled at getting the most out of a computer system by customizing it and providing sophisticated programming to extend the system's capabilities. However, in the 1980s the term has come to mean someone skilled at illegal entry into computerized databases through telecommunications lines. These teenage hackers managed to "break into" more than sixty business and government databases by "cracking" password and other protection schemes. They succeeded in accessing data at the Los Alamos National Laboratory, several large banks, and the Sloan-Kettering Memorial Cancer Center in New York. While nothing was sabotaged or destroyed, this case illustrates the potential for unauthorized entry into sensitive databases. Imagine a doctor going to hospital medical records to assess whether someone has an allergy, or a health educator recommending behavioral changes based on data in a client's files—and the records have been altered. Either case is potentially dangerous, life threatening, and raises the specter of negligence and subsequent liability for the health professional and the institution.

Whenever databases exist that contain sensitive and personal health information, whether coupled with the potential for remote phone access or not, there are certain security techniques that may be utilized to reduce the risk of data loss, compromise, or unauthorized access. There are physical-security strategies as well as direct data-protection devices and techniques. As might be imagined, physical security includes such issues as protecting computers from natural disasters (fireproof and waterproof compartments for machine equipment and software; uninterruptible power sources such as backup generators; surge protectors and line filters) or from physical vandalism, and providing access to authorized users only. Program and data protection become important issues as well as components of what is often called a disaster-recovery strategy. Figures 7.1A and 7.1B illustrate the two primary mechanisms for *data backup*. When data files are updated by rewriting over existing files, backup can

Figure 7.1A. Strategies for backing up data: duplicate copy.

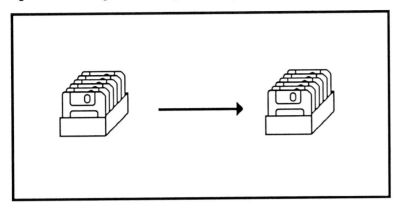

Figure 7.1B. Strategies for backing up data: generations of master files.

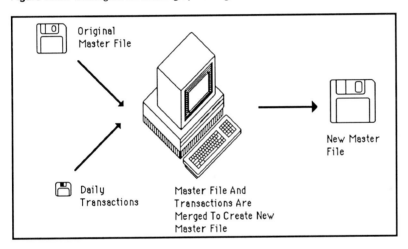

best be accomplished by completely copying the data files. These duplicate files then allow for data recovery in case of loss. In this case simple
copy or backup software will duplicate the files onto additional storage
media. When many transactions occur on a frequent basis, and transaction files are maintained, an efficient scheme uses master files of several generations. At the end of a fixed interval, a master file is updated
by merging it with a transaction file. The updated master file then becomes the new master file. In this scheme, however, the original master
file and transaction file are maintained so that if the new master file is
lost or damaged, it can be recreated again. Each subsequent updated
master file becomes a new-generation data file and the sequences are
often referred to as father/son master files. Some organizations will
maintain at least three to five generations of master and transactions
files as security against lost data.

The most frequently used data-protection schemes are the following:

1. *Anonymity.* In order to make a database anonymous, all personal identifiers must be stripped. In this way anyone gaining access will have access to data, but will not be able to link that data to any individual.

2. *Encryption.* This method is most useful when very sensitive data are maintained in a database or when sensitive data are transmitted over telephone lines. Encryption refers to the encoding of the data in such a way that translation would require a separate decryption algorithm.

3. *Lock-out and dial-back systems.* Both lock-out and dial-back systems are appropriate with phone access to databases. With a lock-out system a user is given only a small number of tries to enter a password correctly. If after this fixed number of tries, the user has not correctly entered the password, the system will disconnect. A dial-back system is one that begins with a user successfully logging onto a system. Once the user has typed a correct password, the system will end the session and look up the password and an authorized phone number for that password. The system will then dial back the authorized number to reestablish the connection.

4. *Passwords.* A password is any string of alphanumeric characters assigned to an individual or group of individuals authorized access to a computer system. When logging onto a computer system, the user must provide the correct combination of letters, numbers, and special characters that constitute a legitimate password. Although passwords provide some security, there are problems—they can be lost, given away, or taken. Any program, agency, or individual setting up a password-protection scheme should recognize the limitations and take steps to reduce the problems by (1) frequently changing passwords; (2) not allowing individuals to select their own passwords (many people tend to select common terms relatively easy to discover); (3) train employees not to divulge passwords under any circumstances.

5. *Segmentation.* The process of segmenting a database divides it into differing levels of sensitivity. With segmentation a person with a certain password may have access to only some information in the database. In order to access more sensitive information, another password with higher security is required.

6. *Transaction auditing.* It is possible to set up a database system in which all requests made of a database are linked to the password of the individual making the request. In this case it is possible for the system managers to monitor the use of each authorized user.

Computer Crime

As of 1986 every state in the United States had enacted specific legislation regarding the use of computers to commit criminal activities. In spite of the dramatic amount of attention given to computer crime, a relatively small number of such crimes have been reported—probably because of the difficulty in detection and the fact that most crimes in general are not reported. However, there are expectations that computer crime will continue to increase as a function of (1) the growing number of individuals using computers for personal and professional purposes; (2) the increasing number of computers in use; (3) the ever-widening diversity of applications being computerized; (4) the growing power of technology; and (5) our continued dependence on computers for basic activities.

Among the most visible computer crimes are those that involve fraud and theft of funds; however, there are several specific categories of computer crime that may have a greater effect on computers used by health educators in professional settings—computer viruses and the unauthorized access, modification, destruction, or theft of information. Because I have already discussed issues related to unauthorized access, and its attendant problems, I will focus here specifically on viruses.

A computer virus is a small section of computer code that is designed to do two things: (1) replicate itself, and (2) conduct some specific activities for which its author intended. When an infected program is introduced into a computer system, the virus duplicates itself and attaches to another piece of program code somewhere else in the system. These pieces of infected code then ordinarily lie dormant until some predetermined time before they begin carrying out their preprogrammed activities. Unfortunately, these preprogrammed activities are often destructive. Viruses are capable of destroying data, erasing files, tying up the system's resources, consuming all available memory, preventing any other program from operating, damaging pertinent system files, preventing access to a hard disk, or simply displaying a message directly at the system users.

One of the first viruses created was programmed simply to print a message on a computer screen on Christmas Day—"Joy to the World." Although this example does not appear to be particularly harmful, it does demonstrate the capacity for infecting computers. This small piece of program code attached itself to the system files, read the date on the internal clock of the computer, and then followed specific actions at the preappointed time—December 25, 1986. Once this capacity was demonstrated, other more dangerous viruses were created. In 1989 a virus called Datacrime was created to activate itself on Friday, October 13. This virus, however, was designed to destroy a special resource in IBM and compatible computers called the "file-allocation table." Once a file-allocation table in such a computer is damaged, the computer cannot use the information stored on its hard-disk drive. The disk drive must be erased and reformatted, causing the loss of all programs and data stored there.

The threat of infection from computer viruses is real. Anyone operating a computer system today needs to understand how to protect the system and its data. As with viruses affecting human and animal populations, a vector for transmission is necessary; in most cases transmission of computer viruses comes from using infected software on a system, or from downloading data or programs from an infected bulletin board, electronic-mail service, or public-access database. As with human virus infections, preventive behavior can minimize some of the problems.

Among the most important steps that a health educator can take are the following:

1. Backup system files, programs, and data. This is important for many reasons, including recovery if a system has been infected by a virus. In order to maintain a virus-free backup, always run virus checks before backing up software. There are commercial, shareware, and public-domain virus-detection applications that are quite effective in identifying all known viruses and replication schemes. Whatever system is used, a user should become familiar with virus-detection software for that system.

2. Whenever new software is obtained, never work with the original disks. It is a relatively easy step to write-protect new software and make a copy. When the software is installed on a system, always use the copy; then if the system or the copy becomes infected, the original is always available to begin with again.

3. If your system is on a network, be aware of the risks associated with virus. Use whatever precautions are available to prevent your files and programs from becoming infected if the server becomes infected. If a system on a network becomes infected, quarantine it by removing it from the network.

4. Do not add unfamiliar software or data files to a hard disk or file server until they have been thoroughly tested for all known viral infections. Run the applications from floppy disks for a period of time to ensure that they are virus free before adding them to a hard disk or server.

5. Be suspicious of all shared software. In order to test software, the following steps will minimize problems: (a) Boot a system from a floppy drive with any hard disk unmounted or disconnected in some way. (b) Record the size of any system and related files; the size of these files should not change over time. If they do get larger, even by only a few bytes, be suspicious. (c) Run the new software from a floppy with system software known to be virus free. If the system files change in any way when running the new software, be suspicious. (d) Modify the dates on the system's clock/calendar. Rerun the new software and observe how it works. Some viruses are programmed to cause damage after specified periods of time determined by the system clock/calendar. (e) Run virus-detection software on the new software.

It is important at this point to identify a substantial problem found in the computer-using community which enhances the prospect of spreading viruses, but which also has other damaging effects. *Software piracy* refers to the unauthorized copying and use of computer programs. If a person buys a piece of software and makes a copy for a friend, or if you use a copy of software that has been copied inappropriately, this is software piracy. Software piracy does not have to involve the exchange of money—just the unauthorized copying and/or use of software. Aside from being against the law and punishable by fine or imprisonment, software piracy has two major effects: It cheats the program author (or authors) out of legitimate revenues, and it contributes to the potential for spreading computer viruses. Whenever software is sold, the author of the software is eligible for royalty payments, in much the same way as is the author of a book. Software piracy thus discourages authors from developing sophisticated software because they are less willing to invest their time. Furthermore, piracy contributes substantially to the possible spreading of computer viruses. Some companies add *copy protection* to software to prevent such piracy.

These steps should minimize the potential dangers associated with viruses. If a system becomes infected in spite of these steps, the hard disk on the system and/or file server on the network should be erased and reformatted or reinitialized. All system software, applications programs, and data files should be reinstalled from virus-free backups.

Moor (1986) defines *computer ethics* as the analysis of the nature and social impact of the use of this technology, and the development of policy regarding its use. Victoroff (1985) suggests three domains for ethical issues with which health educators must struggle when using computers in their professional practice: (1) ethical problems related to the use of a computer for storing, exchanging, and manipulating data; (2) ethical problems related to computers when they are used as devices for reasoning with information; and (3) ethical problems that result from computers making professional judgments that may be affected by values. In an article on the ethical issues associated with the automation of nursing personnel data, Barhyte (1987) accepts these domains but adds another—ethical problems associated with the perception of computers as intimidating or deceptive (p. 171).

ETHICAL ISSUES IN HEALTH COMPUTING

The first of these domains, the issues related to storage, exchange, and manipulation of data, has already been addressed from the legal perspectives of protection of privacy, confidentiality, and anonymity, and the related issues of unauthorized access and computer crime. Added to these, however, are the ethical issues related to "propriety, warranty, liability, realm of application, regulation, use, and abuse" (Victoroff, 1985, p. 644). While these are exasperating issues in the health fields, they are very much the same regardless of whether computers or some other medical and health technology is considered. For example, proprietary software is software protected from unauthorized use or duplication. The term *proprietary* in this sense means that the program code, design, graphic images, or other components of the software are owned by someone and protected by copyright or patent. The unauthorized use or copying of such protected software is a crime. The other terms (warranty, liability, etc.) imply that a product is designed and approved for use within certain standards of practice. If those standards are not adhered to, then the warranties are no longer applicable, and the implied promises of effectiveness of the software cannot be maintained.

The second and third domains raise issues related to the use of expert systems and other artificial-intelligence systems to assist, guide, or direct professional reasoning. These systems go far beyond the presence of information as in a textbook or even in an electronic database, and move

8

EPILOG

By the completion of this chapter, the student will be able to

- respond to questions frequently raised about the application of computer technology;
- describe some of the major technological developments of computer technology to come;
- identify how technological developments will affect health educators using computers

Desktop libraries: Single compact disks that contain enormous amounts of printed materials.

Groupware: Software that is designed to be used by more than one person simultaneously.

High-definition TV (HDTV):   Television that provides resolution three or more times more precise than current television technology.

Integrated Systems Digital Network (ISDN):   A digital network standard being developed that will have the capacity to transfer voice, graphics, video, and sound over telephone lines simultaneously.

Microminiaturization: The capacity to make computer components smaller by miniaturizing different elements and placing many elements on a single chip.

Multitasking: The capacity of a computer to execute several different computer programs and tasks simultaneously.

Neural networks: Computer chips connected in such a way as to simulate the human brain.

SOME FINAL QUESTIONS ANSWERED

Microcomputer Applications in Health Education is a book designed to provide an introduction to the potential uses of microcomputers in the field of health education and related fields. It was written with the following objectives in mind: to provide an overview of the general capabilities and limitations of microcomputers and microcomputer systems; to identify ways in which microcomputers can be used in health-related settings as instructional and/or training tools; and to describe the ways in which microcomputers can be used in health-related settings as an administrative and research tool, and in decision assistance. Each of the chapters has raised questions for discussion but a few more will be presented here, along with some answers. The purpose of this chapter is to provide a global perspective on how the information in earlier chapters can be integrated.

Question: What steps can be taken to increase the use of microcomputers in health education?

Answer: There are several steps that can and should be taken by health educators, professional health-education organizations, and institutions that provide professional preparation and continuing-education programs for health educators. These steps include

- identification of the most fruitful ways in which computer technology can be applied to the needs of health educators;
- examination of the ways in which the early adopters are applying computer technology to various needs of health educators;
- continued use of professional communication mediums (journals, newsletters, professional meetings) to describe potential applications to practitioners;
- support of a general consensus on the priorities for development of applications;
- encouragement (or demand) that institutions with professional preparation programs provide specific training to preservice and in-service professionals.

Question: Should I (my agency) develop a long-range plan for integrating computers and related technology into the practice of health education?

Answer: In general terms long-range plans should be developed. These plans should include the ways in which computer technology is intended to be applied to professional practice. But these plans should not be too specific over a long time because the technology is changing so rapidly. Any implementation plans should be substantive enough to meet needs, yet flexible enough to address changing technological considerations and prospects.

Question: Which microcomputer system is best for health educators?

Answer: This is an impossible question to answer. Acquiring systems begins with the substantive identification of needs, and an assessment of the system characteristics that can best meet those needs. Systems vary dramatically in their capabilities, based on such things as memory, microprocessor capabilities, the use of peripherals, external memory, accessibility characteristics, expandability, and maintenance requirements. Once again, identification of needs is the first step, and this should be followed ultimately with the acquisition of a system designed to meet those needs but with the capacity to grow with changing demands and technological sophistication.

Question: With the costs of computing dropping, is it better to wait before making purchases of equipment and software?

Answer: No. If an individual uses dropping costs or rapid changes in technology as an explanation for not moving forward, then changes will never be made. The technology will continue to change, and the prices will continue to decline per unit of capacity. The person who waits now will wait forever. If your needs call for computerization, then make the best choice you can as soon as you can.

Question: What is the most important thing to look for in software to be used in health-education settings?

Answer: The most important thing is determining if software meets your needs adequately. Terrific software that is not targeted to your professional or personal needs will not be used, no matter how good it is.

Question: How do I know that software is good?

Answer: In the health fields good software has several important characteristics, aside from those already mentioned:

- The best applications are those that use the capabilities of the computer which make it a unique professional medium (e.g., instructional, administrative, research). In other words, the best instructional software will not replicate that which can already be accomplished as effectively without computers.
- The best software always provides a complete description of its intended uses, the basic assumptions under which it operates, and the known limitations.
- The best software that uses either population-based statistics (e.g., health-risk/health-hazard appraisal) or a database of values (e.g., nutritional values of foods) provides adequate updates to maintain constancy as the knowledge base changes.
- The best software doesn't make unreasonable promises about the impact it can have on human cognition and behavioral change.

Question: What kind of information should be expected from a vendor to demonstrate the value of the software offered?

Answer: A vendor should be willing to supply a complete list of the objectives of the software, the assumptions used in its design, a description of the algorithms used in any computational processes, a reasonable license agreement, acceptable documentation for both the professional and the client (if appropriate), and a reasonable plan for updating.

Question: What situations should I be careful with in my use of computers in health education?

Answer: Any time there is the prospect of liability associated with their use, the health educator should be aware of the implications and potential safeguards.

Question: To what extent can computer programs written for one type of microcomputer be used on another?

Answer: Generally, software written for one type of computer cannot be used on another. Many of the most sophisticated software are now produced for several computer platforms, but if a person purchases a piece of software for an IBM-PC, this program cannot be used on another machine. There is, however, a number of ways in which data files and text files created on one machine can be transferred for use on another type. So if someone has a database or a document created on an IBM-PC, it is possible to transfer the database or document to another machine, such as an Apple Macintosh. Usually this type of transfer can be accomplished in any of the following ways:

- Connect the two machines through a cable linking their serial ports; by using communications software on each machine, the data can be transferred from one machine to the other.
- If both machines have modems, one machine can connect to the other through the telephone lines, and the data can be transferred with communications software.
- There are now disk drives available that can read and write formats from different computers. For instance, it is possible to buy a disk drive that can read data from disks formatted for the IBM, then print the data on a disk formatted for an Apple Macintosh.
- There are also commercial services that will effect this transfer for you. You simply provide a disk with the data from one machine and request that the data be transferred to the other machine's format. These services can be found in almost any city.

Question: Will computers ever completely replace health professionals in some settings?

Answer: Although the use of computers in health education settings will undoubtedly continue to increase dramatically, it is highly unlikely that computers will replace health professionals. Health professionals should recognize that the unique contributions they make cannot be replaced by any computer.

Question: Should all health professionals be computer literate?

Answer: There is no question that almost any health professional's practice can be improved with the use of computers. There are so many different ways that computer technology can contribute to the health professions, it is rapidly becoming evident that the failure to use computers for certain applications will be deemed poor practice, and perhaps negligence.

Question: Should health professionals be trained to use computers in their professional settings?

Answer: Randolfi (1986) did most of the early groundwork in this regard, and it is clear that training programs contribute greatly to the literacy of health educators. There will be a time when two health educators competing for the same position will be compared on the basis of their computer expertise as well as other specific health-education competencies. Computer literacy will become a basic competency for all health educators regardless of the setting.

Question: What kind of training and experience should health educators have in order to use computerized health appraisals correctly?

Answer: The most effective training programs will provide a general overview of the capabilities and limitations of computers—not only from a technological perspective, but from an ethical and legal perspective as well. As with other health-education skills, the use of computers must occur within a context of professional ethics and responsibilities.

Question: Should a professional health-education organization that provides support for a code of ethics extend such a code to ethical issues arising from the use of computers in practice?

Answer: Yes, but it should not limit itself to a code of ethics. The Commission on Credentialing for health educators should now examine what basic competencies related to computer technology should be part of the credentialing process.

The future of computers in health education holds many possibilities, some more certain than others: there is no question that we can expect the hardware technology of computing to improve at increasing rates, and that, perhaps, someday software technology will catch up to it. We can probably expect the following developments very soon.

Increasing speed of microprocessors and memories. Desktop computers may equal the computer power of some of today's super computers by the middle of the decade. As we approach the year 2000, the prospect exists for *superconductor* technology to take us to another level of speed and capacity.

Greater memory capacity. Greater memory capacity implies at least two advancements: (1) availability of larger memory chips, and (2) the capacity to use the memory. Current operating systems on microcomputers are very limited in the amount of memory they can access. To accomplish this advance in computing, both hardware and software developments are necessary.

Increased capacity for telecommunications. With the growing use of fiber optics as communication channels, the increasing speed of microprocessors (enabling the computers to receive and understand data at a faster rate), the expanded availability and use of satellite communications, improved communications hardware, and the growing number of users making demands on the system, developments in this field are inevitable and are in fact already taking place. The Integrated Systems

WHAT CAN WE EXPECT IN THE FUTURE FOR HEALTH-EDUCATION APPLICATIONS?

Digital Network (ISDN) will allow for the transmission of video, voice, and data simultaneously over telephone lines (which will be fiber optic). This capacity will allow instantaneous worldwide communications in any medium. If you work in New York, you will be able to read today's *London Times* on your computer. A special television program transmitted in Tokyo will also be available to you on your computer.

Alternative input/output devices. We can expect to see the increasing development of hardware and software that enables people to communicate with computers in many new ways. Speech synthesis and voice recognition are only two examples of leading-edge technology beginning to be available today, but the future will bring even more developments. Imagine this scenario: Your computer scans two thousand video channels based on satellite communications, as well as all of the major bibliographic services, bulletin boards, and digital libraries simultaneously. You walk into your office in the morning and boot up your machine and say: "Get me everything being reported today on current developments in research on an AIDS vaccine." Within moments all the data (video, newspapers, reports, press releases, conferences) are in your computer's memory with the capacity to be displayed selectively, based on your specific needs.

Greater networking capacities. With the increasing use of local- and wide-area networks, greater developments will occur. We can anticipate more rapid network communications, advances in file-server technology, and advances in network software. We are only now beginning to see the potential for *groupware.* Groupware is software that allows more than one individual to operate on a single file within a specific application at one time. For example: Imagine a report is being prepared for an organization, and three people are involved in its writing. The three people live in different cities. Groupware would permit this small work group to log onto a groupware word-processing program that would allow each of them to see the same document on the screen at the same time. And they could jointly edit or write separate parts of the same document simultaneously, or jointly make editorial decisions on the same section simultaneously. This is now possible with some existing multiuser databases that allow more than one person to make changes in a database at the same time.

Greater storage capacity. It is within the realm of reason that erasable optical disks will allow us to access as much as fifty to one hundred times the storage capacity we now have. Such a capability would dramatically change the shape of computing in many ways. Imagine being able to access all studies on smoking and health on a desktop computer, or entire collections of research reports on any topic. The recently introduced NeXT computer already provides erasable optical storage of more than 650 megabytes of space. Furthermore, there are currently a number of devices that allow someone to place up to six or more audio-disks into an audio compact disk player. Imagine, then, the following: very soon an erasable optical disk drive will have the capacity to address six or more CD-ROMs simultaneously, with each one able to store 650 megabytes of information. The math is not complex, but look at the numbers: 4 billion characters of information, approximately 780 million words, or 2.3 million pages of information. The term that will be popularized as a result of this storage revolution will be *desktop libraries,* and by the middle of the 1990s they might be available for less than a thousand dollars. Imagine the capacity to access any piece of information you would want instantly.

Display technology. At the current time *high-definition TV (HDTV)* is becoming increasingly important, offering resolutions of 1,125 lines per screen compared with 525 on traditional technology. This development should allow more realistic images to be displayed, and the increased resolution will permit the display of three-dimensional images more clearly. But by the end of the decade, expect even higher-resolution displays of 2,000 lines or more.

Increased capacity for multitasking. Multitasking is the capacity of a computer to do more than one thing at a time. Imagine having a computer that allows you to work on a final report at the same time that your data are being analyzed in a statistical package, your budgetary spreadsheets are recalculating, and the computer is sending you a facsimile transmission.

Continued advances in microminiaturization. Advances in the area of microminiaturization will allow for increasingly smaller laptop computers that require less energy to operate and ultimately will result in the production of hand-held computers with mainframe power. This will give professionals the freedom to use computer technology in any setting, and under any circumstances.

Artificial intelligence and expert systems. Imagine the day when you can teach an expert system your own work habits and tendencies, so that it can selectively scan information in databases for you. This is how such a capacity might work: You subscribe to three journals and two newsletters and are interested in several others available through your local library. With some coaching you could teach your "intelligent" computer that you read only certain sections of each journal and that you may choose not to read a specific article based on certain key features. Imagine your computer scanning all the journals you are interested in and extracting only the information you are likely to want to read. When the computer has determined which articles you want, it will send an electronic command to the local library to transmit a facsimile of only that subset of articles. All of this can be accomplished in only a few minutes while you are reading your morning messages.

Neural networks. A neural network is a weblike configuration of chips that simulates the structure of a human brain. The connections between the chips operate like synapses, allowing for the transmission of messages on many different pathways. Neural networks, like your brain, have the capacity to learn information, and pathways get stronger with experience. Unlike most current applications, neural networks have the capacity to "remember" information they are taught. These networks are able to perform operations that simulate the kinds of associations made in human reasoning unlike the straight digital processing of a predetermined list of instructions, which most programs perform today. As they learn, neural networks get smarter and improve their operation. Although neural networks are still experimental today, their full potential may be reached by the end of the century.

SOME OF THE POTENTIAL FOR HEALTH EDUCATORS

All of these advances represent developments of incredible magnitude. However, technology is wasted without the appropriate application by professionals. What does this mean for health educators? Here are some possibilities:

1. Data in 1990 are available on a CD-ROM. A single disk contains all the information available in a whole section of the library today. Moreover, the computer is smart enough with database strategies to access that information in a manner that meets your planning needs. If you need to know census-tract data, data on populations at risk for epidemiologic analysis, data on population change for demographic analysis, data on age/gender/ethnicity distributions, household characteristics, or socioeconomic characteristics necessary to plan adequately for community-based health-education programming—all of this will be at your fingertips. Data from these CD-ROMs will also improve survey research, an absolutely essential tool for community-based health promotion/education planning and evaluation.

2. One of the increasingly important assets a health educator can possess is political savvy. If you wish to know, for example, what legislation is pending that will affect the health of Americans, or who has supported specific legislation, or whose campaigns to target for support of health-related issues, or which members of Congress have the most auspicious voting record—all of this is available at the other end of your modem.

3. As most professionals know, keeping up with the health-education literature is a difficult task. Your "intelligent" computer, with access to databases and bibliographic services, can monitor the literature base at any interval, including daily, and extract only the information you want.

4. The increasing sophistication of instructional software will reduce the tedium associated with repetitive instruction, but more than that, will engage students in active learning. The ability of multimedia stations to combine sound, graphics, video, and computer technology will make possible the individualization of any content-oriented instructional sequence in health education. Such programs will involve the educational diagnosis, prescription, implementation, monitoring, and evaluation of instruction.

5. The increasing development of simulations relevant to health education will not only permit enhanced student learning, but improve the skills of professionals as these applications are used in the training of health educators.

6. Access to information, from any source and at any time through improved telecommunications, will improve the effectiveness of health

educators. Few would argue with the basic belief that informed decisions by professionals are better than decisions made in the absence of critical information.

7. Health assessments will become more effective due to several simultaneous developments in hardware and software:

- Rather than operating as independent modules, health assessments will become integrated applications, with health-risk appraisals, dietary analysis, fitness appraisals, stress appraisals, and other assessments dynamically linked to allow the exchange of information.
- These programs will be further enhanced by access to massive knowledge bases, facilitated by telecommunications admission to public-access as well as private-access data (e.g., medical records available on "Smart Cards").
- The development of these integrated programs will also result in the improved preparation of health-education prescriptions (or recommendations to the health professional to guide development of appropriate behavior-change strategies) for those undergoing the assessments.
- These programs will actually be designed to monitor behavior over time and build data sets on clients of health programs. Such monitoring and surveillance will allow for greater evaluation of the system's performance.
- The integration of health assessments with artificial-intelligence and expert-systems technology will improve the programs by providing recommendations and guidance to health professionals using them and by assisting in the interpretation of hard-to-understand health data.

The potential of computers in health education is unlimited, but their promise remains largely unfulfilled today. The National Education Association suggests that computers will become fully integrated into the instructional process only when classroom teachers have been trained and feel competent to use them for this purpose. As health educators we must acquire an understanding of the potential for applying computer technology to our profession. However, this potential can be achieved only if we learn to adapt applications to our purposes, to acquaint health educators with that potential, and to teach them to apply that potential creatively.

SUMMARY

This chapter has reviewed some of the most frequently asked questions about current trends in computer applications in health education, and has concluded with an examination of some of the promises for health-education technology in the near future. The chapter also described the necessity for modifying both the training of health educators and the practice of health education.

DISCUSSION QUESTIONS

1. Where can you seek additional information and training to improve your skills in the application of computer technology to health education?

2. What steps can you take to ensure that your successes and failures in this area will be useful to your colleagues?

RECOMMENDED READINGS

Anderson, D. M., Needle, R. H., Mosow, S. (1988). Evaluation of a microcomputer-enhanced intervention for elementary school children. *Family and Community Health, 11* 1, 36–47.

Deardorff, W. W. (1986). Computerized health education: A comparison with traditional formats. *Health Education Quarterly, 13* 1, 61–72.

Inglis, V., Black, D., Mcnulty, H., & Gibson G. (1987). Micro-computers in interactive health education. *Journal of the Royal Society for Health, 107* (6), 239–241

APPENDIX A
APPLICATIONS EXERCISES

E   X   E   R   C   I   S   E   S

1. Introduction to Database Applications
2. Introduction to Word Processing
3. Introduction to Spreadsheet Applications
4. Additional Capabilities from Spreadsheet Applications
5. Introduction to Graphics Applications
6. Sharing Data between Applications
7. Using Productivity Software for Health Education
8. Database Construction and Use
9. Database Modification
10. Using the Word Processor for Form Letters
11. Adding Spreadsheet Analysis to the Data
12. Adding Graphics to the Data
13. Preparing the Final Report: Desktop Publishing
14. Don't Forget These Skills
15. Introduction to Health-Risk Appraisals
16. Using Results of Health-Risk Appraisals
17. Introduction to Dietary Analysis
18. Conducting a Nutrient Analysis
19. Analysis of Intake for a Specific Nutrient
20. Introduction to Fitness Assessments
21. Simulation—Epidemic Control
22. Simulation—U.S. Population Study

Exercise 1: Introduction to Database Applications

Objective: This exercise is designed to demonstrate some of the basic concepts of database design. To complete this exercise, you may use any database-management program. Plan a simple structure to allow for the entry of data on ten participants (records) of the WellSpirit Health Promotion Program (WSHPP). For each of the ten participants, you will collect information on eight fields (variables). Following is a list of information (data elements) to be used in your database.

NAME	AGE	SEX	HEIGHT	WEIGHT	CHOLESTEROL	SBP*	DBP*
Allen Smith	36	m	69	150	350	195	100
Becky Fyfe	43	f	65	135	220	120	80
Barbara List	29	f	68	127	270	130	85
Cheryl Dent	22	f	62	112	170	120	70
Liz Jones	15	f	73	95	300	125	90
Eve Scott	23	f	66	123	240	120	88
Gail Ice	50	f	58	160	210	130	90
Glen Christo	43	m	74	223	195	140	100
James Deveney	53	m	75	195	280	150	90
Steve Study	29	m	72	156	220	115	75

*SBP = systolic blood pressure; DBP = diastolic blood pressure

1. Decide on the structure you will use for the input format. After creating your input format, define the attributes of each of the fields (e.g., name = text, age = numeric data, gender = text). When you are satisfied with the structure of your database design, save the structure on a disk.

2. Enter the data listed above. Answer the following questions:

   a. Why is it important to enter the data for names in the format "last name, first name," or to enter the names into two separate fields?

   b. Why is it important to identify the attributes of the data in each field?

3. Experiment with different capabilities of the database program you are using. For example:

   a. Sort the data on last name.

   b. Sort the data by gender and age.

   c. Find the first occurrence in the database of a record with a cholesterol level less than 300.

   d. Select all those records with systolic blood pressures less than 140.

   e. Select all those records with systolic blood pressures less than 140 and diastolic blood pressures less than 95.

Exercise 2: Introduction to Word Processing

Objective: This exercise is designed to demonstrate the basic principles underlying the use of word-processing technology, including document entry, editing, formatting, and printing capabilities.

Type in the following document exactly as it appears below within the box.

The WellSpirit Health Promotion Program

The WellSpirit Health Promotion Program (WSHPP) is initiating a worksite wellness program designed to focus on four risk factors for heart disease—weight, cholesterol, systolic blood pressure, and diastolic blood pressure. In order to do this, an initial needs assessment will be conducted in which there is preliminary screening for these four risk factors, followed by programming targeted at maintaining acceptable levels of these risk factors. In those cases where appropriate, an effort will be made at reducing the client's risk. A follow-up will be conducted one year following entry into the program. The purpose of this announcement is to invite all members of the community to an open house at our facility on January 1, 1991.

---

1. After you have typed the document, review it and make all editorial changes (spelling and grammar). Save it on your disk, then print it out exactly as it is without formatting it.
2. Reformat the document in any way (e.g., centering titles, underlining or using bold print for emphasis where necessary) and print another copy.
3. Reformat the document as a letter to go to members of the community, and then as a poster to be displayed on a public bulletin board in a town square.
   a. As a letter, set the document up in the manner depicted below.
   b. As a poster, use any structure you think is attractive.

Exercise 3: Introduction to Spreadsheet Applications

Objective: The objective of this exercise is to enter data into a simple spreadsheet and examine the potential for using formulas to compute simple statistics. The capacity to calculate the mean value of a column of data is found in any spreadsheet.

Enter the data found in exercise 1 into any spreadsheet program. After entering and checking all of the data, enter formulas in the appropriate cells to compute the arithmetic mean (average) for each of the following fields.

FIELD	MEAN VALUE
AGE	
HEIGHT	
WEIGHT	
CHOLESTEROL	
SBP	
DBP	

Exercise 4: Additional Capabilities from Spreadsheet Applications

Objective: The primary purpose of this exercise is to build on your spreadsheet skills by designing a somewhat more complex spreadsheet model for a program budget. Your task is to enter the data into any spreadsheet-application program and then conduct some "what if" analyses.

Listed below are the estimated costs for paying the principal personnel of the WSHPP and some of its expenses in 1990.

PERSONNEL	1990	1991	1992	Total
PROJECT DIRECTOR	$25,000			
ASSISTANT DIRECTOR	$18,500			
SECRETARY	$16,500			
SUB TOTAL				
EXPENSES				
MAILING	$2,500			
TELEPHONE	$12,000			
SUPPLIES	$5,000			
SUBTOTAL				
PROJECT TOTALS				

1. Design your spreadsheet to calculate the subtotals and overall (sum of personnel cost, and expenses) project totals for 1990.
2. Enter formulas in the appropriate cells for 1991 and 1992 to calculate the costs involved in a 7 percent cost-of-living raise for all employees, and an 8 percent increase in expenses. Then repeat the process with an 8 percent cost-of-living raise and expenses.
   a. How much will the total three-year project cost under the first model assumption in part B?
   b. How much more money will have to be raised in order to ensure the program can operate with an 8 percent cost-of-living raise?

Exercise 5: Introduction to Graphics Applications

Objective: The purpose of this exercise is to demonstrate the wide variety of capabilities of graphics software.

With the data from the previous database and spreadsheet problems, create the following graphics using any problem capable of producing charts and graphs.

1. A pie chart illustrating the percentage of total clients in WSHPP who are male and female.
2. A bar chart showing the difference in average cholesterol between men and women.
3. Repeat part 2 for weight, SBP, and DBP.
4. Prepare a line chart illustrating the total cost of running the WSHPP for the years 1990–93.
5. Prepare a combination chart showing the personnel and operating expenses for the three years separately. To do this you may use multiple lines on a line chart, stacked bar charts, multiple bar charts, or combinations.
6. Use a graphics program to design a logo for the WellSpirit Health Promotion Program.

Exercise 6: Sharing Data between Applications

Objective: This exercise is designed to provide an opportunity for a student to experiment with sharing data between applications to produce a single final product. Such an activity is easiest when you use "integrated software" (one package with multiple applications), but this assignment can be completed even with separate applications in the four areas. Using all of the data in exercises 1 through 4, prepare an annual report for the WSHPP to distribute to its clients. Remember that annual reports try to highlight the best qualities of a program and should be done in a professional manner. Do your best to integrate the potential of database, word processing, spreadsheet, and graphics to produce a report you can be proud of.

3. Experiment with global searches to answer questions posed. Regardless of the database program you use, you should be able to answer the following questions by pressing just a few keystrokes:

   a) What are the names of the youngest male and female clients to use the facilities of WSHPP?
   b) Who has the highest-measured blood cholesterol level among the clients tested on intake?
   c) How many clients had systolic blood pressures over 160 on intake?
   d) How many clients had systolic blood pressures over 160 and diastolic blood pressures over 90 on intake?
   e) How many people, who begin the program with elevated cholesterol (e.g., greater than 250) reduced their cholesterol to safer levels by follow-up? (Hint: This type of question involves a search on the original cholesterol level to screen for the first criteria, and then on the follow-up levels to screen for the second.)

Exercise 9: Database Modification

Objective: To demonstrate the importance of database-modification capabilities. Every major database program, whether flat-file or relational, allows for the modification of the structure of the database. The next series of exercises will be based on those capabilities. Examine the documentation available with your database software and experiment with the following.

1. Create a new *calculated field.* A calculated field in a database is a field whose contents are computed automatically by the computer based on a formula that is provided by the user. For example, a new field could be added to any of the database structures which automatically calculates the difference between cholesterol levels on intake and follow-up. The formulas necessary for such calculated fields are generally easy to devise, and often no more than the following:

   CHOL − CHOL2

   Modify your database by adding a calculated field for the difference in cholesterol measures. When you have done this, you will be able to answer the following questions:

   a) Who had the largest positive change (i.e., a change from a higher to a lower number) in cholesterol level from intake to follow-up?
   b) Who had the largest negative change in cholesterol level from intake to follow-up?
   c) How many people who began the program with elevated cholesterol (e.g., greater than 250) reduced their cholesterol to safer levels by follow-up?

2. Create another calculated field—"percent change in cholesterol levels." This field can use a variation of the following formula:

$$(CHOL - CHOL2) / CHOL \times 100$$

By doing this you will produce a number that represents percent change from intake. If this number is positive, it means a change from a higher to a lower cholesterol level; if it is negative, it signifies a higher level at follow-up than at intake. Based on this new calculated field, answer the following questions:

a) Who had the largest positive percentage change from intake to follow-up? Is it the same person who had the largest absolute positive change? What is the difference between absolute change and percentage change?

b) Were there any clients of WSHPP whose cholesterol levels increased more than 20 percent from intake to follow-up?

3. Look for a set of tables that gives guidelines for the height and weight of both men and women. Create a new field called ideal weight (perhaps the most widely used are those distributed by the Metropolitan Life Insurance Company). For each client add the ideal weight for his or her height and gender. Since you do not know frame size, assume all are medium-framed individuals. You have now added an important piece of information that makes it possible to add yet another field—"percent overweight." The formula for this could be as follows:

$$(WGT - IDEAL\ WGT) / IDEAL\ WGT \times 100$$

As you know, obesity is considered an important risk factor for heart disease and other health problems. It is generally believed that anyone more than 20 percent over his or her ideal weight has elevated health risks. We can use such information in making judgments about the clients in WSHPP.

You should create this type of field twice—once for intake and once for follow-up. You will want to be sure to give these two fields different names. With this information in the database, you will be able to answer many questions about clients who have elevated health risks because of their weight.

4. Create two calculated fields for each of the coronary risk factors as you did with cholesterol (i.e., systolic blood pressure, diastolic blood pressure): one that represents the absolute difference between intake and follow-up, and the other for percentage change. For the "weight" fields, you should create a computed field for absolute difference in weight between intake and follow-up, percentage change from intake to follow-up, and then add another computed field that is the absolute difference between the "percent overweight" on intake and "percent overweight" at follow-up. By doing this you will add seven more fields to your database, and you will be able to answer all of the previous

questions on cholesterol for each of these new risk factors. When you have done this, you will be able to compile important statistics for evaluating the WSHPP program.

5. Complete the following table.

Risk Analysis

How many clients were at risk on intake:
        from cholesterol greater than 250? _____
        from systolic BP greater than 160? _____
        from diastolic BP greater than 90? _____
        from being more than 20 percent overweight? _____

How many clients at risk on intake were not at risk on follow-up:
        based on changes in cholesterol? _____
        based on changes in SBP? _____
        based on changes in DBP? _____
        based on changes in weight? _____

How many clients at risk on intake were still at risk on follow-up:
        based on no changes in cholesterol? _____
        based on no changes in SBP? _____
        based on no changes in DBP? _____
        based on no changes in weight? _____

How many clients not at risk on intake were at risk on follow-up:
        from cholesterol greater than 250? _____
        from systolic BP greater than 160? _____
        from diastolic BP greater than 90? _____
        from being more than 20 percent overweight? _____

How many clients have multiple risk factors:
        on intake? _____
        on follow-up? _____

How many clients reduced the number of risk factors from intake to follow-up? _____

How many clients lost more than twenty pounds in one year: _____
        and were still greater than 20 percent?
        and were overweight on follow-up? _____
        and were no longer at risk from weight? _____

Armed with information such as this, a health educator can begin to make informed decisions regarding clientele, their needs, and the effectiveness of programs. What makes this different from simply collecting data to evaluate the program at two points in time, is that the data in the database can continue to be used for many other management decisions.

Exercise 10: Using the Word Processor for Form Letters

Objective: Most of the major word-processing packages allow you to create form letters that use data from a database. This capability is often called "mail merge." The purpose of these exercises is to demonstrate the potential power of mail-merge capabilities.

Examine the documentation for your word-processing package. Carefully review its mail-merge capabilities. Try each of the following tasks:

1. Prepare mailing labels for each client in your database.
2. Prepare a form letter reporting the results of your initial assessment. Each client should receive a letter that is personalized and that reports only personal data.
3. Prepare a form letter only for the clients at increased health risk based on the measured risk factors on intake. This form letter should contain the data that you would be concerned about and that you want your clients to know about. The letter should also contain useful information for follow-up to the clients.
4. Prepare a form letter that reports the level of change at the end of the one-year period. This letter should contain the following:
   a) A congratulatory message if the client demonstrated continued positive behavior.
   b) Information on positive changes and a description of changes still needed.
   c) Information on negative changes.

Exercise 11: Adding Spreadsheet Analysis to the Data

Objective: This set of tasks is designed to demonstrate some important additional information that can be collected from spreadsheets (e.g., Lotus 1-2-3™ and Excel for the IBM, or Excel for the Macintosh) that most databases cannot accomplish.

1. Almost all spreadsheet programs have the capacity to import data from other programs. You should examine the documentation for your spreadsheet program and database program and export your full database to a spreadsheet.
2. After you have imported your database into a spreadsheet program, prepare formulas for all of the fields to create the computations necessary to complete the following table.

MEASURE	MINIMUM	MAXIMUM	MEAN	STD. DEV.
Intake				
Height				
Weight (lbs.)				
Percent overweight				
Cholesterol				
SBP				
DBP				
Follow-Up				
Weight (lbs.)				
Percent overweight				
Cholesterol				
SBP				
DBP				
Difference (intake/follow-up)				
Weight (lbs.)				
Percent overweight				
Cholesterol				
Percent change				
SBP				
Percent change				
DBP				
Percent change				

Exercise 12: Adding Graphics to the Data

Objective: These tasks are designed to allow a user to experiment with the wide variety of ways in which data can be presented graphically.

1. Regardless of the nature of your graphics package, if it is capable of performing simple tasks, you should be able to complete all of the following activities. Summarize each of the following characteristics of WSHPP with the appropriate graphics:

   a) The distribution of males and females.
   b) The number or percentage of clients in each of the following age groups: 15–24; 25–44; 45–64; 65+.
   c) The number or percentage of clients in each age group who have elevated risks in each of the four risk areas (i.e., weight, cholesterol, SBP, DBP).

d) The number or percentage of clients who have one, two, three, or four risk factors.

e) The number or percentage of clients who made improvements in each risk factor.

f) The number or percentage of clients at risk on intake who did not improve by follow-up.

g) Any other summary statistics you think are important in examining the data.

2. Prepare a diagram demonstrating the way WSHPP operates. Include the following:

a) Distribute promotion posters and invitation letters to community members in June 1988.

b) Open the doors to the program in October 1988.

c) Conduct initial client screening during November 1988.

d) Provide feedback to clients and conduct programs from December 1988 to October 1989.

e) Conduct follow-up screening in November 1989.

f) Analyze data in December 1989.

g) Distribute final report to clients and shareholders in February 1990.

For an illustration of how this project might be done, see the graphics section in chapter 2.

Exercise 13: Preparing the Final Report: Desktop Publishing

Objective: To illustrate the mechanism by which data are aggregated from many sources and many different computer programs and used for a single purpose.

By now you have both collected and used a great deal of data on the WSHPP program. It is now time to use it all for one purpose—to prepare a final report to the owners of the company and the community. The purpose of the report is to communicate information effectively, which often means simply and graphically. To do this you may use any word-processing program or any desktop-publishing program. Before you begin, think about the information you want to communicate and then carefully prepare a final report merging text, graphics, statistics, and narrative. Remember the following:

1. Try to design an attractive cover, one that will catch the attention of those whom you want to read the report.

2. Begin the report with an executive summary. Carefully consider the most important information to include in such a summary. Remember, a good executive summary may also include recommendations.

3. Prepare the technical information following the executive summary in a concise way, using graphics wherever possible.

Make sure not only that the graphics are attractive, but that they communicate clear ideas.

4. Where important or necessary, carefully construct narrative to supplement the graphic images.

Exercise 14: Don't Forget These Skills

Objective: The purpose of this section is to illustrate the application of the skills you have gained from the previous exercises for other uses, particularly for individual benefit. You have now used graphics, databases, spreadsheets, and word processors to keep, manage, manipulate, and report data on the WSHPP program. Many of the remaining exercises in this appendix require collecting information about yourself, using a wide variety of health-risk appraisals.

Remember that all the skills you have practiced to this point can be applied to yourself as well. As you conduct a personal health appraisal, keep track of the information. Each time you conduct a subsequent appraisal, update your information. You should now recognize that the data you will be collecting can be maintained in a database for yourself.

Not only should you maintain these data in a database, but every time you visit a health service or a health-care professional, you should keep track of the data you collect. For example, record the date, the purpose of the visit, your symptoms, any tests ordered, test results, the health-care professional's advice, medications ordered, medications taken, and total costs. All of these factors represent data you should be maintaining on yourself.

1. Design a database to last for at least one semester or six months. Structure it in such a way that you can maintain data on your health-care utilization.

2. Design a database to last for at least one semester or six months. Structure it in such a way that you can maintain data on the health assessments you will be using on computers. Each time you conduct an assessment, record the date and results.

3. Design a database to last for at least one semester or six months. Structure it in such a way that you can maintain data on your health-promoting activities, your moods, and your general health.

4. Prepare a report at the end of the semester or six months exactly like the one you did for WSHPP. Use database reporting, manipulation capabilities, spreadsheet analysis, graphics, and word-processing capabilities to write a story on yourself. Maintain these logs over time, and you will be able to track your own health.

Think of the power you put into your own hands with this kind of information.

Exercise 15: Introduction to Health-Risk Appraisals

Objective: To illustrate the potential applications of health-risk appraisal (HRA) software.

1. Using any microcomputer-based HRA, respond to all questions asked. While you are doing that, keep track of the following information:
   a) the basic demographic information collected (e.g., age, gender);
   b) the risk factors specifically mentioned (e.g., smoking, drug use);
   c) the nature of the program's questions (e.g., forced-choice/ multiple-choice, open-ended);
   d) the kind of information provided after the responses are analyzed.

2. Respond to the following questions:
   a) Does the program focus on risk or life expectancy? What is the difference?
   b) Are there any important risk factors that are not covered?
   c) Are there any risk factors that are inadequately covered? (For example, many programs ask for your blood pressure, but may not ask if you are taking medication to regulate your blood pressure. There is a big difference in health risk between a blood pressure of 120/80 without medication and a blood pressure of 120/80 that is achieved with the aid of potent medication.)
   d) If the program you used provides information about appraised age, or health age, how does it differentiate between those terms and chronological age?
   e) Use the program again and when it asks for race or ethnicity, change your answer. Then complete the program. What influence did this have on your results?

Exercise 16: Using Results of Health-Risk Appraisals

Objective: The purpose of this exercise is to identify the ten leading causes of death determined for you based on HRA techniques. If you have a microcomputer-based HRA that provides risks for major causes of death, complete the following table. In these programs, after answering several questions, you will usually get a list of your ten leading causes of death and the risk for each. After completing all the questions in the program, you will ordinarily be told your final specific risks for each based on your responses.

Ten Leading Causes of Death by Age, Gender, and Race

AGE _____   GENDER _____

RACE _____   NAME _____

LEADING CAUSES OF DEATH	INITIAL RISK	FINAL RISK
_____	_____	_____
_____	_____	_____
_____	_____	_____
_____	_____	_____
_____	_____	_____
_____	_____	_____
_____	_____	_____
_____	_____	_____
_____	_____	_____
_____	_____	_____

1. How is the initial risk of cause of death related to demographic characteristics?
2. How did your answers to specific questions result in a modification of your risk?
3. How would you use these results?

Exercise 17: Introduction to Dietary Analysis

Objective: To demonstrate the potential of dietary-analysis software both to provide basic data regarding nutritional requirements and to conduct other sophisticated analyses.

Anyone who has had to do a dietary analysis by hand for even a small set of foods has learned how tedious this activity can be. When the number of foods increases or when the number of days over which you are doing the analysis increases, or when the number of nutrients that you are interested in increases, the difficulties multiply. All of these activities, however, can be made easier by doing these computations and analyses by computer.

The general goal, then, is to explore the capabilities of a dietary-analysis package. Among the specific objectives we will accomplish are:

- the determination of recommended daily allowances;
- the computation of your actual nutrient intake;
- a comparison between your actual and your ideal intakes.

To accomplish these objectives, you may use any dietary-analysis software. It may not be possible to conduct all of these analyses with the software available, but do as many as possible.

In this first exercise you will compute your RDA for each of the nutrients in the following table.

1. Boot the dietary-analysis package and choose the option to compute personal RDAs.
2. Follow the directions to enter data on your age, gender, height, and activity level.
3. Complete the table with the values you are given from the program.

RECOMMENDED DAILY ALLOWANCES FOR _____

YOUR WEIGHT _____ **ACTIVITY LEVEL** _____

YOUR AGE _____ **YOUR SEX** _____

Calories _____ Carbohydr. _____

Protein _____ Cholesterol _____

Fiber _____ Fat—unsat. _____

Vitamin A _____ Fat—total _____

Thiamine _____ Calcium _____

Niacin _____ Iron _____

Vitamin C _____ Vitamin E _____

---

4. Using the same procedures for computing your RDAs, fill in all the blanks in the following table.

Computing RDAs for Fiber and Iron

NAME	AGE	GENDER	HGT.	WGT.	ACTIVITY	FIBER	IRON
A. Smith	36	male	69	150	sedentary	———	———
B. Fyfe	43	female	65	135	very active	———	———
B. List	29	male	68	197	slightly active	———	———
C. Dent	22	female	62	112	very active	———	———
L. Jones	15	female	73	95	slightly active	———	———
E. Scott	23	female	66	123	moderately active	———	———
G. Ice	50	female	58	160	moderately active	———	———
G. Christo	43	male	74	223	very active	———	———
J. Deveney	53	male	75	195	extremely active	———	———
S. Study	29	male	72	156	slightly active	———	———

5. Answer the following questions:
   a) What characteristics (e.g., gender, age) seem to be most important in determining the RDA for these two values?
   b) Where do you see the biggest differences in these requirements?

Exercise 18: Conducting a Nutrient Analysis

Objective: To illustrate how a complete dietary analysis can be conducted using microcomputers.

1. Using the foods and quantities listed in the following table, complete a dietary analysis according to the directions provided with your software.

Dietary-Analysis Food List

QUANTITY	NAME OF FOOD
8 ounces	Fresh orange juice
2	Fried eggs
3 pieces	Cooked Canadian-style bacon
2 slices	Whole-wheat bread/firm
2 TBSP	Butter
1 cup	Brewed coffee
1 TBSP	White powdered sugar
2 ounces	Whole milk

2. Using these same foods, complete the following table.

Final Dietary Analysis for Selected Foods

Calories _____	Carbohydr. _____
Protein _____	Cholesterol _____
Fiber _____	Fat—unsat. _____
Vitamin A _____	Fat—total _____
Thiamine _____	Calcium _____
Riboflavin _____	Iron _____
Niacin _____	Potassium _____
Vitamin C _____	Sodium _____

3. Examine any nutrition resource to find out the total number of calories found in carbohydrates, protein, and fat. What percentage of the total calories consumed came from each of these three nutrients?

Exercise 19: Analysis of Intake for a Specific Nutrient

Objective: In the previous exercises you analyzed the nutrient content of a list of foods for many different nutrients. In this exercise you will use the same list of foods, but find content for a single nutrient—cholesterol.

Examine the documentation for your dietary-analysis program. Almost all published programs afford you the opportunity to examine the single-nutrient content of a list of foods. Using the list of foods in the previous exercise, fill in the following table with the cholesterol content of the foods.

Dietary Analysis for Cholesterol

QUANTITY	NAME OF FOOD	CHOLESTEROL
8 ounces	Fresh orange juice	_____
2	Fried eggs	_____
3 pieces	Cooked Canadian-style bacon	_____
2 slices	Whole-wheat bread/firm	_____
2 TBSP	Butter	_____
1 cup	Brewed coffee	_____
1 TBSP	White powdered sugar	_____
2 ounces	Whole milk	_____

Exercise 20: Introduction to Fitness Assessments

Objective: In this exercise you will compile data that can be used in many different fitness programs (e.g., body composition, fitness assessments). *Warning:* Fitness testing is a sophisticated science. Not only is interpretation of data difficult, but for some individuals strenuous exercise itself may be dangerous. It is therefore recommended that only qualified individuals supervise fitness assessments, and that no individual engage in strenuous physical exercise before some preliminary screening to ensure relative safety.

The following chart is designed to facilitate data collection for use in a wide variety of fitness assessments. Examine the software available to you and complete the appropriate portions of the chart. Reread the previous warning before doing any strenuous exercise.

MEASURE	YOUR DATA	
Blood pressure	Systolic blood pressure	_____
	Diastolic blood pressure	_____
Body measures	Height in inches	_____
	Weight in pounds	_____
	Abdomen circumference	_____
	Iliac circumference	_____
	Buttocks circumference	_____
Skinfolds	Pectoral (mm)	_____
	Abdominal (mm)	_____
	Thigh (mm)	_____
Strength measures	Bent-knee sit-ups	_____
	Push-ups	_____
Flexibility	Sit-and-reach score (inches)	_____
Cardiovascular fitness	Twelve-minute walk/run (miles)	_____

Exercise 21: Simulation—Epidemic Control

Objective: These exercises will give you an opportunity to use the computer to experiment with a simulation. Simulation is a technique that provides an effective means of testing, evaluating, and manipulating a proposed system without any direct action on the real system. Several hours, days, weeks, or even years of operation can be simulated in a matter of minutes on a computer. In this case you will use any simulation program available to experience a "real-life" problem that cannot be provided in a traditional classroom. You should remember that in most cases simulation is not a precise replica of the actual system, but rather reflects a symbolic representation of that system. It can, however, provide experiences and measurements that could not be obtained in any other way.

Goal: To eradicate or minimize the incidence of a communicable disease. For most of the available simulation programs, it is often possible to make use of any combination of several interventions, including the creation and use of hospitals, the use of drugs with those who are ill, some program designed to eradicate the disease vector (the mechanism by which the disease is transmitted: e.g., mosquitos transmit malaria), and preventive drugs for those who are not yet ill.

Curative activities refer to those activities directed at the cure of disease victims. *Preventive activities* are those that are intended to prevent people who are still healthy from getting a disease.

Use any disease-simulation program available to answer the following questions.

1. Can an epidemic be successfully eradicated by using only curative measures, that is, by just setting up hospitals and administering drugs to the ill? Describe the results of using such a plan, and try to explain your results. What implications can you generalize to health education from your results?

2. Can an epidemic be eradicated by using only preventive measures, that is, by just using mosquito control and immunization programs? Describe the results of using such a plan and try to explain your results. What implications can you generalize to health education from your results?

3. If possible, use the program without a financial restriction to determine which of the intervention options is cheapest when applied to the maximum degree. Which of the options is the most effective? Least effective? Is there any relationship between the cost and the effectiveness?

4. Keeping in mind the costs you determined in the last question, devise a control strategy to use with a budget restriction of five hundred thousand dollars. Record your strategy and describe the results obtained when you implemented it using the program.

5. Based on your experiences with this type of simulation, what comments do you have about the program itself and its applicability? What other similar programs do you think should be developed?

Exercise 22: Simulation—U.S. Population Study

Objective: These exercises demonstrate the role that demographic methods can play in forecasting for health planning. The study of population change is called *demography*. Demography was one of the first fields in health to make use of mathematics. It has its origins in census taking and dates back as early as the Roman Empire. Aside from measuring the distribution and composition of populations, however, demographers are also interested in population projection. United States government demographers must be able to estimate populations at least fifty years into the future to enable the government to operate efficiently and anticipate the needs of citizens.

Demographers make such assessments based on the following kinds of data:

- *Fertility.* The average number of children a woman can be expected to have during her life.
- *Birth distribution.* The ages at which females can be expected to have children.
- *Sex ratio of offspring.* Although more males than females are born, as a population ages, the number of females in each age group begins to exceed the number of males at that age.
- *Mortality rate.* The chance that a person will die within a fixed period of time.
- *Population size.*

If you have access to any simulation that allows you to manipulate these and other variables, try to answer the following questions.

1. *What effect will changes in fertility have on population by the year 2010?* The year 2010 is less than twenty years away. Fertility has varied greatly in the last thirty years, particularly due to the trend to reduce family size. Use this information to produce a set of assumptions that you think may hold true for the next twenty years, and then evaluate what effect change in fertility will have on the population in the year 2000.

2. *What effect would delaying the birth of the first child have on population growth?* The most likely time for a birth in a female's life is between the ages of twenty and twenty-four. However, this is not true in other countries. In India women typically have children long before their twenties, while in Ireland the birth of a woman's first child often comes in the early thirties. Would a change in birth distribution alter our population's growth rate? Test this idea using a series of different birthrates. If no change occurred in the birth distribution, what would be the expected population in 2010? Do you feel that lowering the age at which most women have their first child would have much effect on the population? What in your data supports your view?

WSHPP Client Listing

Abbey, Richard
7963 Johnsbury Ln
Washington, D.C. 20015

Abby, Joyce
461 Lincoln Drive
Washington, D.C. 20009

Alice, Diane
763 Ave F
Washington, D.C. 20008

Andrea, Michael
782 Lewis Avenue
Rockville, MD 20850

Ann, Judith
6 Fawnswalk Place
Cabin John, MD 20818

Anna, Jean
9589 Sea Lane
Baltimore, MD 21218

Anne, Rebecca
6379 Seminole Ave
Mt. Rainier, MD 20712

Annette, Marie
7 Dufief Court
Greenbelt, MD 20770

Arthur, Daniel
736 Elm Grove Circle
Beltsville, MD 20705

Arthur, Michel
2270 Colston Road
Silver Spring, MD 20910

Barbara, Mark
6836 Mink Drive
Upper Marlboro, MD 20772

Beatrice Carol
1990 North Fifth Ave
Monterey, MD 21754

Ben, Linda
245 South Street
Rockville, MD 20850

Bernard, Carolyn
71 Ardsley Rd.
Chevy Chase, MD 20815

Betty, Debra
27 Wainwright Road
Columbia, MD 21045

Blanche, Betty
478 Ridge Drive
Apple Falls, MD 22401

Blue, Arthur
9 Lincoln Place
Silver Spring, MD 20910

Brenda, Roxanne
2972 Terrace Dr
Berwyn Heights, MD 20740

Camille, Carolyn
797 Morrison Dr.
Beltsville, MD 20705

Carmine, Jane
947 Park Hall Drive
Wheaton, MD 20902

Carmine, Nina
9 Ruxview Ct
Beltsville, MD 20705

Carol, Bonnie
10 Timber Trail
Silver Spring, MD 20902

Carol, Patricia
74606 Cactus Hill Drive
Los Angeles, CA 90034

Carol, Phyllis
673 Genessee Street
Beltsville, MD 20705

Carol, Stephanie
9 Sand Road
Bowie, MD 20716

Carole, Frankie
6716 69th Street
Washington, D.C. 20002

Carrie, Cassandra
4604 Harling Lane
Annapolis, MD 21401

Catherine, Jamie
67 Crestwood Pl
Burtonsville, MD 20866

Catherine, Leslie
370 Elkader Drive
College Park, MD 20740

Catherine, Sharon
166 Hendrick Lane
Bethesda, MD 20814

Charles, Philipa
9918 St. Andrews Place
Westminster, MD 21157

Cheryl, Stephen
5580 Ashbourne Road
Silver Spring, MD 20910

Christina, Peter
PO Box 665
Columbia, MD 21045

Cook, Cynthia
1599 Bushland Rd.
Washington, D.C. 20015

Corinda, Christine
6647 Wakefield Road
Gaithersburg, MD 20878

Courtney, Ann
1999 Huntwood Drive
College Park, MD 20740

Cynthia, Dennis
810 South Long Ct.
Wilmington, Delaware 19808

Cynthia, Leora
866 Mandan Terrace
College Park, MD 20740

Daisy, Janet
897 Tamar Road
Upper Marlboro, MD 20772

Darlene, Kenneth
8696 Glengyle Dr.
Germantown, MD 20874

David, Brandy
7910 St. Charles Ct
College Park, MD 20740

Deborah, Mary
901 Ave D
Baltimore City, MD 20716

Deitra, Marian
7802 Boyce Street
Takoma Park, MD 20912

Diane, Kathleen
666 F Street
Falls Church, VA 22046

Donald, Marian
647 Champlain Dr
Largo, MD 20772

Donna, Marlin
6824 Valley Lane
Hyattsville, MD 20782

Donna, Nancy
72208 Fuller Street
Annapolis, MD 21403

Donna, Patricia
800 Anniston Drive
Greenbelt, MD 20770

Doris, Barbara
7 Pebble Ave
Takoma Park, MD 20912

Doris, Joan
8600 76th St
Adelphi, MD 20783

Dorothy, Ellen
9102 Washington Ave
Greenbelt, MD 20770

Dorothy, Maria
PO Box 737
Arnold, MD 21012

Downing, Kathryn
7047 St. Michaels Road
Laurel, MD 20707

Edna, Steven
2525 West Ave
Cambridge, MD 21613

Edward, Howard
6008 34th Place, NW
Silver Spring, MD 20902

Eileen, Clara
7 Bonnie Lane
Germantown, MD 20874

Elinore, Emily
996 Muirkirk Drive
Bowie, MD 20716

Elizabeth, Camille
112 Carroll Street
Laurel, MD 20708

Elizabeth, Marilyn
7377 Briarwood Road
Bethesda, MD 20817

Elizabeth, Mark
609 Osage Street
Silver Spring, MD 20904

Ellen, Carol
11876 Vista Drive
Laurel, MD 20707

Eugenia, Courtney
199 St. Johns Place
Bethesda, MD 20817

Evelyn, Marlene
11687 Sourwood Lane
McLean, VA 22102

Frances, Pamela
708 Robinwood Road
Silver Spring, MD 20910

Frances, Rae
19696 Deakins Dr.
Arlington, VA 22207

Francine, Ted
8116 Sondra Ave.
Edgewater, MD 21037

Frank, Linda
PO Box 907
Laurel, MD 20708

George, Ann
2400 76th St, NW
Washington, DC 20007

Geraldine, Mary
PO Box 878
College Park, MD 20740

Glenn, Barry
6599 Mile Dr.
Adelphi, MD 20783

Glenn, Vanessa
70420 Inwood Avenue
Cambridge, MD 21613

Golden, Joseph
27 Heather Rd.
Baltimore, MD 21207

Helen, Joseph
7608 Peyton Court
Norfolk, VA 23502

Hilton, Ann
379 Grace St
Silver Spring, MD 20904

Jack Frances
PO Box 236
Germantown, MD 20874

James, Barbara
PO Box 7002
Timonium, MD 21093

James, Nancy
70 Cinnabar Court
Annandale, VA 22003

James, Patricia
5227 North First Street
Takoma, Park, MD 20912

Jane, Cheryl
72470 Village Terrace
Alexandria, VA 22307

Jane, Marie
875 Nostrand Ave
Greenbelt, MD 20770

Janice, Linda
9 Highview Ave
New York, NY 10011

Jerelyn, Nancy
12 North Street
Riverdale, MD 20737

Jill, Carolyn
16589 Sandy Road
Upper Marlboro, MD 20772

Joan, Barbara
447 Greenwood Rd
Greenbelt, MD 20770

Joan, Chris
16 Sunnypines Circle
Silver Spring, MD 20910

Joan, Kenneth
22 Chantilly Court
Silver Spring, MD 20901

Joan, Roberta
44 Connecticut Ave NW
Laurel, MD 20708

Johanna, Joseph
672 Talisman Lane
Beltsville, MD 20705

Jonathan, Michelle
612 Ridge Road
Alexandria, VA 22314

Jonecia, Maureen
11 Northway
Arlington, VA 22205

Joseph, Philip
191 Greengate Drive
Silver Spring, MD 20902

Juanita, Herbert
6529 Seedling Lane
Baltimore, MD 21204

Judith, Linda
697 Herkos Ct
Upper Marlboro, MD 20772

Judith, Lisa
191 Burlington Dr.
Gaithersburg, MD 20877

Judy, Karen
425 Franklin Ave
Laurel, MD 20708

Julian, Charles
970 Westchester Place
Columbia, MD 21045

Karen, Helen
6291 Osage Street
College Park, MD 20740

Karen, Phyllis
799 E. Buena Vista, Ft.
Washington, MD 20744

Kathleen, Joanne
791 Candlewood Ave.
Sykesville, MD 21784

Kathryn, Patricia
7037 Crestmoor Road
Lehighton, PA 18235

Kevin, Barry
6771 Leatherwood Terrace
Columbia, MD 21045

Larry, Diane
811 Main Street
Silver Spring, MD 20904

Lauren, Maureen
78 Patrick Place
Rockville, MD 20852

Lena, Eileen
254 Shower Terrace
Takoma Park, MD 20912

Leonard, Nova
8 Second Ave
Hyattsville, MD 20782

Liane, Tommy
3474 Dupont Avenue
College Park, MD 20742

Linda, George
1766 Irving Street, NW
Baltimore, MD 21207

Linda, Ronnie
161 Holly Street
Gaithersburg, MD 20879

Lois, Susan
70800 Rose Avenue
Columbia, MD 21045

Londa, Denise
619 Emerson St NW
Columbia, MD 21045

Lori, Susan
2044 85th Street, NW
Cabin John, MD 20818

Lowery, Robert
3404 Tulane Dr
Baltimore, MD 21204

Lynda, Iris
2820 Covington Rd
Rockville, MD 20853

Lynn, Marsha
3662 Alpen Way
Silver Spring, MD 20910

Madden, Joshua
6898 Upton Place
College Park, MD 20740

Major, Marjorie
620 Quiet Terrace
Sykesville, MD 21784

Majors, Jeanne
7366 Briarwood Road
Rockville, MD 20855

Margaret, Johnetta
712 Morrison Drive
Greenbelt, MD 20770

Margaret, Nancy
PO Box 732
Monterey, MD 21754

Margaret, Susan
24 Manor Circle
Kensington, MD 20895

Marianne, Linda
246 Second Street
Baltimore, MD 21207

Marie, Jerry
151 East Main Street
Largo, MD 20772

Marion, Ann
79 Conestoga Road
Fort Meade, MD 20755

Marr, Janet
6882 Norbeck Road
Virginia Beach, VA 23464

Martha, Jerome
8919 Dunleer Rd.
Washington, DC 20037

Martina, Helen
6627 Baron Terrace
Silver Spring, MD 20902

Martina, Josephine
4807 Osage St
Annapolis, MD 21403

Mary, Michelle
8623 Greenbelt Drive
Highland, MD 20777

Mary, Nancy
997 Homer Drive
Rockville, MD 20850

Mary, Sandra
902 Quintana Street
Washington, DC 20008

Mary, Sherri
219 Carroll Lane
Silver Spring, MD 20902

Matthew, Georgiana
150 Ridge Way Circle
Clarksville, MD 21029

Matthew, Mark
897 Isle Royale Ave.
Beltsville, MD 20705

Matthew, Noel
4872 Jasmine Road
Mitchellville, MD 20716

Maurice, Elliot
632 Oakland Drive
Laurel, MD 20708

Melanie, Steven
5570 Columbia Pike
Rockville, MD 20852

Melissa, Edwin
827 Hillspring Dr
Bethesda, MD 20817

Melody, Cheryl
114 East Drive
Jefferson, MD 21755

Michele, Pat
644 Cherry Rd
College Park, MD 20740

Mildred, Laura
4340 Garrison St
Greenbelt, MD 20770

Morgan, Sharon
PO Box 783
Washington, DC 20008

Nancy, Neil
1998 Flowering Terrace
Beltsville, MD 20705

Nova, Stephana
8 Cedar St.
Stevensville, MD 21666

Patricia, Carol
1276 Metzerott Road
Bowie, MD 20715

Patricia, Cathleen
2400 47th Street
Potomac, MD 20804

Patricia, Donald
1276 Metzerott Rd.
Baltimore, MD 21210

Patricia, Donald
1917 Hunziker Ave
Clinton, MD 20735

Patricia, Melinda
171 Elm Circle
Mt. Rainier, MD 20712

Patricia, Vincent
473 Romlon Street
Jefferson, MD 21755

Penelope, Helen
18919 Tweed Lane
Bowie, MD 20715

Phillips, Lonnie
8207 Jeb Stuart Rd
Annapolis, MD 21401

Phyllis, Nanette
4423 Romlon St
Gaithersburg, MD 20878

Randi, Linda
990 Bristol Avenue
Laurel, MD 20707

Raphael, Beverly
207 Victor Pkwy
Washington, D.C. 20009

Renee, Joyce
6024 Needwood Drive
Fort Meade, MD 20755

Richard, Joseph
2908 Carone Road
Ft. Washington, MD 20716

Richard, Patricia
87 Washington Street
Rockville, MD 20850

Richard, Thomas
1299 Nuthatch Ave.
Silver Spring, MD 20902

Robert, Brian
67 Brisbane Street
Riverdale, MD 20737

Robert, Robbie
PO Box 86
Laurel, MD 20707

Roberta, Carole
973 42nd Street
Jefferson, MD 21755

Robyn, Mary
516 High Street
Millersville, MD 21108

Roger Theresa
84 Adelphi Road
Adelphi, MD 20783

Ronald, Mary
597 White Pike
Upper Marlboro, MD 20772

Rosanne, Judd
670 Baltimore Ave
Germantown, MD 20874

Ruth, Beverly
604 Trammell Drive
Baltimore, MD 21221

Sally, Valente
74 Harold Drive
College Park, MD 20740

Sandra, Helen
8890 Seminary Road
Annapolis, MD 21401

Sharan, Philip
72632 Darle Street
Rockville, MD 20852

Sharlene, Mary
4373 Row Road
Chevy Chase, MD 20815

Sharon, Joseph
607 North St
College Park, MD 20740

Sharon, Lanny
6759 Tamar Road
Annapolis, MD 21401

Sheila, Elizabeth
22 Monroe St
Columbia, MD 21045

Sheila, Lisa
922 Bellfall Court
Bethesda, MD 20814

Sheila, Melvin
777 Eastern Drive
Monterey, MD 21754

Sheila, Robyn
9027 Adelphi Drive
Burtonsville, MD 20866

Sheree, Carol
86 First St.
Baltimore, MD 21221

Sidney, David
1190 Sean Court
Columbia, MD 21045

Stella, Charles
9609 Cedar Lane
Hagerstown, MD 21740

Stephen, Roberta
4004 32nd Street
Washington, DC 20016

Steven, Catherine
899 Sollers Road
Vienna, VA 22180

Stuart, Patricia
920 Barron Ave
Silver Spring, MD 20901

Sue, Coral
2 Thorne Drive
Baltimore, MD 21218

Susan, Charlie
222 9th Ave
Cambridge, MD 21613

Susan, Karen
7512 Northampton St.
Cabin John, MD 20818

Susan, Patricia
7562 River Terrace
Accokeek, MD 20607

Susan, Renee
976 Springhill Ct
Rockville, MD 20850

Susan, Robert
888 Burlington Road
Silver Spring, MD 20904

Susan, Roger
292 Colston Road
Accokeek, MD 20607

Theresa, Andrew
7569 Country Sq. Dr.
St. Paul, MD 22117

Thomas, Marian
24 Manor Circle
Rockville, MD 20852

Tice, Edna
3637 Horn Way
College Park, MD 20742

Viola, Martin
743 Monroe St
Lutherville, MD 21093

Virginia, Lowden
5719 Taylor Street
Damascus, MD 20785

Wallace, Edwina
7919 Tanbark Lane
Baltimore, MD 21211

Wanda, Georgie
724 Hunterton Street
Baltimore, MD 21218

Way, Robin
6707 Woodland Dr
Baltimore City, MD 21201

William, Carole
912 Bolling Drive
Alexandria, VA 22307

William, Marea
5668 Darnell Ave
Silver Spring, MD 20904

Zella, Barry
6200 Calvert Hall
Arlington, VA 22205

WellSpirit Health Promotion Program Database

Last	First	Age	Sex	Hgt	Intake	Wgt	Chol	Sys	Dias	Follow	Wgt2	Chol2	Sys2	Dias2
Abbey	Richard	44	male	70	11/22/88	119	221	134	73	11/24/89	120	214	132	76
Abby	Joyce	34	female	69	11/22/88	92	326	134	101	11/24/89	91	281	142	98
Alice	Diane	57	female	73	11/22/88	150	330	107	76	11/23/89	140	286	106	74
Andrea	Michele	36	female	69	11/22/88	127	206	117	114	11/23/89	116	192	126	100
Ann	Judith	62	female	49	11/22/88	160	234	160	99	11/24/89	135	206	150	90
Anna	Jean	20	female	55	11/22/88	176	171	110	103	11/23/89	130	160	106	103
Anne	Rebecca	35	female	64	11/22/88	181	292	96	78	11/23/89	135	249	94	78
Annette	Marie	67	female	59	11/22/88	132	257	103	98	11/23/89	136	249	106	97
Arthur	Daniel	48	male	77	11/22/88	115	270	114	104	11/23/89	115	242	123	104
Arthur	Michel	73	male	71	11/22/88	130	200	119	71	11/24/89	128	206	112	69
Barbara	Mark	40	male	58	11/22/88	158	215	137	77	11/24/89	147	212	137	74
Beatrice	Carol	70	female	66	11/22/88	140	337	115	100	11/23/89	148	275	123	102
Ben	Linda	70	female	51	11/22/88	152	279	111	75	11/24/89	153	242	112	75
Bernard	Carolyn	45	female	71	11/21/88	211	270	115	101	11/24/89	180	249	117	96
Betty	Debra	47	female	62	11/22/88	145	327	118	108	11/23/89	140	277	115	95
Blanche	Betty	66	female	64	11/22/88	126	176	124	83	11/24/89	132	167	114	81
Blue	Arthur	21	male	76	11/22/88	147	236	117	109	11/23/89	151	175	116	78
Brenda	Roxanne	40	female	81	11/22/88	107	305	100	92	11/24/89	106	259	104	93
Camile	Carolyn	70	female	82	11/22/88	126	143	118	106	11/23/89	125	139	118	85
Carmine	Jane	30	female	77	11/21/88	145	159	117	81	11/24/89	135	150	114	82
Carmine	Nina	55	female	69	11/21/88	138	284	137	94	11/23/89	141	248	142	95
Carol	Bonnie	74	female	67	11/21/88	160	305	140	99	11/24/89	148	235	143	98
Carol	Patricia	29	female	77	11/22/88	117	232	128	81	11/24/89	125	225	124	82

WellSpirit Health Promotion Program Database

Last	First	Age	Sex	Hgt	Intake	Wgt	Chol	Sys	Dias	Follow	Wgt2	Chol2	Sys2	Dias2
Carol	Phyllis	54	female	82	11/22/88	114	324	97	69	11/23/89	117	272	102	70
Carol	Stephanie	55	female	80	11/22/88	100	307	128	75	11/23/89	96	254	125	77
Carole	Frankie	67	female	70	11/22/88	190	181	160	112	11/24/89	170	190	101	100
Carrie	Cassandra	32	female	52	11/22/88	95	262	114	66	11/23/89	93	224	112	67
Catherine	Jamie	58	female	72	11/21/88	170	159	109	79	11/24/89	160	158	110	76
Catherine	Leslie	39	female	70	11/22/88	125	288	132	94	11/24/89	125	240	132	94
Catherine	Sharon	35	female	76	11/22/88	87	241	116	80	11/23/89	94	204	117	83
Charles	Phillipa	38	female	72	11/22/88	150	298	114	101	11/23/89	147	231	112	102
Cheryl	Stephen	16	male	80	11/22/88	156	223	146	110	11/24/89	153	229	90	80
Christina	Peter	49	male	74	11/21/88	146	164	122	92	11/23/89	147	166	114	91
Cook	Cynthia	34	female	77	11/22/88	135	311	127	96	11/23/89	145	247	130	95
Corinda	Christine	44	female	58	11/22/88	148	167	127	107	11/24/89	156	170	129	90
Courtney	Ann	52	female	58	11/21/88	121	254	116	77	11/24/89	120	212	110	75
Cynthia	Dennis	17	male	73	11/22/88	210	254	123	95	11/23/89	216	275	122	96
Cynthia	Leora	63	female	53	11/22/88	229	184	91	89	11/24/89	200	180	90	88
Daisy	Janet	60	female	61	11/22/88	193	288	124	70	11/23/89	140	256	119	73
Darlene	Kenneth	19	male	71	11/22/88	203	253	158	111	11/24/89	213	185	107	100
David	Brandy	45	female	76	11/22/88	122	301	101	73	11/24/89	130	238	95	74
Deborah	Mary	70	female	50	11/22/88	162	244	99	71	11/23/89	152	244	99	71
Deitra	Marian	29	female	50	11/22/88	120	203	122	95	11/23/89	119	200	122	100
Diane	Kathleen	45	female	54	11/22/88	170	225	126	99	11/24/89	135	219	120	99
Donald	Marian	35	female	56	11/22/88	150	201	109	77	11/24/89	130	205	103	78
Donna	Marin	46	male	49	11/21/88	154	222	123	89	11/24/89	154	218	129	87

WellSpirit Health Promotion Program Database

Last	First	Age	Sex	Hgt	Intake	Wgt	Chol	Sys	Dias	Follow	Wgt2	Chol2	Sys2	Dias2
Donna	Nancy	41	female	49	11/21/88	130	238	130	112	11/24/89	125	238	116	85
Donna	Patricia	38	female	62	11/22/88	89	244	125	98	11/23/89	92	223	127	94
Doris	Barbara	55	female	54	11/22/88	116	267	112	85	11/24/89	111	212	115	85
Doris	Joan	52	female	67	11/22/88	180	178	126	97	11/24/89	156	187	126	100
Dorothy	Ellen	28	female	51	11/22/88	190	334	122	70	11/24/89	157	262	125	69
Dorothy	Maria	54	female	51	11/22/88	118	226	94	74	11/23/89	119	234	97	73
Downing	Kathryn	38	female	57	11/21/88	124	206	107	72	11/24/89	115	209	106	71
Edna	Steven	70	male	79	11/21/88	123	174	114	97	11/24/89	122	167	108	96
Edward	Howard	26	male	82	11/22/88	117	333	127	91	11/24/89	112	260	125	93
Eileen	Carla	54	female	56	11/22/88	161	282	127	100	11/24/89	171	215	123	105
Elinore	Emily	73	female	80	11/22/88	96	209	135	105	11/23/89	98	213	135	107
Elizabeth	Camile	46	female	81	11/22/88	142	220	91	80	11/24/89	144	212	89	79
Elizabeth	Marilyn	65	female	48	11/22/88	125	251	119	66	11/24/89	122	205	124	63
Elizabeth	Mark	56	male	82	11/22/88	120	188	135	101	11/24/89	126	205	134	101
Ellen	Carol	57	female	80	11/22/88	118	165	124	113	11/24/89	117	164	127	105
Eugenia	Courtney	16	male	80	11/22/88	148	235	123	115	11/23/89	150	200	131	95
Evelyn	Marene	16	female	72	11/22/88	137	256	121	99	11/24/89	149	233	117	95
Frances	Pamela	36	female	72	11/22/88	175	267	122	71	11/24/89	184	212	122	68
Frances	Rae	37	female	78	11/22/88	137	186	135	89	11/23/89	129	198	128	87
Francine	Ted	66	male	57	11/21/88	117	188	135	85	11/23/89	114	200	136	90
Frank	Linda	22	female	80	11/22/88	89	153	102	79	11/24/89	82	155	100	79
George	Ann	51	female	51	11/22/88	148	261	117	110	11/24/89	147	220	124	80
Geraldine	Mary	59	female	59	11/22/88	97	237	115	97	11/24/89	92	239	112	97

WellSpirit Health Promotion Program Database

Last	First	Age	Sex	Hgt	Intake	Wgt	Chol	Sys	Dias	Follow	Wgt2	Chol2	Sys2	Dias2
Glenn	Barry	29	male	50	11/22/88	86	321	93	85	11/23/89	83	210	94	86
Glenn	Vanessa	37	female	64	11/22/88	158	218	91	86	11/24/89	151	221	94	86
Golden	Joseph	46	male	61	11/22/88	191	281	125	87	11/23/89	196	250	127	87
Helen	Joseph	51	male	74	11/22/88	192	312	108	99	11/24/89	196	290	109	100
Hilton	Ann	29	female	69	11/22/88	124	184	139	68	11/23/89	120	172	135	69
Jack	Frances	72	female	53	11/22/88	109	265	103	78	11/24/89	104	229	99	77
James	Barbara	29	female	57	11/22/88	175	321	94	88	11/23/89	160	270	94	92
James	Nancy	47	female	67	11/22/88	104	264	133	113	11/23/89	105	227	124	110
James	Patricia	57	female	75	11/22/88	164	294	180	108	11/24/89	147	250	104	75
Jane	Cheryl	43	female	55	11/21/88	125	309	134	89	11/24/89	123	242	141	84
Jane	Marie	37	female	49	11/22/88	182	240	132	104	11/24/89	148	226	130	103
Janice	Linda	15	female	65	11/21/88	137	313	135	95	11/23/89	138	268	140	96
Jereyn	Nancy	46	female	72	11/22/88	153	248	145	103	11/24/89	139	248	140	102
Ji	Carolyn	26	female	77	11/22/88	107	315	114	79	11/23/89	99	273	114	82
Joan	Barbara	41	female	61	11/22/88	100	253	126	106	11/23/89	99	208	120	85
Joan	Chris	28	male	64	11/22/88	107	269	195	113	11/23/89	104	220	106	90
Joan	Kenneth	19	male	55	11/22/88	128	209	133	115	11/23/89	127	196	126	100
Joan	Roberta	36	female	58	11/22/88	130	332	190	113	11/23/89	127	290	98	90
Johanna	Joseph	56	male	70	11/22/88	215	146	135	77	11/24/89	226	145	133	76
Jonathan	Michele	53	female	51	11/22/88	163	189	127	110	11/23/89	138	195	127	88
Jonecia	Maureen	64	female	72	11/22/88	114	269	138	78	11/23/89	116	224	140	76
Joseph	Phillip	68	male	54	11/22/88	179	232	120	81	11/23/89	175	230	119	80
Juanita	Herbert	34	male	69	11/22/88	92	326	134	101	11/24/89	91	225	142	98

Last	First	Age	Sex	Hgt	Intake	Wgt	Chol	Sys	Dias	Follow	Wgt2	Chol2	Sys2	Dias2
Judith	Linda	44	female	75	11/22/88	190	189	130	90	11/24/89	143	182	135	88
Judith	Lisa	23	female	67	11/21/88	202	306	139	82	11/23/89	197	253	139	81
Judy	Karen	71	female	74	11/22/88	152	261	131	66	11/23/89	135	219	134	67
Julian	Charles	67	male	74	11/22/88	117	203	124	89	11/24/89	118	230	128	85
Karen	Helen	36	female	59	11/22/88	101	231	114	94	11/24/89	104	221	111	96
Karen	Phyllis	68	female	58	11/22/88	163	286	116	70	11/23/89	200	240	116	67
Kathleen	Joanne	39	female	52	11/22/88	186	212	124	88	11/24/89	155	213	132	87
Kathryn	Patricia	43	female	80	11/22/88	137	322	125	69	11/23/89	130	269	122	69
Kevin	Barry	48	male	71	11/22/88	185	304	120	112	11/23/89	182	250	117	85
Larry	Diane	69	female	68	11/22/88	153	275	122	97	11/24/89	141	225	125	96
Lauren	Maureen	38	female	72	11/22/88	113	244	133	93	11/23/89	114	237	124	93
Lena	Eileen	54	female	58	11/22/88	114	281	131	110	11/23/89	112	236	130	100
Leonard	Nova	39	female	83	11/22/88	93	246	115	90	11/24/89	93	249	120	91
Liane	Tommy	21	female	56	11/22/88	227	213	220	114	11/24/89	213	228	150	95
Linda	George	66	female	71	11/22/88	152	290	137	83	11/24/89	158	247	144	83
Linda	Ronnie	25	female	50	11/22/88	215	215	115	108	11/23/89	180	211	118	90
Lois	Susan	43	female	51	11/22/88	154	152	139	96	11/24/89	124	146	132	98
Londa	Denise	56	female	70	11/22/88	88	302	112	75	11/24/89	88	229	120	73
Lori	Susan	27	female	58	11/22/88	195	309	113	90	11/23/89	195	261	112	88
Lowery	Robert	34	male	69	11/22/88	220	310	121	66	11/24/89	219	190	123	67
Lynda	Iris	42	female	72	11/22/88	211	214	95	76	11/24/89	230	212	96	75
Lynn	Marsha	54	female	53	11/21/88	83	154	125	107	11/23/89	85	148	122	105
Madden	Joshua	45	male	67	11/22/88	227	147	127	69	11/23/89	235	139	131	70

WellSpirit Health Promotion Program Database

Last	First	Age	Sex	Hgt	Intake	Wgt	Chol	Sys	Dias	Follow	Wgt2	Chol2	Sys2	Dias2
Major	Marjorie	48	female	56	11/22/88	155	288	112	106	11/23/89	152	224	112	85
Majors	Jeanne	53	female	50	11/22/88	117	268	139	83	11/23/89	113	224	140	83
Margaret	Johnetta	19	female	67	11/22/88	192	272	109	78	11/23/89	178	216	110	81
Margaret	Nancy	51	female	71	11/21/88	109	183	190	110	11/23/89	113	188	88	88
Margaret	Susan	17	female	53	11/21/88	125	239	107	77	11/23/89	130	232	111	76
Marianne	Linda	33	female	82	11/22/88	122	168	125	98	11/24/89	128	170	122	96
Marie	Jerry	31	male	75	11/22/88	149	197	155	104	11/24/89	147	192	140	108
Marion	Ann	32	female	70	11/22/88	185	241	176	105	11/23/89	164	246	140	100
Marr	Janet	25	female	52	11/22/88	147	284	190	107	11/23/89	136	224	97	80
Martha	Jerome	30	male	60	11/22/88	145	142	136	86	11/24/89	148	142	136	83
Martina	Helen	46	female	49	11/21/88	190	231	108	79	11/24/89	140	231	105	79
Martina	Josephine	47	female	71	11/21/88	119	284	117	68	11/24/89	112	240	110	67
Mary	Michele	68	female	65	11/22/88	183	263	120	86	11/23/89	181	216	122	86
Mary	Nancy	29	female	58	11/22/88	84	247	109	105	11/23/89	90	206	107	101
Mary	Sandra	43	female	54	11/22/88	211	224	115	94	11/23/89	156	209	117	93
Mary	Sherri	23	female	80	11/22/88	137	266	103	70	11/23/89	152	225	106	72
Matthew	Georgiana	25	female	75	11/22/88	147	220	122	67	11/24/89	138	216	122	64
Matthew	Mark	57	male	69	11/22/88	183	183	165	114	11/23/89	185	178	107	80
Matthew	Noel	21	female	53	11/22/88	140	190	116	81	11/23/89	145	182	120	78
Maurice	Elliot	61	male	73	11/22/88	194	302	135	102	11/24/89	197	195	139	101
Melanie	Steven	19	female	61	11/22/88	172	146	156	108	11/23/89	145	148	102	75
Melissa	Edwin	30	male	60	11/22/88	112	305	126	92	11/24/89	114	220	129	96
Melody	Cheryl	47	female	51	11/22/88	108	201	134	70	11/24/89	106	202	138	72

WellSpirit Health Promotion Program Database

Last	First	Age	Sex	Hgt	Intake	Wgt	Chol	Sys	Dias	Follow	Wgt2	Chol2	Sys2	Dias2
Michele	Pat	48	male	53	11/22/88	194	160	137	103	11/23/89	202	47	139	103
Mildred	Laura	39	female	50	11/22/88	154	300	140	99	11/24/89	185	260	98	95
Morgan	Sharon	27	female	50	11/22/88	158	320	112	95	11/23/89	160	220	115	91
Nancy	Neil	25	male	77	11/22/88	204	237	190	100	11/24/89	207	185	160	95
Nova	Stephana	68	female	65	11/22/88	163	248	95	82	11/24/89	134	243	92	83
Patricia	Carol	59	female	56	11/22/88	116	280	140	111	11/24/89	113	250	148	110
Patricia	Cathleen	46	female	56	11/21/88	152	310	97	72	11/24/89	120	210	98	73
Patricia	Donald	54	male	54	11/21/88	127	279	139	112	11/24/89	128	250	141	110
Patricia	Donald	64	male	70	11/22/88	97	232	111	82	11/23/89	91	200	110	85
Patricia	Melinda	65	female	60	11/22/88	119	301	130	101	11/24/89	112	240	130	101
Patricia	Vincent	44	male	54	11/22/88	180	176	132	89	11/24/89	183	173	130	89
Penelope	Helen	60	female	73	11/22/88	138	329	136	112	11/24/89	132	229	137	105
Phillips	Lonnie	47	male	71	11/22/88	136	178	123	71	11/24/89	135	169	117	69
Phyllis	Nanette	16	female	48	11/22/88	96	240	95	68	11/23/89	96	225	91	65
Randi	Linda	27	female	70	11/22/88	115	326	160	105	11/23/89	123	270	140	101
Raphael	Beverly	53	female	59	11/22/88	145	185	138	95	11/23/89	144	188	138	95
Renee	Joyce	19	female	68	11/22/88	126	254	132	110	11/24/89	124	200	131	110
Richard	Josephine	27	female	66	11/22/88	172	336	145	114	11/24/89	135	210	112	85
Richard	Patricia	27	female	68	11/21/88	164	215	136	71	11/24/89	159	201	139	74
Richard	Thomas	26	male	63	11/22/88	182	186	108	104	11/23/89	182	177	115	103
Robert	Brian	24	male	67	11/22/88	151	285	96	79	11/23/89	148	220	98	78
Robert	Robbie	38	female	77	11/21/88	140	337	123	68	11/24/89	151	300	122	70
Roberta	Carole	44	female	54	11/21/88	94	311	127	71	11/23/89	100	190	125	69

Appendix A

WellSpirit Health Promotion Program Database

Last	First	Age	Sex	Hgt	Intake	Wgt	Chol	Sys	Dias	Follow	Wgt2	Chol2	Sys2	Dias2
Robyn	Mary	67	female	65	11/22/88	140	331	136	82	11/23/89	139	240	133	81
Roger	Theresa	43	female	62	11/22/88	113	251	117	75	11/24/89	111	180	119	76
Ronald	Mary	44	female	58	11/22/88	100	140	140	104	11/24/89	98	144	141	105
Rosanne	Judd	23	male	50	11/22/88	129	337	136	112	11/24/89	128	255	136	100
Ruth	Beverly	48	female	80	11/22/88	144	183	136	83	11/24/89	143	187	146	82
Sally	Valente	26	male	78	11/22/88	211	314	95	83	11/23/89	217	290	93	83
Sandra	Helen	29	female	83	11/22/88	165	219	111	108	11/24/89	150	228	107	80
Sharan	Phillip	24	male	49	11/21/88	127	325	119	114	11/23/89	124	190	119	95
Sharene	Mary	33	female	54	11/21/88	218	287	109	89	11/24/89	220	220	109	90
Sharon	Joseph	32	male	57	11/22/88	193	314	118	71	11/24/89	187	265	121	71
Sharon	Lanny	46	male	78	11/22/88	151	305	130	78	11/24/89	141	250	131	82
Sheila	Elizabeth	25	female	77	11/22/88	126	329	138	111	11/23/89	115	210	137	95
Sheila	Lisa	33	female	56	11/21/88	133	145	132	109	11/23/89	131	139	128	95
Sheila	Melvin	72	male	63	11/22/88	86	207	130	73	11/23/89	84	200	135	73
Sheila	Robyn	72	female	49	11/22/88	145	184	123	93	11/24/89	123	184	122	92
Sheree	Carol	66	female	76	11/22/88	227	270	130	97	11/24/89	215	250	133	95
Sidney	David	20	male	55	11/22/88	176	171	110	103	11/23/89	173	160	106	103
Steal	Chares	60	male	78	11/22/88	194	202	174	112	11/24/89	204	200	100	75
Stephen	Roberta	41	female	77	11/22/88	144	240	92	66	11/24/89	143	243	88	65
Steven	Catherine	37	female	58	11/22/88	130	222	110	82	11/24/89	135	214	109	79
Stuart	Patricia	15	female	76	11/21/88	158	267	160	104	11/24/89	169	250	150	100
Sue	Coral	34	female	57	11/21/88	107	292	92	88	11/24/89	106	195	92	88
Susan	Charie	19	female	57	11/22/88	224	212	175	107	11/24/89	233	219	94	85

WellSpirit Health Promotion Program Database

Last	First	Age	Sex	Hgt	Intake	Wgt	Chol	Sys	Dias	Follow	Wgt2	Chol2	Sys2	Dias2
Susan	Karen	60	female	61	11/22/88	120	222	160	114	11/24/89	112	223	91	75
Susan	Patricia	54	female	73	11/22/88	114	281	131	110	11/23/89	112	320	130	90
Susan	Renee	73	female	74	11/22/88	104	232	200	93	11/23/89	104	240	160	93
Susan	Robert	35	male	52	11/22/88	226	179	129	105	11/24/89	228	188	137	105
Susan	Roger	57	male	49	11/22/88	211	284	130	66	11/23/89	211	180	131	64
Theresa	Andrew	52	male	48	11/22/88	90	205	110	77	11/23/89	94	197	111	79
Thomas	Marian	28	female	73	11/22/88	83	254	190	113	11/24/89	88	170	109	80
Tice	Edna	16	female	81	11/22/88	158	157	99	68	11/24/89	152	158	95	66
Viola	Martin	21	male	67	11/21/88	223	257	95	92	11/23/89	227	190	95	90
Virginia	Lowden	60	female	62	11/21/88	110	261	118	79	11/24/89	120	246	119	80
Wallace	Edwina	37	female	60	11/21/88	185	277	108	70	11/24/89	175	250	102	70
Wanda	Georgie	44	female	75	11/22/88	160	332	128	113	11/24/89	167	190	121	92
Way	Robin	32	female	76	11/22/88	150	310	180	103	11/24/89	153	175	150	106
William	Carole	37	female	78	11/22/88	150	197	105	74	11/23/89	146	201	99	74
William	Marea	26	female	56	11/22/88	157	210	100	90	11/23/89	157	200	103	93
Zeal	Barry	55	male	53	11/22/88	116	176	107	97	11/23/89	111	172	112	96

Appendix B
References Cited

Chapter 1

Anderson, D. M., Needle, R. H., Mosow, S. (1988). Evaluation of a microcomputer-enhanced intervention for elementary school children. *Family and Community Health, 11,* 1, 36–47.

Bailey & Pigg (1983).

Brown, R. L., McDermott, R. J., & Marty, P. J. (1981a). A conversational information computer system for health and safety operation: The OSIS. *American Industrial Hygiene Association Journal, 42* (11), 824–830.

Brown, R. L., McDermott, R. J., Marty, P. J. (1981b).

Chen, M., Houston, T., Burson, J. (1983). Microcomputer-based health education in the waiting room: A feasibility study. *Journal of Computer-Based Instruction, 9,* 90.

Dorf, R. C. (1974). *Computers and man.* San Francisco: Boyd & Fraser.

Ellis, L. B. M., Raines, J. R. & Hakanson, N. (1981). Health education using microcomputers: I. Initial acceptability. Preventive Medicine, 10, 77–84.

Ellis, L. B. M., Raines, J. R., & Hakanson, N. (1982). Health education using microcomputers: II. One year in the clinic. *Preventive Medicine, 11,* 212–224.

Gold, R. S., & Duncan, D. F. (1980a). Computers and health education. *The Journal of School Health, 50,* 503–505.

Gold, R. S., & Duncan, D. F. (1980b). Potential uses of microprocessors for home health education. *Health Values: Achieving High Level Wellness, 4* (2), 69–70.

Hahn, J. S., & Nicholson, T. (1986). The role of computers in health education: Some lessons from instructional technology. *Journal of Family and Community Health, 9* (2), 64–67.

Hawkins, G. S. (June, 1964). The secret of Stonehenge. *Harper's Magazine,* pp. 96–99.

Hawkins, W. E., Duncan, D. F., & McDermott, R. J. (1986). Can high technology make self-care a social movement? *Journal of Family and Community Health, 9* (2), 37–45.

McDermott & Belcastro (1983).

Randolfi, E. A. (1986). *The diffusion of a curriculum innovation in higher education: A course in microcomputer applications for health educators.* Unpublished doctoral dissertation, University of Oregon, Eugene.

Randolfi, E. A., Irvine, A. B., & Davis, L. G. (1986). A course in microcomputer applications for the health educator. *Journal of Family and Community Health, 9* (2), 51–59.

Randolfi, Irvine & Davis (1985).

Shoderbek, C. G., Shoderbek, P. P., & Lefales, A. G. (1980). *Management Systems: Conceptual considerations.* Dallas: Business Publishers.

Simkin, M. G. (1987) *Introduction to Computer Information Systems for Business.* Dubuque, IA: W. C. Brown Publishers.

Simkin, M. G., & Dependahl, R. H., Jr. (1987). *Microcomputer principles and applications.* Dubuque: Wm. C. Brown.

Sullivan, D. R., Lewis, T. G., & Cook, C. R. (1985). *Computing today: Microcomputer concepts and applications.* Boston: Houghton Mifflin.

Tom, (1981).

Chapter 2

Collen, M. F. (1983). General requirements for clinical departmental systems. In J. H. Ban Bemmel, M. J. Ball, & O. Wigertz (Eds.), *MEDINFO 83* (pp. 61–64) Amsterdam: North-Holland.

Conklin, G. S., McCormack, M., Andersen, E. G., & Libenson, D. D. (1987). Database management systems into the 1980's: A review. *Topics in Health Management, 7* (3), 1–11.

Demel, John T., & Miller, Michael J. (1984). *Introduction to computer graphics.* Monterey, CA: Brooks/Cole Engineering Division (a division of Wadsworth, Inc.).

Graves, J. R. (1987). Personal library management. *Computers in Nursing, 5* (6), 225–230.

Hammond, W. E., & Stead, W. W. (1988, November). *Database concepts.* Workshop session presented at the twelfth Annual Symposium on Computer Applications in Medical Care, Washington, DC.

Holmes, Nigel. (1984). *Designer's guide to creating charts and diagrams.* New York: Watson-Guptill.

Lefferts, Robert. (1981). *Elements of graphics: How to prepare charts and graphs for effective reports.* New York: Harper & Row.

Meilach, Dona Z. (1986). *Dynamics of presentation graphics.* Homewood, Illinois: Dow Jones-Irwin.

Sandler, Corey. (1984). *Desktop graphics for the IBM PC.* Morris Plains, NJ: Creative Computing Press.

Simkin, M. G., & Dependahl, R. H., Jr. (1987). *Microcomputers principles and applications.* Dubuque, IA; Wm. C. Brown.

White, Jan V. (1984). *Using charts and graphs.* New York: R. R. Bowker.

Chapter 3

Carrasco, N. J., Testi, N., Montgomery, W., et al. (1986). An integrated perinatal information system and telecommunications networking. *American Journal of Perinatology 3* (2), 141–143.

Connell, C. M., Smyer, M. A. (1986). Telephone conference networks for training in mental health. *Gerontologist, 26* (4), 339–341.

Evans, R. L., Smith, K. M., Werkhoven, W. S., et al. (1986). Cognitive telephone group therapy with physically disabled elderly persons. *Gerontologist, 26* (1), 8–11.

Homan, J. M. (1986). End-user information utilities in the health sciences. *Bulletin of the Medical Library Association, 74* (1), 31–35.

Howard, E. H., & Jankowski, T. A. (1986). Reference services via electronic mail. *Bulletin of the Medical Library Association, 74* (1), 41–44.

LaPorte, R. E., Rewers, M., Tuomilehto, J., et al. (1988). Telecommunication and international health research. *American Journal of Epidemiology, 128* (2) 439–443.

Online databases in the medical and life sciences. (1987). New York: Cuadra/ Elsevier.

Radwin, H. M. (1986). Telecommunications in urology. *Urology Clinica North America, 13* (1), 59–64.

Schneider, S. J., & Tooley, J. (1986). Self-help computer conferencing. *Computers in Biomedical Research, 19* (3), 274–281.

Simkin, M. G. (1987). *Introduction to Computer Information Systems for Business.* Dubuque, IA: Wm. C. Brown.

Simkin, M. G., & Dependahl, R. H., Jr. (1987). *Microcomputer principles and applications.* Dubuque, IA: Wm. C. Brown.

Weinstein, R. S., Bloom, K. J., & Rozek, L. S. (1987). Telepathology and the networking of pathology diagnostic services. *Archives of Pathology Laboratory Medicine, 111* (7), 646–652.

Chapter 4

Anderson, D. M., Needle, R. H., & Mosow, S. (1986). Evaluation of a microcomputer-enhanced intervention for elementary school children. *Family and Community Health, 11* (1), 36–47.

Coggan, P. G., Hoppe, M., & Hadac, R. (1984). Educational applications of computers in medical education. *Journal of Family Practice, 19* (1), 66–71.

Cook, G. (1982). The microcomputer: Physician's aid for patient education in cancer. In *Proceedings of the Sixth Annual Symposium on Computer Applications in Medical Care* (p. 656). New York: Institute of Electrical and Electronic Engineers.

Dennison, D. (1982). *The DINE system: The nutritional plan for better health.* Amherst, New York: DINESystem, Inc.

Eberts, R. E. (1986). Computer-aided education. *MD Computing, 3,* 20–28.

Ellis, L. B. M., Raines, J. R., Hakanson, N. (1981). Health education using microcomputers. I. Initial acceptability. *Preventive Medicine, 10* (1), 77–84.

Greenes, R. A., & Seigel, E. R. (1987). Characterization of an emerging field: Approaches to defining the literature and disciplinary boundaries of medical informatics. In *Proceedings of the Eleventh Annual Symposium on Computer Applications in Medical Care* (pp. 411–414). New York: Institute of Electrical and Electronic Engineers.

Gross, C. R., & Ellis, L. B. M. (1987). Teaching health professionals to use the computer: Options for the transition years. In *Proceedings of the Eleventh Annual Symposium on Computer Applications in Medical Care* (pp. 437–441). New York: Institute of Electrical and Electronic Engineers.

Kadden, R., Wetstone, S. (1982). Teaching coping skills to alcoholics using computer based education. In *Proceedings of the Sixth Annual Symposium on Computer Applications in Medical Care* (p. 635). New York: Institute of Electrical and Electronic Engineers.

LaVenture, M., Davis, J., Faulkner, J., et al. (1982). Wisconsin epidemiology disease surveillance system. User control of data-base management technology. In *Proceedings of the Sixth Annual Symposium on Computer Applications in Medical Care* (p. 156). New York: Institute of Electrical and Electronic Engineers.

Lyons, C., Krasnowski, J., Greenstein, A., et al. (1982). Interactive computerized patient education. *Heart Lung, 11,* 340–341.

Mazzola, F., Rowe, B., Rowe, D. (1983). Video diabetes: A teaching tool for children with insulin-dependent diabetes. In *Proceedings of the Seventh Annual Symposium on Computer Applications in Medical Care* (p. 182). New York: Institute of Electrical and Electronic Engineers.

Naditch, M. (1983). PLATO STAYWELL: A behavioral medicine microcomputer program of health behavior change. In *Proceedings of the Seventh Annual Symposium on Computer Applications in Medical Care* (pp. 363–365). New York: Institute of Electrical and Electronic Engineers.

O'Grady, B. V. (1984). Computerized documentation of community health nursing—What shall it be? *Computers in Nursing, 2* (3), 98–101.

Piemme, T. E. (1988). Computer-assisted learning and evaluation in medicine. *Journal of the American Medical Association, 260* (3), 367–372.

Piggins, J. L., Barnett, G. O., Foster, E. A., et al. (1987). Experience with information technology at Harvard Medical School. In *Proceedings of the Eleventh Annual Symposium on Computer Applications in Medical Care* (pp. 445–449). New York: Institute of Electrical and Electronic Engineers.

Randolfi, E. A. (1986). *The diffusion of a curriculum innovation in higher education: A course in microcomputer applications for health educators.* Unpublished doctoral dissertation, University of Oregon, Eugene.

Robertson, L. H., McDonnell, K., Scott, J. (1976). Nursing health assessment of preschool children in Perth County. *Canadian Journal of Public Health, 67,* 300–304.

Romano, C. A., & Heller, B. R. (1988). Curriculum model for graduate specialization in nursing informatics. In *Proceedings of the Twelfth Annual Symposium on Computer Applications in Medical Care* (pp. 343–349). New York: Institute of Electrical and Electronic Engineers.

Saba, V. K., & McCormick, K. A. (1986). *Essentials of computers for nurses.* Philadelphia: J. B. Lippincott.

Slack, W. V., Slack, C. W. (1977). Talking to a computer about emotional problems: A comparative study. *Psychotherapy: Theory, Research and Practice, 14* (2), 156–164.

Somand, M. E. (1981). PIES: Patient instruction in the physician's office. In *Proceedings of the Fifth Annual Symposium on Computer Applications in Medical Care* (pp. 356–357). New York: Institute of Electrical and Electronic Engineers.

Van Cura, L. J., et al. (1975). Venereal disease: Interviewing and teaching by computer. *American Journal of Public Health, 65,* 1159–1164.

Wheeler, L., Wheeler, M., Ours, P., & Swider, C. (1983). Use of CAI/video in diabetes patient nutritional education. In *Proceedings of the Seventh Annual Symposium on Computer Applications in Medical Care* (pp. 961–964). New York: Institute of Electrical and Electronic Engineers.

Yates, W. R. (1982). Computer assisted patient prenatal education. In *Proceedings of the Sixth Annual Symposium on Computer Applications in Medical Care* (p. 633). New York: Institute of Electrical and Electronic Engineers.

Chapter 5

Beery, W. L., et al. (1981). *Description analysis and assessment of health hazard/health risk appraisal programs. Final report.* Washington, DC: National Center for Health Services Research.

Beery, W. L., Schoenbach, V. J., Wagner, E. H., et al. (1986). *Health risk appraisal: Methods and programs with annotated bibliography* (DHHS Publication No. PHS 86–3396). Washington, DC: National Center for Health Services Research.

Charlesworth, E. A., & Nathan, R. S. (1982). *Stress management: A comprehensive guide to wellness.* Houston: Biobehavioral Publisher & Distributors.

Dunton, S. M., & Perkins, D. D. (1985). *Health risk appraisal and safety belt use* (Contract No. DTNH22–84–07323). Washington, DC: USDOT, National Highway Traffic Safety Administration.

Fielding, J. E. (1982). Appraising the health of health risk appraisal. *American Journal of Public Health, 72* (4).

Gersham, L. & Clouser, R. A. (1974). Treating insomnia with relaxation and desensitization in a group setting by an automated approach. *Behavioral Therapy and Experimental Psychiatry, 5,* 31–35.

Imrey, H. H. (1985). *Evaluation of HHA programs. An annotated bibliography.* Urbana, IL: Regional Health Resource Center.

Lauzon, R. J. (1977). *A randomized controlled trial on the ability of health hazard appraisal to stimulate appropriate risk-reduction behavior.* Unpublished doctoral dissertation, University of Oregon, Eugene.

Lepanto, J. D. & Jenkins, C. F. (1984). *Exercise: For the health of it (3rd ed.).* Dubuque, IA: Kendall/Hunt.

Mullen, K. D., Gold, R. S., Belcastro, P. A., & McDermott, R. J. (1986). *Connections for health.* Dubuque, IA: Wm. C. Brown.

Potter, P. A., & Perry, A. G. (1987). *Basic nursing: Theory and practice.* St. Louis: C. V. Mosby.

Quick, J. C., & Quick, J. D. (1984). *Organizational stress and preventive management.* New York: McGraw-Hill.

Reitman, R. (1984). *Coping with stress.* Woodland Hills, CA: Psycomp.

Selmi, P. M. (1983). Computer-assisted cognitive-behavior therapy in the treatment of depression. *Dissertation Abstracts International, 44,* 3943B–3944B.

Smith, J. J. (1987). The effectiveness of a computerized self-help stress coping program with adult males. *Computers in Human Services, 2* (1/2), 37–49.

Wagner, E. H., Beery, W. L., Schoenbach, V. J., & Graham, R. M. (1982). An assessment of health hazard/health risk appraisal. *American Journal of Public Health, 72*(4), 347–352.

Chapter 6

Bowerman, R. G., & Glover, D. E. (1988). *Putting expert systems into practice.* New York: Van Nostrand Reinhold.

Brodman, E. (1985). Computers and the historic millieu of health services libraries. *Behavioral and Social Sciences Librarian, 4*(4), 15–20.

Feldman, J. A., & Ballard, D. H. (1982). Connectionist models and their properties. *Cognitive Science, 6,* 205–254.

Gold, R. S., & Kelly, M. A. (1988). Is knowledge really power? *Health Education, 19*(4), 40–46.

Hinton, G. E., & Anderson, J. A. (1981). *Parallel models of associative memory.* Hillsdale, NJ: Erlbaum.

Jewell, J. A., Abraham, I. L., & Fitzpatrick, J. J. (1987). Selecting an appropriate problem for nursing expert system development. In *Proceedings of the Eleventh Annual Symposium on Computer Applications in Medical Care* (pp. 85–87). New York: Institute of Electrical and Electronic Engineers.

Parsaye, K., & Chignell, M. (1988). *Expert systems for experts.* New York: John Wiley and Sons.

Pople, H. E. (1982). Heuristic methods for imposing structure on ill-structured problems: The structuring of medical diagnostics. In P. Szolovits (Ed.) *Artificial intelligence in medicine.* (pp. 119–190). Boulder: Westview Press.

Rumelhart, D. E. & McClelland, J. L. (1986). *Parallel distributed processing: Explorations in the microstructure of cognition* (Vol. 1.). Cambridge, MA: The MIT Press.

Shangraw, R. F. (1986). Telephone surveying with computers: Administrative, methodological and research issues. *Evaluation and Program Planning 9*(2), 107–111.

Chapter 7

Barhyte, D. Y. (1987). Ethical issues in automating nursing personnel data. *Computers in Nursing, 5*(5), 171–174.

Brannigan, V. (1987). The regulation of medical computer software as a "device" under the Food, Drug and Cosmetic Act. In *Proceedings of the Eleventh Annual Symposium on Computer Applications in Medical Care* (pp. 347–354). New York: Institute of Electrical and Electronic Engineers.

Brannigan, V. M. & Dayhoff, R. E. (1981). Liability for personal injuries caused by defective medical computer programs. *American Journal of Law and Medicine, 7*(2), 123–144.

Brannigan, V. M., & Dayhoff, R. E. (1986). Medical informatics: The revolution in law, technology, and medicine. *The Journal of Legal Medicine, 7*(1), 1–53.

Hiller, M. D. & Beyda, V. (1981). Computers, medical records, and the right to privacy. *Journal of Health Politics, Policy, and Law, 6*(3), 463–488.

Hsiao, D. K., Kerr, D. S., & Madnick, S. E. (1979). *Computer security.* New York: Academic Press.

Moor, J. H. (1986). What is computer ethics? *Metaphilosophy, 16,* 266–275.

Romano, C. A. (1987). Privacy, confidentiality, and security of computerized systems. *Computers in Nursing, 5*(3), 99–104.

Simkin, M. G., & Dependahl, R. H., Jr. (1987). *Microcomputer principles and applications.* Dubuque, IA: Wm. C. Brown.

U.S. Department of Health and Human Services. (1984). Basic HHS Policy for Protection of Human Research Subjects, 45 C. F. R, §46, 101.

Victoroff, M. S. (1985). Ethical expert systems. In *Proceedings of the Ninth Annual Symposium on Computer Applications in Medical Care* (pp. 644–648). New York: Institute of Electrical and Electronic Engineers.

Watson, B. L., & Bernstein, J. M. (1988). Liability for not using computers in medicine. In *Proceedings of the Twelfth Annual Symposium on Computer Applications in Medical Care* (pp. 898–901). New York: Institute of Electrical and Electronic Engineers.

Watson, D. (1981). Disclosure of computerized health care information: Provider privacy under supply side competition. *American Journal of Law and Medicine, 7,* 265–300.

Whalen v. Roe, 429 U.S. 589, 605 (1977).

Winslade, W. L. (1982). Confidentiality of medical records. *The Journal of Legal Medicine, 3*(4), 497–533.

Chapter 8

Randolfi, E. A. (1986). *The diffusion of a curriculum innovation in higher education: A course in microcomputer applications for health educators.* Unpublished doctoral dissertation, University of Oregon, Eugene.

Appendix C
Vendors of Health-Promotion Software

Actronics, Inc.
810 River Avenue
Pittsburg, PA 15212

Albion Software
562 Boston Avenue
Bridgeport, CT 06610

ALSoft
PO Box 927
Sprint, TX 77383

Am. Alliance For Health, Phys. Educ.,
Recreation and Dance
1900 Association Drive
Reston, VA 22091

American Diabetes Center Inc.
Waukegan, IL

American Wellness Systems, Inc.
6400 Lake Forrest Drive, NW., Suite 255
Atlanta, GA 30328

Ames Division of Miles Laboratories, Inc.
PO Box 70
Elkhart, IN 46515

Andent, Inc.
1000 North Avenue
Waukegan, IL 60085

Anderson-Bell Corporation
11479 South Pine Drive, Suite 438
Parker, CO 80134

Artificial Intelligence Research Group
921 North La Jolla Avenue
Los Angeles, CA 90046

Baumgartner, T.
University of Georgia
PE Building
Athens, GA 30602

Besserman, R.
Besserman Corporation
1728 West Glendale Avenue
Phoenix, AZ 85021

Biosource Software
2105 S. Franklin, Suite B
Kirksville, MO 63501

BMDP Statistical Software, Inc.
1440 Sepulveda Blvd., Suite 316
Los Angeles, CA 90025

BrainPower, Inc.
24009 Ventura Blvd., Suite 250
Calabasas, CA 91302

CAMDE Corporation
4435 South Rural Road, Suite 331
Tempe, AZ 85282

Center for Corporate Health Promotion
1850 Centennial Park Drive, Suite 520
Reston, VA 22091

Center for Science In The Public Interest
1501 Sixteenth Street NW
Washington, DC 20036

Christensen, CL
San Jose State University
San Jose, CA 95192

Circle Systems
1001 Fourth Avenue., Suite 3200
Seattle, WA 98154

Clear Lake Research
5615 Morningside, Suite 127
Houston, TX 77005

Clinical Nursing Software
PO Box 172
Middleton, WI 53562

Clinical Reference Systems, Inc.
600 South Cherry Street
Suite 20
Denver, CO 80222

Clinical Reference Systems, Ltd.
5613 DTC Parkway, Suite 350
Englewood, CO 80111

Cognitive Development Inc.
12345 Lake City Way, NE, Suite 141
Seattle, WA 98125

CompTech Systems Design
Box 516
Hastings, MN 55033

Computer And Media Services
Spencer S. Eccles Health Sciences
    Library
University of Utah, Building 589
Salt Lake City, UT 84112–1185

Computerized Educational Systems
Florida Hospital Association
    Management Corporation
PO Box 536905
Orlando, FL 32853–6905

Computerized Health Appraisals
15431 SE 82nd Drive
Clakamas, OR 97015

Computrition Inc.
21049 Devonshire Street
Chatsworth, CA 91311

CompYOUtr-cize Inc.
13003 Cohassett Lane
Woodbridge, VA 22192

Constructive Leisure
511 N. La Cienega Blvd.
Los Angeles, CA 90048

Couldry, W.
4525 Downs Drive
St. Joseph, MO 64507

Crunch Software
5335 College Avenue, Suite 27
Oakland, CA 94618

Custom Medical Software
42 Walnut Lane
Davis, CA 95616

Cybermedic, Inc.
740 South Pierce Avenue
Louisville, CO 80027

DG Systems
322 Prospect Avenue
Hartford, CT 06016

Dick Dodge, PhD
Corporate Health Center, Inc.
11754 Terrace View Drive
Grand Terrace, CA 92324

Digital Diagnostics, Inc.
601 University Avenue, Suite 255
Sacramento, CA 95825

Digitealth
4304 West Bay
Lake Oswego, OR 97034

DINESystems, Inc.
2211 Main Street, Building C
Buffalo, NY 14314

Donabedian, Professor D.
University of Michigan School of Nursing
400 North Ingalis
Ann Arbor, MI 48109

DW Software, Inc.
Box 705
Quincy, IL 62306

Educational Images
PO Box 3456
West Side Station
Elmira, NY 14905

Educational Media Center
UN. of Texas at El Paso College of
    Nursing
1101 North Campbell
El Paso, TX 79902

Educational Software
10037 Mastin
Overland Park, KS 66212

Elsevier Science Publishing Co.
PO Box 1663, Grand Central Station
New York, NY 10164–0028

Epic Systems Corporation
5609 Medical Circle
Madison, WI 53719

ESHA Research-Nutrition Systems
606 Juntura Way Southeast
Salem, OR 97302

Family Life Software
1401 South 11th Avenue
St. Cloud, MN 66301

Goldman, M.
198 Echo Cove Road
S. Hamilton, MA 01982

Gross Anatomy By Computer, Inc.
PO Box 791
Lee's Summit, MO 64063

Hartley Courseware
133 Bridge Street
Dimondale, MI 48821

Health and Fitness Systems
8423 W. Gregory, Suite 301
Chicago, IL 60656

Healthcare Data
5311 Mt. Pleasant North Drive
Greenwood, IN 46142

Heshi Computing
PO Drawer M
Hitchcock, TX 77563

HMC Software
4200 North Macarthur Boulevard
Irving, TX 75038

Hospital for Sick Children
Toronto, Ontario, Canada

HRM Software
175 Tompkins Avenue
Pleasantville, NY 10570

Human Factors Software
3731 Dell Road
Carmichael, CA 95608

Immunization Alert
PO Box 406
Storrs, CT 06268

Instructional Systems Company
14 East 4th Street
Suite 602
New York, NY 10012

Int. Medical Products Corporation
4503 Moorland Avenue
Minneapolis, MN 55424

Intellectual Software
562 Boston Ave.
Bridgeport, CT 06610

IRL Press, Inc.
PO Box Q
McLean, VA 22101–0850

ISC Consultants
14 East 4th Street, Suite 602
New York, NY 10012

ISI Software
3501 Market Street
Philadelphia, PA 19104

Jeffries, R. DO
Harrisburg, PA

Keyes, L. and M. Simons
8637 Pebble Hills Drive
Sandy, UT 84070

Laboratory Consulting, Inc.
PO Box 1763, 2702 International Lane
Madison, WI 53701

Landa, R.
BrainBank, Inc.
220 Fifth Avenue
New York, NY 10001

Lea & Febiger
600 S. Washington Square
Philadelphia, PA 19106–4198

Leahy, E.
BIOSOFT
PO Box 580
Milltown, NJ 08850

Lippincott Company
East Washington Square
Philadelphia, PA 19105

Mac-Medic Publications
Houston, TX

Macmillan Software
630 Third Avenue
New York, NY 10017

MCE Inc.
157 S. Kalamazoo Mall, Suite 250
Kalamazoo, MI 49007

MECC Distribution Center
MN Educational Computing Consortium
3490 Lexington Avenue North
St. Paul, MN 55112

MEDI-SIM, Inc.
PO Box 13267
Edwardsville, KS 66113

Media Distribution
Box 734 Mayo
420 Delaware St. SE
Minneapolis, MN 55455

Medical Data Analysis Company
85 Woodhaven Park
Storrs, CT 06268

Medical Logic International
5 Pathfinder Drive
Sumter, SC 29150

Medical Software Consortium
PO Box 76069
St. Peters, MO 63376

Medichart Corporation
799 Broadway, Suite 325
New York, NY 10003

MEDMICRO
The Center for Medical Microcomputing
6701 Seybold Road
Madison, WI 53719

MEDx Systems, Lts.
Springdale Court, Box 2000
Dover, MA 02030

MicroHealth Software
PO Box 471783
Tulsa, OK 74147

Micromedx
187 Gardiners Ave
Levittown, NY 11756

Milesis, CA
2228 Lee Street
Augusta, GA 30904

Mindscape, Inc.
3444 Dundee Road
Northbrook, IL 60062

MOSBYSYSTEMS
11830 Westline Industrial Drive
St. Louis, MO 63146

Muse Software
Baltimore, MD

N-Squared Computing Analytic Software
5318 Forest Ridge Road
Silverton, OR 97381

Nat. Res. for Comp. In Life Science Educ
Stop PR-70 University of Washington
Seattle, WA 98195

National Wellness Institute
1319 Fremont Street-UWSP
Stevens Point, WI 54482

National Wellness Institute
University of Wisconsin-Stevens Point
South hall
Stevens Point, WI 54481

Nordic Software
3939 N. 48th Street
Lincoln, NE 68504–1401

Northwest Analytical, Inc.
520 NW Davis Street
Portland, OR 97209

NursePerfect Software
PO Box 471783
Tulsa, OK 74147

NutriMed, Inc.
1701 North Greenville Avenue, Suite 712
Richardson, TX 75081

Nutrition Services Division of Health
Development Inc.
1165 West Third Avenue, PO Box 12299
Columbia, OH 43212

Nutritional Consultants, Inc.
PO Box 1513
Norman, OK 73070

Nutritional Data Resources
PO Box 540
Willoughby, OH 44904

Occidental Computer Systems, Inc.
21201 Oxnard Street
Woodland Hills, CA 91367

Persimmon Software
910 Memory Lane
Mobile, AL 36608

Personal Bibliographic Software, Inc.
PO Box 4250
Ann Arbor, MI 48106

Peters, HF
University of British Columbia
    Department of Health Care
Mather Building, 5804 Fairview Crescent
Vancouver, British Columbia V5T 1W5

Pine Rest Christian Hospital
Staff Education Department
300 68th Street, SE
Grand Rapids, MI 49508–6999

Planetree Medical Systems, Inc.
3519 South 1200 East
Salt Lake City, UT 84106

Programs For Health and Fitness
3851 Orleans Road
Birmingham, AL 35243

Psychological Psoftware Company
312 Los Altos Drive
Aptos, CA 95003

Public Interest Software
1501 Sixteenth St. NW
Washington, DC 20035

Randall, JE
609 South Jordan
Bloomington, IN 47401

Research Information Systems, Inc.
1991 Village Partway, Suite 206
Encinitas, CA 92024

Rhode Island Department of Health
75 Davis Street
Providence, RI 02908

Right On Programs
1737 Veterans Highway
Central Islip, NY 11727

Ruppert, K. & B. Fernhall
Arizona State University
HPE Department
Tempe, AZ 85282

Smolin, R.
C. R. Smolin, Inc.
7760 Fay Avenue, Suite J
La Jolla, CA 92037

Soft Bite, Inc.
PO Box 1484
East Lansing, MI 48823

Softech Computing Company
264 Morris Street
Pewaukee, WI 53072

Software Toolworks
13557 Ventura Boulevard
Sherman Oaks, CA 91423

SPSS Inc.
444 N. Michigan Ave.
Chicago, IL 60611

Statsoft Software
2325 East 13th Street
Tulsa, OK 74104

STSC Inc.
2115 E. Jefferson St.
Rockville, MD 20852

Substance Abuse Education, Inc.
670 South 4th Street
Edwardsville, KS 66113

Systat, Inc.
1800 Sherman Avenue
Evanston, IL 60201

The MedSoft Company
1105 Arondale Drive
Fircrest, WA 98466

Thought Technology Ltd.
2180 Belgrave Avenue
Montreal, Quebec, Canada H4A 2L8

TJ Designs
5905 Ironwood
Ranchos Palos Verdes, CA 90274

Un. of CT Multipurpose Arthritis Center
School of Medicine
Farmington, CT 06032–9984

Vacumed
2261 Palma Drive
Ventura, CA 93003–5789

Walonick Associates
6500 Nicollet Avenue S.
Minneapolis, MN 55423

Wanda Monthey
Department of Education
700 Pringle Parkway SE
Salem, OR 97310

WB Saunders Company
West Washington Square
Philadelphia, PA 19105

Wellsource
15431 Southeast 82nd Drive, Suite E
Clackamas, OR 97015

Wholebody Health Management
18653 Ventura Blvd., Suite 137
Tarzana, CA 91354

Williams & Wilkins
428 East Preston Street
Baltimore, MD 21202

Willoughby, L.
UMKC Software Series
2411 Holmes Street
Kansas City, MO 64108-2792

Wm. C. Brown Publishers
2460 Kerper Blvd.
Dubuque, IA 52004-0539

Appendix D: Sources of Information on Health Applications

Journals

Advances for Medicine (Hewlett-Packard Corporation)
Algorithm (Journal of Computer Applications in Allied Health)
Computer-Disability News (National Easter Seal Society)
Computer Methods and Programs in Biomedicine (Elsevier Science Publishers)
Computers in Biology and Medicine (Pergamon Press)
Computers and Biomedical Research (Academic Press)
Computers and Medicine (Medit Associates)
Computers in Healthcare (Cardiff Communications)
Computer Medicine (Associates)
Computer Medicine (Computer Medicine Society)
Computers in Nursing (J. B. Lippincott)
Computer Programs in Biomedicine (North Holland)
Computers in Psychiatry/Psychology
Healthcare Computing and Communications (Health Data Analysis)
International Journal of Bio-medical Computing (Elsevier)
Journal of Clinical Computing (Journal of Clinical Computing)
Journal of Dietetic Software for Nutrition (Quarterly Report of Software for Nutrition and Food Service Professionals)
Journal of Medical Systems (Plenum)
MD Computing: Computers in Medical Practice (Springer-Verlag)
Medical Computer Journal (Medical Computer Journal)
Medicine and Computer (American Association for Medical Systems and Informatics)
Methods of Information in Medicine (European Federation for Medical Information)
Micro MD Journal (Micro MD Publishers)
Physicians and Computers (Physicians and Computers)
Software in Healthcare (Software in Healthcare Publishing)
Update: Computers in Medicine (Medical Marketing Communications)

Information On Software On Health Education

Directory of Computer Software with Application to Sports, Science, Health, and Dance (2nd ed.) (AAHPERD)

Directory of Educational Software for Nursing (National League For Nursing)

The Educational Software Selector 1986/87 (TESS) (Educational Products Information Exchange)

The FNIC Software Collection (Food and Nutrition Information Center of the National Agricultural Library)

Health Risk Appraisals (ODPHP National Health Information Center)

Mental Health Systems Software Directory (American Association of Medical Systems and Informatics: AAMSI)

Menu—The International Software Database (Dialog Information Services)

Online Microcomputer Software Guide and Directory (BRS Information Technologies)

The Software Catalog: Health Professions (Elsevier Science Publishing)

SpecialWare Directory: A Guide to Software for Special Education (LINC Associates)

Appendix E
Selected References

Anonymous. (1986). Interactive medical telecomputing [letter]. *New England Journal of Medicine, 315* (14), 899–900.

Abbey, L. M. (1987). An expert system for oral diagnosis. *Journal of Dental Education, 51* (8), 475–480.

Abernathy, W. B. (1979). The microcomputer as a community mental public information tool. *Community Mental Health Journal, 15* (3), 192–202.

Adams, G. A. (1986). Computer technology: Its impact on nursing practice. *Nursing Administration Quarterly, 10* (2), 21–33.

Adelman, M., Dwyer, J. T., Woods, M., Bohn, E., & Otradove, C. L. (1983). Computerized dietary analysis systems. *Continuing Education, 83* (4), 421–429.

Adlassnig, K. P., Kolarz, G., Scheithauer, W., Kolarz, G., Scheitha, W., Effeuberg, H., & Grabner, G. (1985). CADIAG: Approaches to computer-assisted medical diagnosis. *Computers in Biological Medicine, 15* (5), 315–335.

Agamalian, R. G. (1987). Computers, clinical applications, and the CCU nurse. *Focus on Critical Care? 14* (3), 29–37.

Ahijevych, K., Boyle, K. K., & Burger, K. (1985). Microcomputers enhance student health fairs. *Journal of Nursing Education, 24* (1), 16–20.

Allan, D. M. E., & Walraven, G. (1986). Issues in the adoption of new educational technology. In *Proceedings of the Tenth Annual Symposium on Computer Applications in Medical Care* (pp. 194–200). New York: Institute of Electrical and Electronics Engineers.

Amatetti, S. L. (1987). The use of computer models to evaluate prevention strategies: An interview with Harold Holder. *Alcohol Health and Research World,* Fall, 18–21, 47.

Anderson, D. M., Needle, R. H., & Mosow, S. (1986). Evaluation of a microcomputer-enhanced intervention for elementary school children. *Family and Community Health, 11* (1), 36–47.

Arnold, J. M., & Bauer, C. A. (1984). A collaborative proposal for advanced computer literacy. In *Proceedings of the Eighth Annual Symposium on Computer Applications in Medical Care* (pp. 662–667). New York: Institute of Electrical and Electronics Engineers.

Arnold, J. M., & Bauer, C. A. (1988). Meeting the needs of the computer age in continuing education. *Computers in Nursing, 6* (2), 66–69.

Ascione, F. J., & Fish, C. A. (1986). Computer health/medication information software—Compilation for pharmacists. *American Pharmacy,* NS26, 2, 45–50.

Austin, C. J., & Greene, B. R. (1978). Hospital information systems: A current perspective. *Inquiry, 15,* 95–112.

Auvert, B., Aegerter, P., Van Look, K., Du, L. T. H., Boutin, P., & Monier, J. L. (1986). A hand-held decision-aid system designed for rural health workers. *Computers in Biomedical Research, 19* (1), 80–89.

Aveney, B., & Conneen, S. (1986). The atomization of information. *Bulletin of the Medical Library Association, 74* (1), 22–26.

Barhyte, D. Y. (1987). Ethical issues in automating nursing personnel data. *Computers in Nursing, 5* (5), 171–174.

Barnett, G. O. (1982). The computer and clinical judgment. *The New England Journal of Medicine, 307* (8), 493–494.

Barnett, G. O., Cimino, J. J., Hupp, J. A., & Hoffer, E. P. 1987. DXplain: An evolving diagnostic decision-support system. *Journal of the American Medical Association, 258,* 67–74.

Bartlett, E. E. (1986). Patient education meets the desktop computer revolution. *Patient Education and Counseling, 8,* 345–348.

Basch, C. E., & Gold, R. S. (1988). The potential contribution of computerized school-based record systems to the monitoring of the disease. *Health Education Quarterly, 15* (1), 35–51.

Beck, R. J., Ellis, L. B. M., Scott, D. M., Raines, J. R., Hakanson. (1982). Microcomputer as patient educator. *American Journal of Hospital Pharmacy, 39* (12), 2105–2108.

Beier, B. (1986). Liability and responsibility for clinical medical software in the Federal Republic of Germany. In *Proceedings of the Tenth Annual Symposium on Computer Applications in Medical Care,* (pp. 364–368). New York: Institute of Electrical and Electronics Engineers.

Beier, B. R. (1983). Medical computing law—The way to correct information and documentation. In *Proceedings of the Seventh Annual Symposium on Computer Applications in Medical Care,* (pp. 645–649). New York: Institute of Electrical and Electronics Engineers.

Bell, J. A. (1986). The role of microcomputers in patient education. *Computers in Nursing, 4* (6), 255–258.

Billings, D. M. (1986). Advantages and disadvantages of computer-assisted instruction. *Dimensions of Critical Care Nursing, 5* (6), 356–362.

Billings, D. M. (1984). Evaluating computer-assisted instruction. *Nursing Outlook, 32* (1), 50–53.

Birkett, N. J. (1988). Computer-aided personal interviewing: A new technique for data collection in epidemiologic surveys. *American Journal of Epidemiology, 127* (3), 684–690.

Bischoff, M. B. (1983). Integration of a computer-based consultant into the clinical setting. In *Proceedings of the Seventh Annual Symposium on Computer Applications in Medical Care,* (pp. 149–152). New York: Institute of Electrical and Electronics Engineers.

Bishop, D. (1986). Information overload and how to lighten it. *Mobius, 6* (3), 47–53.

Bissen, C. A. (1988). Data security: Protecting a corporate asset. *Topics in Health Records Management, 9* (1), 13–23.

Bitonti, C. (1987). On coping with stress. *Computers in Human Services, 2* (1/2), 93–97.

Bloom, K. C., Leitner, J. E., & Solano, J. L. (1987). Development of an expert system prototype to generate nursing care plans based on nursing diagnoses. *Computers in Nursing, 5* (5), 140–145.

Bolinger, R. E., Price, S., & Kyner, J. L. (1971). Computerized management of the outpatient diabetic. *Journal of the American Medical Association, 216,* 1779–1982.

Borenstein, M., Kane, J., & Buchbinder, J. (1987). Monte Carlo simulation of statistical power. *Psychopharmacology Bulletin, 23* (2), 300–302.

Boutwell, B., & Sandefur, R. R. (1987). Biomedical communication: The next chapter. *Journal of Biocommunications, 14* (2), 4–6.

Boykin, P., & Romano, C. A. (1985). The process of evaluating the clinical application of computerized instruction. In *Proceedings of the Ninth Annual Symposium on Computer Applications in Medical Care.* (pp. 772–775). New York: Institute of Electrical and Electronics Engineers.

Boyle, K. K., & Ahijevych, K. (1987). Using computers to promote health behavior of nursing students. *Nurse Educator, 12* (3), 33–37.

Bradstock, M. K., Marks, J. S., Forman, M. R., Gentry, E. M., Hogelin, G. C., Binkin, N. J., & Trowbird, F. L. (1987). Drinking-driving and health lifestyle in the United States: Behavioral risk factors surveys. *Journal of Studies on Alcohol, 48* (2), 147–151.

Brannigan, V. (1985). Acceptance testing: The critical problem in software acquisition. *IEEE Transactions on Biomedical Engineering, 32* (4), 295–299.

Brannigan, V. (1986). The regulation of medical computer software as a "device" under the Food, Drug, and Cosmetic Act. In *Proceedings of the Tenth Annual Meeting of the Symposium on Computer Applications in Medical Care,* (pp. 347–354). New York: Institute of Electrical and Electronics Engineers.

Brannigan, V. M. (1986). Can the computer commit medical malpractice? *Professional Liability Newsletter, 8,* 2–5, 12.

Brannigan, V. M., Dayhoff, R. E. (1981). Liability for personal injuries caused by defective medical computer programs. *American Journal of Law and Medicine, 7* (2), 123–144.

Brannigan, W. M., Dayhoff, R. E. (1981). Liability for personal injuries caused by defective medical computer programs. *American Journal of Law and Medicine, 7* (2), 123–144.

Bratt, E. M., & Vockell, E. L. (1987). Using the microcomputer to give students personalized feedback on preparing patient health histories. *Computers in Nursing, 5* (4), 146–151.

Breckon, D. J., & Pennington, R. M. (1986). Interactive videodiscs: A new generation of computer assisted instruction. *Health Values, 10* (6), 52–55.

Breese, M. S., Welch, A. C., & Schimpfhauser, F. (1977). Computer-simulated clinical encounters. *Journal of the American Dietetic Association, 70* (4), 382–384.

Brink, M. M. (1977). FOINANA: Food intake analysis. *Agricultural Extension Service. Extension Folder 454.* Minneapolis: University of Minnesota.

Briscoe, C. (1987). Catering and nutrition: An educational approach to support a healthier diet. *Human Nutrition Applied Nutrition, 41* (3), 212–219.

Brown, R. L., McDermott, R. J., & Marty, P. J. (1981). A conversational information computer system for health and safety operation: The OSIS. *American Industrial Hygiene Association Journal, 42* (11), 824–830.

Buchanan, B., & Shortliffe, E. (1984). *Rule based expert systems: The MYCIN experiments of the Stanford Heuristic Programming Project.* Reading, MA: Addison-Wesley.

Burnett, K. F., Taylor, C. B., & Agras, W. S. (1987). Computer-assisted management of weight, diet, and exercise in the treatment of Type II diabetes. *Diabetes Education, 13* (Suppl.), 234–236.

Buyse, M. L., & Edwards, C. N. (1987). The birth defects information system. A computer-based information system for diagnostic support, education, and research. *American Journal of Perinatology, 4* (1), 8–11.

Byrd-Bredbenner, A., Lewis, M., Davis, B., & Antanitis, R. (1988). Computer-analyzed dietary intake printouts: Guidelines for their design and student comprehension. *Journal of the American Diet Association, 88* (3), 311–316.

Byrd-Bredbenner, C., & Pelican, S. (1984). Software: How do you choose? *Journal of Nutrition Education, 16* (2), 77–79.

Cage, G. W. (1986). Computer hardware. *Dermatolgic Clinics* (Philadelphia) *4* (4), 533–543.

Caine, C., & Kaplan, R. M. (1984). Experimental evaluation of computer-assisted diabetes education. *Diabetes, 34* (Suppl. 1), 33, 121A (Abs. 470).

Carpenter, J., Deloria, D., & Morganstein, D. (1984). Statistical software for microcomputers. *BYTE, 9,* 234.

Carpenter, T. E. (1986). Epidemiologic programs for computers and calculators. Decision-tree analysis using a microcomputer. *American Journal of Epidemiology, 124* (5), 843–50.

Chase, S. K. (1988). Knowledge representation in expert systems: Nursing diagnosis applications. *Computers in Nursing, 6* (2), 58–64.

Chen, M., Houston, T., & Burson, J. (1983). Microcomputer-based health education in the waiting room: A feasibility study. *Journal of Computer-Based Instruction, 9,* 90.

Chen, M. S., Burson, J. L., & Comer, R. C. (1987). Reflections: A hierarchy of criteria for evaluating microcomputer-based health education. *Health Values, 11* (2), 44–45.

Chen, M. S., Houston, T. P., Burson, J. L., Comer, R. C. (1984). Microcomputer-based patient education programs for family practice. *Journal of Family Practice, 18* (1), 149–150.

Clancey, W. J., & Shortliffe, E. H. (1984). *Readings in medical artificial intelligence: The first decade.* New York: Addison-Wesley.

Clochesy, J. M. (1987). Computer use and nursing research: Statistical packages for microcomputers. *Western Journal of Nursing Research, 9* (1), 138–141.

Cohen, J. (1985). Computers in patient education. *Postgraduate Medicine, 77* (4), 71–72.

Cohen, M. E., Cecil, J. C., & Schroeder, D. C. (1984). Computerized method for the graphic representation of multivariate periodontal data. *Community Dentistry and Oral Epidemiology, 12,* 123–127.

Collen, M. F. (1985). Full-text medical literature retrieval by computer. A pilot test. *Journal of the American Medical Association, 254,* 2768–2774.

Collier, P. A. (1986). Computers and education. *Minnesota Nursing Accent, 58* (6), 245–246.

Connell, C. M., Smyer, M. A. (1986). Telephone conference networks for training in mental health. *Gerontologist, 26* (4), 339–341.

Conrad, W. H. (1988). Body systems II series: The blood system: A liquid of life. *Science and Children, 25* (5), 41.

Cook, G. B. (1987). A computer program for teaching and auditing patients' knowledge of diabetes. *Diabetes Education, 13* (3), 306–308.

Cook, G. B. (1982). The microcomputer: An extension of the diabetes educator. *Diabetes Education 7* (4), 12–14.

Cook, M. (1982). Using computers to exchange professional practice. *Nursing Times, 77* (37), 1542–1544.

Cooper, G. (1984). NESTOR: A medical decision support system that integrates causal, temporal and probabilistic knowledge. Unpublished doctoral dissertation, Stanford University.

De Rosis, F., Pizzutilo, S., Greco, D. (1986). MICRO-IDEA: Improving decisions in epidemiological analysis by microcomputer. *Medical Informatics (London), 11,* (3), 225–236.

Deardorff, W. W. (1986). Computerized health education: A comparison with traditional formats. *Health Education Quarterly, 13* (1), 61–72.

Dedmon, R., Smith, T., & Swanson, A. (1988). Database management in a corporate health promotion program. *Corporate Commentary,* 34–39.

DeLeeuw, E. R. (1987). Computers in diabetes nutrition education: A perspective. *Diabetes Education, 13* (Suppl.), 240–244.

Dizard, W. P., Jr. (1982). *The coming information age: An overview of technology, economics and politics.* New York: Longman.

Dobberstein, K. (1987). Computer-assisted patient education. *American Journal of Nursing, 87* (5), 697.

Donabedian, D. (1976). Computer-taught epidemiology. *Nursing Outlook, 24* (12), 749–751.

Dooling, S. L. (1986). Designing computer simulations for staff nurse education. *Journal of Medical Systems, 10* (2), 139–149.

Dowey, J. A. (1987). Computer games for dental health education in primary schools. *Health Education Journal, 46,* 3.

Dozier, J. A., Hammond, W. E., & Stead, W. W. (1985). Creating a link between medical and analytical databases. In *Proceedings of the Ninth Annual Symposium on Computer Applications in Medical Care,* (pp. 478–482). New York: Institute of Electrical and Electronics Engineers.

Droste-Bielak, E. M. (1986). Two techniques for teaching interviewing: A comparative study. *Computers in Nursing, 4* (4), 152–157.

DuBois, D., Jacobson, M., & Moyer, G. (1983, November). Eat by numbers: Nutrition programs byte off more than they can chew. *Nutrition Action,* pp. 10–13.

Duda, R. O., & Shortliffe, E. H. (1983). Expert systems research. *Science, 220,* 261–268.

Dunn, T. G., Lushene, R. E., & O'Neil, H. F. (1972). Complete automation of the MMPI and a study of its response latencies. *Journal of Consulting and Clinical Psychology, 39* (3), 381–387.

Edmunds, L. (1982). Computer-assisted nursing care. *American Journal of Nursing, 82* (7), 1076–1079.

Edmunds, L. (1984). Computers for inpatient nursing care: What can be accomplished? *Computers in Nursing, 2* (3), 102–108.

Eklund, S. A. (1984). Is it time for CONFER, a computer-based conference for dental public health? *Journal of Public Health Dentistry, 44* (2), 73–77.

Ellis, L. B., Raines, J. R., & Hakanson, N. (1982). Health education using microcomputers: II One year in the clinic. *Preventive Medicine, 11,* 212–224.

Ellis, L. B. M. (1981). Computer-based patient education: Problems and opportunities. In *Proceedings of the Fifth Annual Symposium on Computer Applications in Medical Care* (p. 196). New York: Institute of Electrical and Electronics Engineers.

Ellis, L. B. M., Raines, J. R., & Hakanson, N. (1979). Teaching health risk concepts using microcomputers. In *Proceedings of the Third Annual Symposium on Computer Applications in Medical Care,* (pp. 158–163). New York: Institute of Electrical and Electronics Engineers.

Ellis, L. B. M., Raines, J. R., & Hakanson, N. (1980). The microcomputer in the waiting room. In *Proceedings of the Fourth Annual Symposium on Computer Applications in Medical Care,* (pp. 1412–1415). New York: Institute of Electrical and Electronics Engineers.

Ellis, L. B. M., Petzel, S. V., & Asp, E.H. (1983). Computer-assisted instruction for the chronically ill child. In *Proceedings of the Seventh Annual Symposium on Computer Applications in Medical Care,* (pp. 366–369). New York: Institute of Electrical and Electronics Engineers.

Ellis, L. B. M., Raines, J. R., & Hakanson, N. (1981). Health education using microcomputers: I. Initial acceptability. *Preventive Medicine, 10* (1), 77–84.

Evans, S. (1984). A computer-based nursing diagnosis consultant. In *Proceedings of the Eighth Annual Symposium on Computer Applications in Medical Care,* (pp. 658–661). New York: Institute of Electrical and Electronics Engineers.

Farrant, S., Dowlatshahi, D., Ellwood-Russell, M., & Wise, P. H. (1984). Computer-based learning and assessment for diabetic patients. *Diabetic Medicine 1* (4), 309–315.

Fetonti, R. (1987). The science professor series: Muscles and bones. *Science and Children, 25* (2), 40.

Feurzeig, W. (1984). The first expert CAI system. In *Proceedings of the Eighth Annual Symposium on Computer Applications in Medical Care,* (pp. 980–986). New York: Institute of Electrical and Electronics Engineers.

Fielding, J. E. (1982). Appraising the health of health risk appraisal. *American Journal of Public Health, 72* (4), 337–339.

First, M. B., Soffer, L. J., & Miller, R. A. (1985). QUICK: Using the Internist-1/Caduceus Knowledge Base as an electronic textbook of medicine. *Computers and Biomedical Research, 18,* 137–165.

Fisher, L. A., Johnson, S., Porter, D., Bleich, H. L., & Slack, W. V. (1977). Collection of clean voided urine specimen: Comparison among spoken, written, and computer-based instructions. *American Journal of Public Health, 67* (7), 640–644.

Flaugher, P. D. (1986). Computer training for nursing personnel: Suggestions for training sessions. *Computers in Nursing, 4* (3), 105–108.

Forrest, J. L., Williams, C., & Gurenlian, J. R. (1986, December). Improved communication through computer technology. *Dental Hygiene,* pp. 558–561.

Fowler, R. D. (1967). Computer interpretation of personality tests: The automated psychologist. *Comprehensive Psychology, 8* (6), 455–467.

Foxman, B., & Edington, D. W. (1987). The accuracy of health risk appraisal in predicting mortality. *American Journal of Public Health, 77* (8), 971–974.

Francis, K. T. (1988). Upper extremity fitness training. *Clinical Computing, 5* (1), 29–32.

Frank, G. C. (1985, February–March). Nutrient profile on personal computers: A comparison of DINE with mainframe computers. *Health Education,* pp. 16–19.

Freeman, A. W. (1987). Computer use in allied health programs. *Journal of Allied Health, 16* (2), 177–83.

French, D. (1986). Influence on smoking cessation with computer-assisted instruction. *American Association of Occupational Health Nursing Journal, 34* (8), 391–394.

Gabler, J. M., Albright, J. W., & Pickton, R. J. (1986). A management model for a hospital information system. *Health Care Computing and Communication 3,* 48–54.

Gelernter, D., & Gelernter, J. (1984). Expert systems and diagnostic monitors in psychiatry. In *Proceedings of the Eighth Annual Symposium on Computer Applications in Medical Care* (pp. 45–48). New York: Institute of Electrical and Electronics Engineers.

Gianturco, D. T., & Ramm, D. (1971). Use of the computer in caring for the elderly. *Postgraduate Medicine, 59,* 140–149.

Gillett, J. D. (1987). The harnessing of artificial satellites for the prevention of disease in the tropics: Flights of fancy or of fact. *Transactions of the Royal Society of Tropical Medicine and Hygiene, 81* (2), 350–351.

Glaser, W. (1974). Computer diagnosis. *American Journal of Diseases of Children, 127,* 793–794.

Goetz, A., & Bernstein, J. (1987, Oct.). Computer developments in health risk management. *Corporate Commentary,* 26–33.

Gold, R. S. (1984). Computing health: Alcohol metabolism rate—Part 1. *Health Education, 15* (3), 35–36.

Gold, R. S. (1984). Computing health: Alcohol metabolism rate—Part 2. *Health Education 15* (4), 23–24.

Gold, R. S. (1983). Computing health: Choosing statistical software for microcomputers. *Health Education 14* (7), 33–35.

Gold, R. S. (1984). Computing health: Current initiatives. *Health Education, 15,* 5.

Gold, R. S. (1985). Computing health: Programming problem 3—Computing peak blood alcohol levels. *Health Education, 15* (7), 15–16.

Gold, R. S. (1985). Computing health: Programming problem 4—Completing the program. *Health Education, 16* (1), 20–21.

Gold, R. S. (1984). Computing health: Sources of information for educators. *Health Education, 15* (2), 39–40.

Gold, R. S., & Duncan, D. F. (1980). Computers and health education. *The Journal of School Health,* Nov, 503–505.

Gold, R. S., & Duncan, D. F. (1980). Potential uses of microprocessors for home health education. *Health Values: Achieving High Level Wellness, 4* (2), 69–70.

Goldman, L., Cook, E. F., Brand, D. A., & Lee, T. H., (1988). A computer protocol to predict myocardial infarction in emergency department patients with chest pain. *The New England Journal of Medicine, 318* (13), 797–802.

Goodwin, J., Ozbolt, J. G., & Edwards, B. S. (1975). Developing a computer program to assist the nursing process: Phase I—From systems analysis to program. *Nursing Research, 24,* 299–305.

Green, R. S., Gastfriend, D. R., Kolondner, R. M., & Fowler, R. D. (1984). Personal computer application for psychiatry and psychology. In *Proceedings of the Eighth Annual Symposium on Computer Applications in Medical Care,* (pp. 280–285). New York: Institute of Electrical and Electronics Engineers.

Griesser, G. (1984). The issue of data protection in computer-aided health care information systems. In K. J. Hannah, E. J. Guillemin, & D. N. Conklins (Eds.), *Nursing uses of computers and information science* (pp. 113–117). North Holland: Elsevier.

Griest, J. H., & Klein, M. H. (1980). Computer programs for patients, clinicians, and researchers in psychiatry. In J. H. Johnson & T. A. Williams (Eds.), *Technology in mental health care delivery systems,* (pp. 161–181). Norwood, NJ: Ablex.

Grobe, S. J. (1984). *Computer primer and resource guide for nurses.* Philadelphia: Lippincott.

Grundner, T. M., & Garrett, R. E. (1986). Interactive medical telecomputing: An alternative approach to community health education. *The New England Journal of Medicine, 314* (15), 982–985.

Gustafson, D. H., (1981). A computer-based system for identifying suicide attemptors. *Computers and Biomedical Research, 14,* 144–157.

Gustafson, D. H., Bosworth, K., Chewning, B., & Hawkins, R. P. (1987). Computer-based health promotion: Combining technological advances with problem-solving techniques to effect successful health behavior changes. *Annual Review of Public Health, 8,* 387–415.

Hahn, J. S., & Nicholson, T. (1986). The role of computers in health education: Some lessons from instructional technology. *Journal of Family and Community Health, 9* (2), 64–67.

Hardt, S. L., & MacFadden, D. H. (1987). Computer assisted psychiatric diagnosis: Experiments in software design. *Computers in Biological Medicine, 17* (4), 229–237.

Harman, C. E., & Meinhardt, K. (1972). A computer system for treatment evaluation at the community mental health center. *American Journal of Public Health, 62* (12), 1596–1601.

Hasman, A. (1987). Medical applications of computers: An overview. *International Journal of BioMedical Computing, 20,* 239–251.

Hedlund, J. L., Vieweg, B. W., & Cho, D. W. (1987). Computer consultation for emotional crises: An expert system for "non-experts." *Computers in Human Behavior, 3,* 109–127.

Heller, B. R., Romano, C. A., & Damrosch, S. (1985). Computer applications in nursing: Implications for the curriculum. *Computers in Nursing, 3,* 14.

Henningson, K. A., Gold, R. S., & Duncan, D. F., (1986). A computerized marijuana decision maze: Expert opinion regarding its use in health education. *Journal of Drug Education, 16* (3), 243–281.

Hershberger, R. D., (1979). Computers: Physician's tool, patient's friend. *Medical World News, 20* (18), 65–68.

Hersher, B. S. (1985). The job search and information systems opportunities for nurses. *Nursing Clinics of North America, 20* (3), 585–594.

Hettler, B. (1988). Every little byte helps: Computers have found their place in health promotion. *Health Action Managers, 2,* 6–10.

Hickam, D. (1985). The treatment advice of a computer-based cancer chemotherapy protocol advisor. *Annals of Internal Medicine, 6,* 928–936.

Hickam, D. H., Shortliffe, E. H., Bischoff, M. B., Scott, A. C., & Jacobs, C. D. (1985). The treatment advice of a computer-based cancer chemotherapy protocol advisor. *Annals of Internal Medicine, 103,* 928–936.

Hill, M. (1986). BMDPC: BMDP statistical software for microcomputers. *Psychopharmacology Bulletin, 22* (1), 301–306.

Hill, M. (1986). Why a statistical package on a micro? *Psychopharmacology Bulletin, 22* (1), 65–72.

Hiller, M. D., & Beyda, V. (1981). Computers, medical records, and the right to privacy. *Journal of Health Politics, Policy, and Law, 6* (3), 463–488.

Appendix E

Holder, H. D., & Blose, J. O. (1983). Prevention of alcohol-related traffic problems: Computer simulation of alternative strategies. *Journal of Safety Research, 14,* 115–129.

Holder, H. D., & Blose, J. O. (1987). Reduction of community alcohol problems: Computer simulation experiments in three counties. *Journal of Studies on Alcohol, 48* (2), 124–135.

Homan, J. M. (1986). End-user information utilities in the health sciences. *Bulletin of the Medical Library Association, 74* (1), 31–35.

Hon, D. (1982, June). Interactive training in cardiopulmonary resuscitation. *BYTE,* pp. 108–140.

Horne, D. A., & Gold, R. S. (1983). Guidelines for developing health education software. *Health Education/Microcomputers, 10,* 85–86.

Howard, E. H., & Jankowski, T. A. (1986). Reference services via electronic mail. *Bulletin of the Medical Library Association, 74* (1), 41–44.

Howe, R. C., & Layman, E. B. (1981). Clinical cancer education package in medicine. In *Proceedings of the Fifth Annual Symposium on Computer Applications in Medical Care,* (pp. 692–694). New York: Institute of Electrical and Electronics Engineers.

Hudson, D. L., Estrin, T. (1981). Microcomputer-based expert system for clinical decision making. In *Proceedings of the Fifth Annual Symposium on Computer Applications in Medical Care* (pp. 976–978). New York: Institute of Electrical and Electronics Engineers.

Hurst, A. K., Noguchi, J. K., & Besinque, K. M. (1988). Use of computer-assisted case presentations in a clinical therapeutics course. *American Journal of Pharmaceutical Education, 52,* 56–58.

Irving, J. M., & Crombie, I. K. (1986). The use of microcomputers for data management in a large epidemiological survey. *Computers in Biomedical Research, 19* (5), 487–495.

Jacobsen, B. S., Tulman, L., Lowery, B. J., & Garson, C. (1988). Experiencing the research process using statistical software on microcomputers. *Nursing Research, 37* (1), 56–59.

Janssen, H. F. (1986). Experimental design and data evaluation in orthopaedic research. *Journal of Orthopaedic Research, 4* (4), 504–509.

Jason, H. (1984). Will computers dehumanize medical care and education? *Journal of Family Practice, 18* (4), 525–527.

Jervis, C. K., (1988). Genetics. *Science and Children, 25* (4), 49.

Johnson, J. H. (Ed.). (1981). Computer technology in clinical psychology, psychiatry and behavioral medicine. *Behavior Research Methods and Instrumentation, 13,* 4.

Johnson, J. H., Giannetti, R. A., & Williams, T. A. (1975). Real-time psychological assessment and evaluation of psychiatric patients. *Behavior Research Methods and Instrumentation, 7,* 199–200.

Jorgens, J., III. (1983). Computer hardware and software as medical devices. *Medical Device and Diagnostics Industry,* May, pages 62–64 and 88.

Juckett, M., & Spratt, J. S. (1987). What is the value of the computer for the physician? *Journal of Surgical Oncology, 34* (1), 1–5.

Kalisman, M., & Studin, J. R. (1986). Basic principles of computer technology. *Clinics in Plastic Surgery, 13* (3), 355–366.

Kann, L. K. (1987). Effects of computer-assisted instruction on selected interaction skills related to responsible sexuality. *Journal of School Health, 57* (7), 282–286.

Kehm, S. (1987). Public access computing in health science libraries. *Journal of Biocommunications, 14,* (2), 7–12.

Kinney, E. L. (1986). Expert system detection of drug interactions: Results in consecutive inpatients. *Computers and Biomedical Research, 19,* 462–467.

Kinney, E. L., Brafman, D., & Wright, R. J., II. (1988). An expert system on the diagnosis of ascites. *Computers and Biomedical Research, 21,* 169–173.

Kirchhoff, K. T., & Holzemer, W. L. (1979). Student learning and a computer-assisted instructional program. *Journal of Nursing Education, 18,* 22–30.

Koh, D., & Lee, J. (1987). A microcomputer program for significance testing of the difference between statistically adjusted rates obtained by direct standardization. *Asia Pacific Journal of Public Health, 1* (3), 49–54.

Korpman, R. A. (1987). Using the computer to optimize human performance in health care delivery. The pathologist as medical information specialist. *Archives Pathology Laboratory Medicine, 111* (7), 637–645.

Kosidlak, J. G., & Kerpelman, K. B. (1987). Managing community health nursing. *Computers in Nursing, 5* (5), 175–180.

Kuhl, P. W. (1988). Safety first. *Science and Children, 25* (7), 45.

Kulikowski, C. A. (1983). Expert medical consultation systems. *Journal of Medical Systems, 7* (3), 229–234.

Kulikowski, C. A. (1986). Knowledge-based systems in biomedicine: A ten year retrospective. In *Proceedings of the Tenth Annual Symposium on Computer Applications in Medical Care* (pp. 423–424). New York: Institute of Electrical and Electronic Engineers.

Kunz, J. (1984). Use of AI, simple mathematics, and a physiological model for making medical diagnoses and treatment plans. Unpublished doctoral dissertation, Stanford Heuristic Programming Project.

Laborde, M. J. (1984). Expert systems for nursing? *Computers in Nursing, 2* (1), 130–135.

LaPorte, R. E., Rewers, M., Tuomilehto, J., Tajima, N., Akimoto, Y., Aiso, M., Grabausk, V. J., & Williams, J. G. (1988). Telecommunication and international health research. *American Journal of Epidemiology, 128* (2), 439–443.

Leonard, M. S., & Goldman, J. (1981). Health information system transferability evaluation. *Computers and Biomedical Research, 14,* 559–569.

Leung, F. K., & Kwang, P. C. (1985). A computer management program for diabetes mellitus. *Diabetes, 34* (Suppl. 1), 34A (Abs. 136).

Levenson, P. M., & Morrow, J. R., Jr. (1987). Learner characteristics associated with responses to film and interactive video lessons on smokeless tobacco. *Preventive Medicine, 16* (1), 52–62.

Lincoln, T. L., & Korpman, R. A. (1980). Computers, health care, and medical information science. *Science, 210,* 257–263.

Lindberg, D. A., & Riecken, H. W. (1986). Future programs at the National Library of Medicine. *Bulletin of the Medical Library Association, 74* (4), 344–352.

Lipkin, M. (1984). Historical background on the origin of computer medicine. In *Proceedings of the Eighth Annual Symposium on Computer Applications in Medical Care,* (pp. 987–989). New York: Institute of Electrical and Electronics Engineers.

Lipman, A. (1987). Drug alert. *Science and Children, 25* (2), 41.

Litton, J., Morris, M., & Friedman, M. (1985). Education enhancement with CAI. *Diabetes, 34* (Suppl. 1), 36A (Abs. 142).

Lundsgaarde, H. P. (1987). Evaluating medical expert systems. *Social Science in Medicine, 24* (10), 805–819.

Lunin, L. F., & Stein, R. S. (1987). CHID: A unique health information and education database. *Bulletin of the Medical Library Association, 75* (2), 95–100.

Lyons, C., Krasnowski, J., Greenstein, A. L., Maloney, D., & Tatarezu, J. (1982). Interactive computerized patient education. *Heart and Lung, 11* (4), 330–341.

MacDonald, C. J. (1983). Computer technology and continuing medical education. *Mobius, 3* (2), 7–12.

MacDonald, F. (1987). Computer applications in diabetes management and education. *Computers in Nursing, 5* (5), 181–185.

Malik, R., Horwitz, D. L., & Smyth-Staruch, K. (1987). Energy metabolism in diabetes: Computer-assisted instruction for persons with diabetes. *Diabetes Education, 13* (Suppl.), 203–205.

Malik, R. L., & Smyth-Staruch, K. (1985). Computer-assisted instruction for the intensive management of diabetes mellitus. *Diabetes, 34* (Suppl. 1), 36A (Abs. 143).

Markushewski, W. T., & Baker, R. W., Jr. (1985). Software maintenance in the health care environment. In *Proceedings of the Ninth Annual Symposium on Computer Applications in Medical Care* (pp. 649–654). New York: Institute of Electrical and Electronics Engineers.

Mars, N. J., & Miller, P. L. (1987). Knowledge acquisition and verification tools for medical expert systems. *Medical Decision Making, 7* (1), 6–11.

Masarie, F. E., Miller, R. A., & Myers, J. D. (1985). INTERNIST-I Properties: Representing common sense and good medical practice in a computerized medical knowledge base. *Computers and Biomedical Research, 18,* 458–479.

Mattes, R. D., & Gabriel, S. J. (1988). A comparison of results from two microcomputer nutrient analysis software packages and a mainframe. *Journal of Nutrition Education, 20* (2), 70–76.

Mayer, P. A., & Eddy, J. M. (1986, June–July). Using microcomputers to develop a personalized health fitness student workbook. *Computing Health,* pp. 24–25.

McAlister, N. H., Correy, H. D., Munkman, E. J., & Wigle, E. D. (1980). Community hypertension management project: A randomized controlled clinical trial to test a computer-supported hypertension management system in primary care. In *Proceedings of the Fourth Annual Symposium on Computer Applications in Medical Care,* pp. 1135–1142. New York: Institute of Electrical and Electronics Engineers.

McCool, A. C. (1987). Computerized information management: Is it cost-effective for diabetes care? *Diabetes Education, 13* (Suppl.), 193–197.

McCormick, K. A. (1984). Nursing in the computer revolution. *Computers in Nursing, 2,* 30.

McCullough, L. (1981). Systematic evaluation of the impact of computer-acquired data on psychiatric care. In *Proceedings of Fifth Annual Symposium on Computer Applications in Medical Care,* 426–430. New York: Institute of Electrical and Electronics Engineers.

McGee, D. L. (1986). A program for logistic regression on the IBM PC. *American Journal of Epidemiology, 124* (4), 702–705.

McNeill, D. G. (1979). Developing the complete computer-based information system. *Journal of Nursing Administration, 9* (11), 34–35.

McWilliams, A. T. (1988). Introducing expert systems to medical students using ESTA, expert system teaching aid. *Medical Education, 22* (2), 99–103.

Meade, C. D., & Wittbrot, R. (1988). Computerized readability analysis of written materials. *Computers in Nursing, 6* (1), 30–36.

Meadow, D., & Rosenthal, M. A. (1983). A corporation-based computerized preventative dentistry program. *Journal of the American Dental Association, 106,* 467–470.

Meadows, K. A., Fromson, B., & Gillespie, C. (1988). Development, validation and application of computer-linked knowledge questionnaires in diabetes education. *Diabetic Medicine, 5* (1), 61–67.

Meineke, I. (1987). A simple BASIC program for the calculation of nonparametric confidence intervals in bioequivalence testing. *Computer Methods Programs Biomedicine, 24* (1), 65–71.

Mikan, K. (1984). Computer integration: A challenge for nursing education. *Nursing Outlook, 32* (1), 6.

Miller, L. V., Goldstein, J., & Nicolaisen, G. (1978). Computerized assessment of diabetes patient education. *Journal of Medical Systems, 2* (3), 223–240.

Miller, P. L. (1984). *A critiquing approach to expert computer advice.* Boston: Pitman.

Miller, P. L. (1985). Goal-directed critiquing by computer: Ventilator management. *Computers and Biomedical Research, 18,* 422–438.

Miller, P. L. (1985). Medical information science; What academic role should it play? In *Proceedings of the Ninth Annual Symposium on Computer Applications in Medical Care,* (pp. 169–171). New York: Institute of Electrical and Electronics Engineers.

Miller, P. L., Blumenfrucht, S. J., Rose, J. R., Roth, M., Swett, H. A., Weltin, G., & Mars, N. J. (1987). HYDRA: A knowledge acquisition tool for expert systems that critique medical workup. *Medical Decision Making, 7* (1), 12–21.

Miller, R. A. (1987). From automated medical records to expert system knowledge bases: Common problems in representing and processing patient data. *Topics in Health Records Management, 7* (3), 23–36.

Miller, R. A. (1984). INTERNIST-1/Caduceus: Problems facing expert consultant programs. *Methods Inform Medicine, 1,* 9–14.

Miller, R. A., McNeil, M. A., Challinor, S. M., Bonnadonn, C., Valagusse, P., & Nicolini, C. (1986). The INTERNIST-1/QUICK MEDICAL REFERENCE project: Status report. *The Western Journal of Medicine, 145* (6), 816–822.

Miller, R. A., Pople, H. E., & Jyers, J. D. (1982). INTERNIST-1, an experimental computer-based diagnostic consultant for general internal medicine. *The New England Journal of Medicine, 307* (8), 468–476.

Miller, R. A., Schaffner, K. F., & Meisel, A. (1985). Ethical and legal issues related to the use of computer programs in medicine. *Annals of Internal Medicine, 102,* 529–536.

Mitchell, B. (1987, May). Fault tolerant hardware takes an evolutionary step. *Computers in Healthcare,* pp. 27, 30, 32, 36.

Moody, L. E., & Rienzo, B. A. (1981). A computerized health profile model for adolescents. *Health Education, 12* (4), 15–19.

Morelli, R. A., Bronzino, J. D., & Goethe, J. W. (1987). Expert systems in psychiatry. A review. *Journal of Medical Systems, 11* (2–3), 57–68.

Mulsant, B., & Servan-Schrieber, D. (1984). Knowledge engineering: A daily activity on a hospital ward. *Computers and Biomedical Research, 17,* 71–91.

Murphy, M. A. (1984). Computer-based education in nursing: Factors influencing its utilization. *Computers in Nursing, 2* (6), 218–223.

Murphy, M. A. (1987). Preparing faculty to use and develop computer-based instructional materials in nursing. *Computers in Nursing, 5* (2), 59–63.

Myers, J. D. (1983). Caduceus and continuing medical education. *Mobius, 3* (2), 13–16.

Nadelson, T. (1978). The inhuman computer/the too-human psychotherapist. *American Journal of Psychotherapy, 41* (4), 489–98.

Naditch, M. (1987). Computer-assisted worksite health promotion: The fit between workers and programs. *Corporate Commentary,* pp. 40–48.

Naditch, M. P. (1983). PLATO Staywell: A behavioral medicine micro-computer program of health behavior change. In *Proceedings of the Seventh Annual Symposium on Computer Applications in Medical Care,* (pp. 363–365). New York: Institute of Electrical and Electronics Engineers.

Nanson, E. M. (1977). The potential of an educational computer in medical education. *Australian and New Zealand Journal of Surgery, 47* (4), 545–547.

Nichols, R. C., & Kauffman, C. (1986). Computer-assisted instruction for identifying enterobacteriaceae and other gram-negative rods. *Laboratory Medicine, 17* (10), 613–615.

Niland-Weiss, J., Azen, S. P., Odom-Maryon, T., Liu, F., & Hagerty, C. (1987). A microcomputer-based distributed data management system for a large cooperative study of transfusion associated acquired immunodeficiency syndrome. *Computers in Biomedical Research, 20* (3), 225–243.

Norton, M. L., & Norton, J. D. (1986). Medical computers—from the manufacturer's viewpoint. In *Proceedings of the Tenth Annual Symposium on Computer Applications in Medical Care* (pp. 358–363). New York: Institute of Electrical and Electronics Engineers.

O'Malley, D. T., Heger, J. B., Trudgett, M., & Mayo, S. T. (1987). Computerized nutrition education in the supermarket. *Journal of Nutrition Education, 19* (4), 159–162.

Olivieri, P., & Sweeney, M. (1980). Evaluation of clinical learning: By computer. *Nurse Educator, 5* (4), 26–31.

Ozbolt, J. G. (1982). A prototype information system to aid nursing decisions. In *Proceedings of the Sixth Annual Symposium on Computer Applications in Medical Care.* (pp. 653–657). New York: Institute of Electrical and Electronics Engineers.

Ozbolt, J. G. (1987). Developing decision support systems for nursing: Theoretical bases for advanced computer systems. *Computers in Nursing, 5* (3), 105–111.

Ozbolt, J. G., Schultz, S., Swain, M. A. P., Stein, K. F., & Abraham, I. L. (1984). Developing expert systems for nursing practice. In *Proceedings of the Eighth Annual Symposium on Computer Applications in Medical Care* (pp. 654–657). New York: Institute of Electrical and Electronics Engineers.

Ozbolt, J. G., Schultz, S., Swain, M. A., Stein, K. F., & Abraham, I. L. (1985). A proposed expert system for nursing practice. *Journal of Medical Systems, 9,* 57–68.

Packer, C. L., (1987). Use of personal computers increase 40 percent in '86. *Hospitals, 61* (4), 98.

Pass, T. M., & Goldstein, L. P. (1979). A computerized aid for medical cost-effectiveness analysis. In *Proceedings of the Fifth Annual Symposium on Computer Applications in Medical Care* (pp. 219–221). New York: Institute of Electrical and Electronics Engineers.

Patil, R. S. (1987). Causal reasoning in computer programs for medical diagnosis. *Computer Methods Programs Biomedicine, 25* (2), 117–123.

Patil, R. S. (1986). Review of causal reasoning in medical diagnosis. In *Proceedings of the Tenth Annual Symposium on Computer Applications in Medical Care* (pp. 11–16). New York: Institute of Electrical and Electronics Engineers.

Pauker, S. G., & Kassirer, J. P. (1981). Clinical decision analysis by computer. *Archives of Internal Medicine, 141,* 1831–1837.

Payton, J., & Asbuty, A. J. (1983). ABCs of computing: Computer security. *British Medical Journal, 287* (6397), 965–967.

Pelican, S. (1987). Evaluating computer nutrition education software for clients. *Diabetes Education, 13* (Suppl.), 182.

Penfield, M. P., & Costello, C. A. (1988). Microcomputer programs for diet analysis: A comparative evaluation. *Journal of the American Dietetic Association, 88* (2), 209–211.

Perrone, J. (1988). Breaking barriers: Computerized teen questionnaire eases discomfort with sex issues. *American Medical News,* 15–17.

Petzel, S. V., Ellis, L. B. M., & Miller M. (1984). A computer-based approach to improving problem-solving skills for parents of children with chronic illness. In *Proceedings of the Eighth Annual Symposium on Computer Applications in Medical Care* (pp. 908–916). New York: Institute of Electrical and Electronics Engineers.

Phelps, J., & Dennison, D. (1982). Using microcomputers for health education research. *Health Education, 13* (3), 27–29.

Pople, H. E. (1982). Heuristic methods for imposing structure on ill-structured problems: The structuring of medical diagnostics. In P. Szolovits, (Ed.), *Artificial intelligence in medicine* (pp. 119–190). Boulder: Westview Press.

Powills, S. (1988). Computers communicate with voice/data links. *Hospitals, 62* (1), 50–52.

Protti, D. J., & Brunelle, F. W. (1985). Protecting the privacy of patient information: Fact or fiction? In K. J. Hannah, E. J. Gullemin, & D. N. Conklin (Eds.), *Nursing uses of computers and information science,* (pp. 97–102). North Holland: Elsevier.

Pursley, R. J., Neutens, J. J. (1986). Can microcomputers identify differences in health status between different groups? *Health Education,* 37–42.

Quaglini, S., & Stefanelli, M. (1986). ANEMIA: An expert consultation system. *Computers and Biomedical Research, 19,* 13–17.

Quinn, C. A. (1986). Computer-assisted instruction: Is it really your best choice? *Nurse Educator, 11* (6), 34–38.

Radwin, H. M. (1986). Telecommunications in urology. *Urologic Clinics of North America, 13* (1), 59–64.

Rappaport, W., & Steen, C. (1981). FLOW GEMINI: An occupational health information system. In *Proceedings of the Fifth Annual Symposium on Computer Applications in Medical Care.* New York: Institute of Electrical and Electronics Engineers.

Reeves, D. M., & Underly, N. K. (1982). Computerization of nursing. *Nursing Management, 13* (8), 50–53.

Rennels, G. D. (1986). A computational model of reasoning from the clinical literature. In *Proceedings of the Tenth Annual Symposium on Computer Applications in Medical Care* (pp. 373–380). New York: Institute of Electrical and Electronics Engineers.

Reynolds, A., & Pontious, S. (1986). CAI enhances the medication dosage calculation competency of nursing students. *Computers in Nursing, 4* (4), 158–165.

Rippey, R. M., Abeles, M., Day, J., Downing, D. S., Pfeiffer, C. A., Thal, S. E., Wetstone, S. L. (1987). Computer-based patient education for older persons with osteoarthritis. *Arthritis and Rheumatism, 30* (8), 932–935.

Riser, M. C., & Dick, W. (1972). Computer-managed instruction for prospective health teachers. *School Health Review, 3* (3), 16–18, 38.

Rizzolo, M. A. (1987). Guidelines for creating test question banks. *Computers in Nursing, 5* (2), 65–69.

Roberts, B. (1980). A computerized diagnostic evaluation of a psychiatric problem. *American Journal of Psychiatry, 137* (1), 12–15.

Robinson, T. N., & Walters, P. A., Jr. (1986). Health-Net: An interactive computer network for campus health promotion. *Journal of the American College Health Association, 34,* 284–285.

Romano, C. (1984). A computerized approach to discharge care planning. *Nursing Outlook, 32* (1), 23–25.

Romano, C. (1983). Developing the nursing database. *Computer Technology and Nursing. First National Conference.* USDHHS, NIH Publication No. 83–2142.

Romano, C. A. (1985). Computer technology in nursing: A futuristic view. *Computers in Nursing, 3* (2), 85–87.

Romano, C. A. (1987). Privacy, confidentiality, and security of computerized systems: The nursing responsibility. *Computers in Nursing, 5* (3),99–104.

Romano, C. A. (1986). The development of computer-assisted instruction for drug dosage calculations: A group endeavor. *Computers in Nursing, 4* (3), 114–118.

Romano, C. A., Ryan, L., Harris, J., et al. (1985). A decade of decisions: Focus perspectives of computerization in nursing practice. *Computers in Nursing, 3* (2), 64–76.

Ronald, J. S. (1982). Attitudes and learning need of nursing educators with respect to computers. Unpublished doctoral dissertation, State University of New York, Buffalo.

Ronald, J. S. (1982). Computer and undergraduate nursing education: A report on an experimental introductory course. *Journal of Nursing Education, 18,* 4–9.

Ross, S., & McBride, B. (1985). Computer sweetens diabetes management. *Quest, 2* (3), 1–2.

Rossman, P. (1983). The future of sex education: Computerizing the facts of life. *Futurist, 17* (6), 69–73.

Rosson, M. B., & Hewit, T. T. (1988). Computer use by psychology professionals: Electronic spreadsheet as a professional productivity tool. *Behavior Research Methods, Instruments and Computers, 20* (2), 231–235.

Rubinson, L., & Warner, W. (1980). An evaluation of a computer-based instruction program in health education. *International Journal of Instructional Media, 7* (3), 229–236.

Ruby, G. (1984). The elderly's use of computers for health purposes. In *Proceedings of the Eighth Annual Symposium on Computer Applications in Medical Care* (pp. 912–916). New York: Institute of Electrical and Electronics Engineers.

Ryan, S. (1983). Applications of a nursing knowledge based system for nursing practice, inservice, continuing education and standards of care. In *Proceedings of the Seventh Annual Symposium on Computer Applications in Medical Care* (pp. 491–494). New York: Institute of Electrical and Electronics Engineers.

Ryan, S. A. (1985). An expert system for nursing practice: Clinical decision support. *Computers in Nursing, 3,* 77–84.

Safir, A., Kashdan, N. R., & Scherer, J. R. (1981). Teaching computer science to health professionals. *Journal of Medical Education, 56,* 858–860.

Sager, R. A., (1987). Microcomputer software: The hard part. *Health Education, 18* (3), 52–56.

Salvaggio, J. L. (Ed.). (1983). *Telecommunications: Issues and choices for society.* New York: Longman.

Schank, M. J., Doney, L. D., & Seizyk, J. (1988). The potential of expert systems in nursing. *Journal of Nursing Administration, 18* (6), 26–31.

Schartz, W. B., Patil, R. S., & Szolovits, P. (1987). Artificial intelligence in medicine: Where do we stand? *New England Journal of Medicine, 316,* 685–688.

Schliack, M. (1987). Reading, storing and statistical calculation of weight data. *Computer Methods Programs Biomedicine, 24* (1), 73–75.

Schneider, R. H. (1986). The regulation of medical software under the Food, Drug, and Cosmetic Act: A perspective from the government. In *Proceedings of the Tenth Annual Symposium on Computer Applications in Medical Care* (pp. 355–357). New York: Institute of Electrical and Electronics Engineers.

Schoeffel, P. R. (1988). A personal computer database system for head and neck cancer records. *Journal of Medical Systems, 12* (1), 43–55.

Schultz, S. (1984). Languages, DBMSs and expert systems software for nurse decision making. *The Journal of Nursing Administration, 14* (12), 15–23.

Schwartz, M. D. (Ed.). (1984). *Using computers in clinical practice: Psychotherapy and mental health applications.* New York: Haworth Press.

Scott, A. A., & Boehm, L. A. (1988). Continuing education through Telemedicine for Ontario [letter]. *Canadian Medical Association Journal, 138* (1), 10–11.

Scott, H. D., & Cabral, R. M. (1988). Predicting hazardous lifestyles among adolescents based on health-risk assessment data. *American Journal of Health Promotion, 2* (4), 23–28.

Shortliffe, E. (1981). Clinical consultation systems: Designing for the physician as computer user. In *Proceedings of the Fifth Annual Symposium on Computer Applications in Medical Care.* New York: Institute of Electrical and Electronics Engineers, 236.

Shortliffe, E. H. (1976). *Computer-based medical consultations: MYCIN.* New York: American Elsevier.

Shortliffe, E. H. (1987). Computer programs to support clinical decision making. *Journal of the American Medical Association, 258* (1), 61–66.

Shortliffe, E. H. (1986). Medical expert systems: Knowledge tools for physicians. *Western Journal of Medicine, 145,* 830–839.

Shortliffe, E. H. (1984). The science of biomedical computing. *Medical Informatics, 9,* 185–193.

Shumaker, R. C. (1986). PKCALC: A BASIC interactive computer program for statistical and pharmacokinetic analysis of data. *Drug Metabolism Review, 17* (3–4) 331–48.

Sidowski, J. E., Johnson, J. H., & Williams, T. A. (Eds.). (1980). *Technology in mental health care delivery systems.* Norwood, NJ: Ablex.

Siegel, C., & Alexander, M. J. (1984). Evaluation of a computerized drug review system: Impact, attitudes and interactions. *Computers and Biomedical Research, 17,* 419–435.

Siegel, J. D., & Parrino, T. A. (1988). Computerized diagnosis: Implications for clinical education. *Medical Education, 22* (1), 47–54.

Siemon, J. E., & Robertson, J. S. (1987). Databases and report writers: An introduction to basic concepts for health care professionals. *Topics in Health Records Management 7* (3), 13–21.

Simborg, D. (1983). Local area networks and the hospital. *Computers and Biomedical Research, 16,* 247–259.

Skiba, D. J. (1984). Evaluation criteria for computer-assisted instruction courseware in nursing. In *Proceedings of the Eighth Annual Symposium on Computer Applications in Medical Care* (pp. 929–932). New York: Institute of Electrical and Electronics Engineers.

Skinner, H. A., Palmer, W., Sanchez-Craig, M., & McIntosh, M. (1987). Reliability of a lifestyle assessment using microcomputers. *Canadian Journal of Public Health, 78* (5), 329–334.

Slack, W. V. (1971). Computer-based interviewing systems dealing with nonverbal behavior as well as keyboard responses. *Science, 171,* 84–87.

Slack, W. V., & Slack, C. W. (1972). Patient-computer dialogue. *New England Journal of Medicine, 286,* 1304–1309.

Slack, W. V., & Slack, C. W. (1977). Talking to a computer about emotional problems: A comparative study. *Psychotherapy: Theory, Research and Practice, 14,* (2), 156–164.

Slack, W. V., & Van Cura, L. J. (1968). Patient reaction to computer-based medical interviewing. *Computers in Biomedical Research, 1,* 527–531.

Smith, M. J. (1982). Computers in nursing. *Journal of the Operating Room Research Institute, 2* (9), 4–12.

Snyder, A. A. (1987). Computer competence for school nurses. *Journal of School Health, 57* (1), 35–36.

Somand, M. E. (1981). PIES: Patient instruction in the physician's office. In *Proceedings of the Fifth Annual Symposium on Computer Applications in Medical Care* (pp. 356–357). New York: Institute of Electrical and Electronics Engineers.

Sprigings, E. J. (1988). Sport biomechanics: Data collection, modelling, and implementation stages of development. *Canadian Journal of Sport Science, 13* (1), 3–7.

Staggers, N. (1988). Using computers in nursing: Documented benefits and needed studies. *Computers in Nursing, 6* (4), 164–170.

Starn, J. R. (1987). Enhancing adolescent sex education through computer-assisted instruction: An exploratory study. Unpublished doctoral dissertation: University of Hawaii.

Starpoli, C. J., & Waltz, C. F. (1978). *Developing and evaluating educational programs for healthcare providers.* Philadelphia: F. A. Davic Company.

Steele, A. A., Davis, P. J., Hoffer, E. P., & Famiglietti, K. T. (1978). A computer-assisted instruction (CAI) program in diseases of the thyroid gland (THYROID). *Computers and Biomedical Research, 11,* 133–146.

Stein, R. F. (1969). An exploratory study in the development and use of automated nursing reports. *Nursing Research, 18* (1), 14–21.

Stolar, M. H. (1987). Developing drug-use indicators with a computerized drug database and a personal computer software package. *American Journal of Hospital Pharmacy, 44* (5), 1075–1086.

Szolovits, P. (Ed.). (1982). Artificial intelligence in medicine. *AAAS Selected Symposium Series, V 51.* Boulder, CO: Westview Press.

Taintor, Z. C. (1980). Computers and diagnosis. *American Journal of Psychiatry, 137* (1), 61–63.

Teach, R. L., & Shortliffe, E. H. (1981). An analysis of physician attitudes regarding computer-based clinical consultation systems. *Computers and Biomedical Research, 14,* 542–558.

Terry, P. E. (1987). The role of health risk appraisal in the workplace: Assessment versus behavior change. *American Journal of Health Promotion, 2* (2), 18–21, 36.

Thomas, B. S. (1985). A survey study of computers in nursing education. *Computers in Nursing, 3,* 173–179.

Thorne, B. S., & Gloninger, M. (1981). "How good is my diet?"—A nutrition analysis program that young cystic fibrosis patients can run themselves. In *Proceedings of the Fifth Annual Symposium on Computer Applications in Medical Care* (pp. 356–357). New York: Institute of Electrical and Electronics Engineers.

Tira, D. E. (1980). A computer-based dental diagnostic case simulation (DDS) system. *Computers in Biology and Medicine, 10,* 23.

Tolbert, S. H., & Pertuz, A. E. (1977). Study shows how computerization affects nursing activities in ICU. *Hospitals, 51,* 79–84.

Trollor, J. (1987). A drug information system. *Australian Family Physician, 16* (7), 930, 932.

Turner, R. E., & Evers, W. D. (1987). Development and testing of a microcomputer nutrition lesson for preschoolers. *Journal of Nutrition Education, 19* (3), 104–108.

van Bemmel, J. H. (1987). Computer-assisted care in nursing: Computers at the bedside. *Computers in Nursing, 5* (4), 132–139.

van Bemmel, J. H., Hasman, A., Sollet, P. C. G. M., & Veth, A. F. L. (1983). Training in medical informatics. *Computers in Biomedical Research, 16,* 414–432.

Vanker, A. D., & VanStoecker, W. (1984). An expert diagnostic program for dermatology. *Computers and Biomedical Research, 17,* 241–247.

Victoroff, M. S. (1985). Ethical expert systems. In *Proceedings of the Ninth Annual Symposium on Computer Applications in Medical Care* (pp. 644–648). New York: Institute of Electrical and Electronics Engineers.

Vockell, E. L., & Bratt, E. (1985). Computerized review of factual information in nursing education. *Computers in Nursing, 3* (4), 159–165.

Wagner, E., Berry, W. L., Schoenback, V. J., & Graham, R. M. (1982). An assessment of health hazard/health risk appraisal. *American Journal of Public Health, 72* (4), 347–351.

Wallace, D., Slichter, M., & Bolwell, C. (1985). Evaluation criteria for Micro-CAI: A psychometric approach. In *Proceedings of the Ninth Annual Symposium on Computer Applications in Medical Care* (pp. 558–564). New York: Institute of Electrical and Electronics Engineers.

Walton, J. D., Musen, M. A., Combs, D. M., Lane, C. D., Shortliffe, E. H., & Fagan, L. M. (1987). Graphical access to medical expert systems: III. Design of a knowledge acquisition environment. *Methods Information Medicine, 26* (3), 78–88.

Ware, J. H. (1987). Statistical practice and statistical education in cardiology. *Circulation, 75* (2), 307–310.

Watson, J. E. (1983). Impact of technology on the future of health illness education. *Health Education Quarterly, 10,* 99.

Watzlaf, V. J. M. (1987). The medical record as an epidemiological database. *Topics in Health Records Management, 7* (3), 61–67.

Weed, L. L. (1983). Can the promise be kept? *Mobius, 3* (2), 17–24.

Weinstein, R. S., Bloom, K. J., & Rozek, L. S. (1987). Telepathology and the networking of pathology diagnostic services. *Archives of Pathology Laboratory Medicine, 111* (7), 646–652.

Weiss, S., Kulikowski, C., Amarel, S., & Safir, A. (1978). A model-based method for computer-aided medical decision making. *Artificial Intelligence, 11,* 145–172.

Weiss, S. M., Kulikowski, C. A., & Safir, A. (1977). A model based consultation system for the long-term management of glaucoma. *International Joint Conference on Artificial Intelligence, 5,* 826–832.

Wenzel, A., & Gotfredsen, E. (1987). Retention after computer-assisted instruction in intraoral radiography. *Journal of Dental Education, 51* (5), 244–245.

Werner, G. (1987). Methuselah—An expert system for diagnosis in geriatric psychiatry. *Computers and Biomedical Research, 20,* 477–488.

Whiteside, M. F., & Whiteside, J. A. (1988). Microcomputer authoring systems: Valuable tools for health educators. *Health Education, 18* (6), 4–6.

Whiteside, M. F., & Whiteside, J. A. (1987). Preparing allied health faculty to use and develop computer-assisted instruction. *Journal of Allied Health, 16* (3), 247–254.

Whyte, A. A. (1983). What's new in health information systems? *Occupational Health and Safety,* June, 48–50.

Wiist, W. H. (1987). Update on computer-assisted video instruction in the health sciences. *Health Education,* 8–12.

Wilkinson, R. (1987). Telemedicine picks up steam. *Hospitals, 61* (2), 80–82.

Willard, R. (1982). Computers in dietetics. *Dietetic Currents, 9* (3), 7–14.

Williams, F. (1982). *The communications revolution.* Beverly Hills, CA: Sage.

Winters, D. M. (1988). CD-ROM and its application in the storage of health information. *Topics in Health Records Management, 9* (1), 24–31.

Wise, P. H., Dowlatshahi, D. C., Farrant, S., Fromson, S., & Meadows, K. A. (1986). Effect of computer-based learning on diabetes knowledge and control. *Diabetes Care, 9* (5), 504–508.

Woodward, J., Carnine, D., & Gersten, R. (1988). Teaching problem solving through computer simulation. *American Educational Research Journal, 25* (1), 72–86.

Woodward, J. P., Carnine, D., & Davis, L. G. (1986). Healthways: A computer simulation for problem solving in personal health management. *Journal of Family and Community Health, 9* (2), 60–63.

Wright, C. (1985). Computer-aided nursing diagnosis for community health nurses. *Nursing Clinics of North America, 20* (3), 487–494.

Yates, W. R. (1982). Computer-assisted patient prenatal education. In *Proceedings of the Sixth Annual Symposium on Computer Applications in Medical Care* (p. 633). New York: Institute of Electrical and Electronics Engineers.

Young, F. E. (1987). Validation of medical software: Present policy of the Food and Drug Administration. *Annals of Internal Medicine, 106,* 628–629.

Glossary

Acoustic coupler. A hardware device that connects a computer to the headset of a telephone for the purposes of transmitting information.

Address. The specific memory location of a piece of information.

Analog-to-digital conversion. The conversion of continuous signals (e.g., temperature) into discrete signals (a series of numbers) so the data can be used by a computer.

Analog. Continuous signals analogous to real-world events.

Anonymity. A situation in which the identity of a person providing information is unknown.

Anthropometric measures. Measures of either size or girth of different parts of the body, or the capacity of different body systems.

Applications software. Computer programs that are created for a specific purpose, such as word processing or data analysis.

Arithmetic logic unit. A high-speed circuit in the brain of a computer which is responsible for the computations.

Artificial intelligence. A broad name for a family of computer applications that mimic human intelligence and/or behavior.

ASCII. American Standard Code for Information Interchange. An agreement to assign specific code numbers to represent characters of information. For example, the capital letter *A* is represented by the code *65.*

Assembly languages. Programming languages that are only one step away from the languages that computers understand directly.

Asynchronous. In communications terms, asynchronous refers to the transmission of information in one direction at a time.

Auxiliary memory. Also called storage, auxiliary memory is necessary for computers to maintain information after the power is turned off.

Bandwidth. The capacity of a communications channel or computer to transmit information.

Bar charts. A graphic format consisting of either horizontal or vertical bars representing numerical information to compare data.

Baud rate. The transmission speed of communications.

Bits (*BI*nary digi*TS*). The primary component of computer memory, a byte, is composed of a group of these smaller elements.

Body composition. Measures of the physical stature of the human body, particularly percentage of body fat.

Boot. Start up a computer.

Bug. Any error found in hardware or software.

Bus. A pathway between components of a computer system. A bus is the information channel within a computer.

Byte. The primary storage unit in the memory of a computer. One byte of memory holds the equivalent of one character of information (e.g., any letter, number, or symbol).

CD-ROM. Compact-disk read-only memory. A form of optical storage device capable of holding more than six hundred megabytes of information. Rather than information being stored magnetically, it is stored in a format that can be read by laser.

Cell. The term *cell* in a spreadsheet refers to a single location at the intersection of any column and row. Data, values, or formulas may be entered into a cell.

Central processing unit (CPU). The main computer circuit that acts as the brain for the computer and controls its actions.

Channel. See *communications channel*.

Chip. A miniaturized electronic circuit found in computers.

Clock speed. A clock is the internal timing device that governs the speed at which the computer can process instructions—the faster the clock speed, the faster the computer can operate. Clock speed is measured in cycles per second, and the term *megaherz* is million cycles per second.

Communications channels. The pathway over which information flows in computer communications. May be either physical devices (e.g., telephone lines, fiber optics) or carrier frequency (e.g., microwave).

Communications protocol. A set of agreements or standards by which two computer systems communicate.

Communications software. An application that allows for transmission and receipt of information between computers.

Communications. The exchange of information from one computer to another.

Compilers. A software program that translates other computer languages into a form the computer can understand directly.

Computer-assisted instruction (CAI). The use of computer technology to provide instruction, assist in the instructional process, or manage data necessary to improve the instructional process. Related terms include computer-assisted learning (CAL), computer-based instruction (CBI), and computer-managed instruction (CMI).

Computer crime. The use of computers to access, modify, or change data unlawfully. Any such activity is against the law and subject to prosecution.

Computer ethics. Standards of practice that set the guidelines within which computers should be used professionally.

Computer literacy. The understanding and recognition of the capabilities and limitations of computer technology, including hardware and software. For health educators computer literacy also implies a recognition of the potential applications of this technology to the practice of health education and the training of health educators.

Computer system. A combination of computer components, including central processing unit, input/output devices, and storage.

Computer virus. A section of program code that attaches itself to a computer's operating system and does subsequent damage to the information stored in the computer.

Computer. A general-purpose machine that processes data based on some instructions.

Computerized health assessments. The application of computerized strategies to assess different levels of health or risk to health.

Confidentiality. Assurance that data collected from persons will not be reported in any manner that allows the individual to be identified by others.

Configuration. The manner in which the components of a computer system are connected and used. Also refers to the capabilities of the computer system.

Copy protection. The process of adding hardware or software devices to prevent a software application from being copied inappropriately or illegally.

Crash. Unplanned interruption of the operation of a computer program or computer system.

Creation and text entry. One of the capabilities of productivity software (e.g., word-processing programs allow for the ''creation and entry of text information'').

Critical Path Methods. A strategy for assessing implementation of a project. The critical path is the sequence of events that must occur on time for the project to be completed as planned.

Cursor. Any blinking character on a computer screen that indicates where the next character typed at a keyboard will appear.

Cut and paste. The movement of a section of information from one location in a document to another, or from one application to another.

Data acquisition. The use of computers to accumulate or acquire raw data.

Data backup. The process and product of making copies of electronic information to protect against loss.

Data presentation. The use of a variety of strategies to present information in the most concise and easily understood manner.

Data security. Methods and procedures for protecting data against unauthorized access or loss.

Data transmission rate. The speed at which data is transmitted over a communication channel.

Database. Any collection of information.

Database-management software. A program that allows a user to store, manage, manipulate, and retrieve data from a database.

Decision assistance. A computer system that provides a user with information useful in making difficult administrative, practice, or other programmatic decisions. A related term is *decision-support systems* (DSS).

Dedicated word-processing system. A computerized system that is limiting in its use to word processing.

Delimiter. Any character or set of characters that is used to separate data (e.g., a comma).

Demographics. Information describing a sample population (e.g., gender, age, ethnicity, level of education, annual income).

Desktop libraries. Enormous amounts of printed materials on single compact disks.

Desktop publishing. Production of publication-quality output from a personal computer.

Diagram. A visual representation of relationships of elements to a whole.

Dietary analyses. Assessments of dietary behavior, including nutritional composition of someone's diet, or assessments of personal recommended daily allowances of different nutrients.

Digital. Coming from the word *digit* (which means finger), digital refers to counting. Modern usage, however, has led to the word *digital* being associated with the word *computer.* A digital computer is one that operates with discrete numerical information.

Disk drive. A device attached to a computer system which allows a user to store information. See *diskettes.*

Diskettes. A storage medium used in disk drives. Diskettes store information in magnetic form.

Dissertation Abstracts International. A bibliographic retrieval service that contains the abstracts and key information on all doctoral dissertations completed in the United States.

Distributed processing. The use of separate microcomputers, usually networked together, rather than one large mainframe computer with terminals.

Download. The receipt of information to a user's computer from a remote location.

Drill and practice. A format in which computer-assisted instruction is provided. In drill-and-practice programs, learners are given the opportunity to answer questions about material presented. The process is continued until a learner displays mastery of the material.

Edit. The process of changing existing information in a text, data, or graphic document.

Electrical. A mechanical device using electricity as its power source (see *electronic*).

Electronic bulletin board. A computer system that acts as a central location for storage of information.

Electronic mail. Transmission of information (letters, memos, reports) over a communications network.

Electronic. The use of electricity in sophisticated devices.

Element. A single piece of data in a database.

Encryption. The translation of information into a format not easily interpretable or understandable by unintended or unauthorized users of the data. Encryption is a procedure used to protect or secure information.

End-users. The final user of the information output by a computer.

ENIAC. Electronic Numerical Integrator and Calculator, was the first computer that was considered operational. Based on vacuum-tube technology, ENIAC was housed at the University of Pennsylvania in 1946.

Entity. A collection of information about a single person in a database (see *record*).

ERIC. A bibliographic retrieval service that covers the domain of educational resources and materials.

Exercise prescriptions. A sophisticated mechanism for providing a recommendation for exercise following an appropriate assessment of an individual's needs and exercise capacity.

Expert systems. A subset of artificial intelligence, expert systems are designed to mimic the behavior and problem-solving ability of experts in a field.

Export. To prepare information kept in one applications format (e.g., spreadsheet) for use by another program or another type of application (e.g., database).

Facsimile (FAX). Communication of printed information between locations. A fax machine scans a printed page and converts the information on the page into information that can be transmitted over phone lines.

Fever charts. A graphic format in which points are plotted along coordinates of time and quantity. A line is usually drawn to connect the points.

Field. Location reserved for a specific type of data—including text, numbers, or special characters.

Fifth-generation machines. Computers designed specifically to use artificial intelligence strategies and applications.

File server. A central computer on a network that stores programs and files for the users on the network.

File. Any collection of information electronically stored.

Fitness appraisals. Assessment of different aspects of individual fitness (e.g., cardiorespiratory fitness, body composition).

Flat file. A type of database structure. A flat file is a database that is self-contained, that is, has no physical connection with other databases.

Font. The particular design of a set of characters, numbers, and symbols (e.g., Helvetica, Times).

Format. The graphic style selected to portray different types of data. Examples include pie charts, bar charts, fever charts, and tables.

Formula. A set of instructions, ordinarily in algebraic form, that directs the computer to manipulate a set of data in a specific way. Used primarily in spreadsheet and database applications, the formula describes how the computer should use the data in a field.

Full-duplex. A term used in communications, referring to the capacity to send and receive information simultaneously.

Games. A special form of simulation program used for recreation and learning. Games take many forms, but most often involve competition between learners or between a learner and the computer.

Gantt Charting. A family of strategies and procedures for tracking the flow of operation of large projects or programs.

Global search and replace. Usually used in word processing and other productivity applications, this term refers to searching an entire document for a specific set of information (e.g., a word) and exchanging all occurrences with another set of information.

Graphic. Visual information as opposed to textual information.

Graphical user interface (GUI). A term used to describe a computer display that is based on pictures and objects rather than entirely on textual information. Although developed by Xerox at the Palo Alto Research Center, the graphical user interface was commercially popularized by Apple Computer in 1984 with the introduction of the Macintosh Computer.

Graphics software. Any computer program capable of creating or processing pictures or images.

Groupware. Software that is designed to be used by more than one person simultaneously.

Hacker. A person who is very knowledgeable about the technical characteristics and operation of computer systems.

Half-duplex. A term used in communications, referring to the ability to transmit information along a channel in only one direction at a time.

Hardware. A computer and all the physical equipment that is part of a computer system.

Health Education Electronic Forum (HEEF). Developed by Dr. Michael Pejsach, the first electronic bulletin board specifically devoted to health-education issues and concerns.

Health-risk appraisals. Assessment of an individual's overall health risk based on life-style choices, genetic predisposition, health behaviors, and other measures.

Healthfinders. A series of publications produced by the U.S. Office of Disease Prevention and Health Promotion (ODPHP) Health Information Center. Three such publications were produced on microcomputer technology in health education: health promotion software, health-risk appraisals, and on-line information.

High-definition TV (HDTV). Television that provides resolution three or more times more precise than current television technology.

High-level languages. Computer programming languages that are close to natural language (e.g., Basic, Fortran, C).

Hypercard. A database program using *hypertext* strategies produced for Apple Macintosh computers. Using the graphical interface of the Macintosh, Hypercard allows for the linkage of text, graphics, and sound.

Hypertext. A technique that allows for the free-form linkage of information. The connections between words and their definitions, or between events and the precedents, or between concepts and their descriptions, are invisible to the user.

I/O. An acronym for input/output. Refers to the transfer of data from any computer component to any other computer component.

Import. Transporting elements into a software application.

Informatics. A field of study that examines the use of information in a discipline.

Input. The entry of any information into a computer. Input devices refer to the hardware necessary to enter the data.

Integrated Systems Digital Network (ISDN). A digital network standard being developed which will have the capacity to transfer voice, graphics, video, and sound over telephone lines simultaneously.

Integrated circuit. The combinations of many electronic components on a single computer chip.

Integrated package. A software program that includes the functions of several different types of productivity software (e.g., word processing, database, spreadsheet, communications, or graphics).

Interactive applications. Computer software designed to respond to input provided by a computer user.

Interpreters. A program that translates higher-level language programs into a form the computer can understand. This is done one line at a time while the program is running.

Kilobytes (KB). In computer terminology the term *kilo* refers to 1,024. A kilobyte is 1,024 bytes of computer memory.

Labels. A type of data that can be entered into a spreadsheet cell. Often used as titles for columns or row of information.

Laptop computer. A microcomputer whose circuitry has been made small enough to be easily carried and placed on a lap to use. It generally refers to a microcomputer whose weight is not more than ten to fifteen pounds.

Liability. Legal responsibility for producing goods or services as promised and in a manner that is not harmful to the recipient.

Line graph. (Also called a line chart). See *fever chart*.

Local-area network (LAN). A communications network that is confined to a small geographic area such as an office complex.

Lock-out and dial-back systems. A form of security measure taken to protect against unauthorized access to database information. When a user calls a remote-access database by modem over telephone lines, the system will record the call, hang up on the user, check the phone number that the authorized user has listed in the system, and then dial back the authorized phone number. If the number from which the caller is dialing is not on the authorized phone number list, access will be denied.

Machine languages. The language that a computer understands directly. Machine language is entirely numeric, with no words or special symbols. Before any other computer program can be run by a computer, it has to be translated into machine language by another program (see *compilers, interpreters*).

Mail merge. A function found on most intermediate and advanced word-processing applications, mail merge allows for a form letter to be created and the computer to access information in a database to personalize any letter.

Mainframe computer. Large-scale computer system capable of storing hundreds of millions of bytes of information. Mainframe computers have the capacity to handle as many as several thousand users simultaneously.

Mechanical. Having to do with machines or tools, mechanical devices have moving parts that wear out through use.

Medline. A bibliographic retrieval service that covers the medical literature.

Megahertz (MHZ). Million cycles per second on a computer clock.

Meta-systems. In communications, metasystems are systems that provide many different services to potential users (e.g., electronic bulletin boards, electronic mail).

Microcomputer. A small desktop-size computer, often called personal computer. Although capable of doing many of the same things as other computers, it is designed for use by one person. Generally costs less than ten thousand dollars.

Microelectronics. The miniaturization of electronic components.

Microminiaturization. The capacity to make computer components smaller by miniaturizing different elements and placing many elements on a single chip.

Microprocessors. The central processing unit or brain of the microcomputer. The microprocessor is responsible for overseeing the operation of the microcomputer's resources.

Minicomputer. A midrange computer between mainframe and microcomputer. Minicomputers can support up to several hundred users. Cost in the range of twenty thousand dollars to two hundred thousand dollars.

Mnemonic codes. A symbol or code for some computer function. Mnemonic codes are used in assembly-language programming to make program construction more manageable.

Modem. Modulator-demodulator. A piece of equipment that translates electronic information in one computer into signals that can be transmitted to another computer. At the other end of the transmission, another modem converts the signals back into electronic form.

Motherboard. The main circuit board in electronic computers, a motherboard provides the mechanism for connecting all other components of the computer system.

Multipoint. In communications refers to a single-line channel with connections for multiple users.

Multiprocessing. The simultaneous use of two or more microprocessors in a computer.

Multitasking. The capacity of a computer to execute several different computer programs and tasks simultaneously.

Multiuser. The capacity of two or more individuals to use a single computer simultaneously.

Negligence. Failure to comply with a set of standards or rules that govern professional behavior. Negligence may result from inadequate training, loss of skill or judgment through inadequate upkeep of skills, or carelessness. A professional may be held legally responsible for not adhering to standards of practice.

Network. A communications path between computers.

Neural networks. Computer chips connected in such a way as to simulate the human brain.

Nodes. Points on a network where connections to computers or terminals, or other peripheral devices, are physically attached.

Open-architecture machine. In computer terminology *open architecture* refers to two issues: (1) the publication of technical specifications of a computer system; and (2) the ability of an individual user to open the machine and modify its configuration without voiding warranties.

Operating system. In a computer system the operating system is the software program that controls all operations.

Optical scanner. A computer device able to translate text or graphic information on a printed page into signals that can be used by a computer. Several different types of scanners are in use: (1) mark-sense scanners used to pick up responses to questions on IBM-type answer sheets; (2) optical-character-recognition devices, able to read text information on a printed page; (3) graphics scanners, able to transfer images from a printed page to a computer.

Output. Information produced by a computer for use by the user.

Parallel. The simultaneous transmission of one or more bytes of information.

Password. A word or code used to identify an authorized user of a computer system, programs, or data files. When a user attempts to use a password-protected system, if the password provided is incorrect, access is denied.

Pie chart. Shows the relationship of parts to the whole, usually in a circular shape.

Point to point. A computer network configuration in which the computers are attached in a series.

Points. In publishing terminology a point is equal to 1/72 of an inch and is used to measure the vertical height of characters and spaces between lines of text.

Printing. A form of computer output.

Privacy. The legal right to control information about oneself.

Problem solving. A form of instructional software in which the computer is used as a tool by a learner to solve complex problems.

Productivity software. A group of software-applications programs that enhance the speed and capabilities of individual professional activities (e.g., word processing, database management).

Program Evaluation Review Techniques (PERT). A tool for planning and monitoring large projects.

Project-management software. A name given to a variety of computer applications that assist in the planning, management, monitoring, surveillance, or evaluation of large projects. Among the components found in such software are Gannt Charting, PERT, and CPM techniques.

Public-access databases. Databases that are maintained in such a way as to be accessed by the general public from remote locations by telecommunications.

Public domain. Software that has been made available to anyone in the general public who wants it.

RAM. Random-access memory in a computer system. RAM is the primary memory in which information is stored by a user.

Real-time conferencing. Communication that occurs between remote locations as if the participants were all in the same location.

Record. A group of fields in a database containing information about one subject or other *entity*.

Relational database. A database made up of more than one file, linked together based on common data.

Ring network. A network configuration in which the computers are connected in circular fashion.

ROM. Read-only memory. ROM is memory that contains information that cannot be changed by the computer user. It generally contains information needed by the computer system to operate.

Search strategy. The plan used to selectively identify records in a database satisfying specific criteria.

Segmentation. The breaking down of any file or computer program into smaller, logical units.

Serial transmission. A mode of communication in which information (e.g., byte) is broken down into its smallest physical unit (e.g., bits) and transmitted as a single file stream of these units.

Shareware software. Software for microcomputers that is distributed at no cost to potential users. After the software is evaluated by the individual user, if it is considered to be of value and used, a charge for the program is requested by the authors/distributors.

Simulation. A model that represents real-world situations or problems. Computerized simulations are often used for training professionals (e.g., flight simulators) or testing skills (e.g., driving simulators). Computerized simulations of health-related scenarios (e.g., spread of pollution in the environment) help train health educators to solve problems or to study how events can be altered by changing important elements of the problem.

Site licenses. A discount purchase agreement between an organization and a software company. Such agreements give the organization the right to make up to a predetermined number of copies of the software for workers in the organization. The cost of the site license is determined by the number of copies to be made. In the case of site licenses, the cost is always lower than the cost of buying a comparable number of original copies.

Smart card. A credit-card-size card that contains personal health information encoded on a magnetic strip.

Software. Set of instructions that the computer follows. A series of instructions designed to serve a particular purpose or solve a particular problem is called *software program or program.*

Sort. The process of ordering a set of data according to specified criteria (e.g., in database applications, a group of records may be ordered based on the age of the clients from youngest to oldest).

Speech synthesis. The production of vocal sounds by a computer. See also *voice recognition.*

Spreadsheet software. An application program that mimics a table with columns and rows. Any operations on numbers or text that can be performed in such a table can be done electronically in spreadsheet software.

Star network. A network configuration in which the computers are all connected directly to a central computer.

Statistical analysis. Use of the computer to conduct a variety of descriptive or analytic procedures on a set of data.

Stress assessment. Measurement of sources and stress on an individual and/or coping skills.

Supercomputer. The fastest computers currently available. Capable of executing hundreds of millions of instructions per second, supercomputers are used only for solving complex problems.

Superconductor. A material able to conduct electrical current with almost no resistance. Such material allows for the extremely rapid transmission of currents without losing energy or generating heat.

Switch network. A network configuration in which any computer can send a message to any other computer in the network.

Synchronous. A communications protocol in which data are transmitted in blocks of fixed size.

Syntax errors. A grammatical error in a computer program. As in natural language, computer languages have rules for construction of statements. Any violation of these construction rules makes it impossible for the computer to understand the nature of the command.

System software. Computer programs that control the operation of the computer and any devices attached to it.

Table. A listing of text or graphics in columnar format.

Telecommunications. The communication of any form of information—data, text, video, and sound.

Time-shared word-processing systems. A system in which one computer serves the word-processing needs of several users simultaneously.

Transistor. An important component of a computer's logic, transistors act as switches for electrical impulses passing through the system.

Transmission characteristics. The characteristics of the protocol used in a telecommunications session.

Tutorials. A form of CAI, tutorials are used to present new information to a learner.

Unauthorized access. Occurs when any security measures are breached or overridden in order to secure access to data.

Upload. To send information from a user's computer to some other location.

Virus. See *computer virus*.

Voice recognition. The ability of a computer system to interpret and understand the spoken voice.

What-if projections. The ability to test changing assumptions in spreadsheet models.

Wide-area network (WAN). A communication network between computers at remote locations. A WAN may be citywide, statewide, nationwide, or worldwide.

Word processing. An application program that allows a user to enter, store, manipulate, and print text information.

Workstations. A single-user computer with very high performance characteristics and graphical user interface.

CREDITS

Chapter 1   Page 5 top left: Paul Shambroom/Courtesy of Cray Research, Inc.; top right: Courtesy of Control Data Corporation; middle left: Courtesy of Digital Equipment Corporation; middle right: Courtesy of IBM; bottom: Courtesy of Apple Computer, Inc.; Page 11: Courtesy of IBM; 1.3a: Courtesy of Apple Computer, Inc.; 1.3b: Courtesy of Microsoft Corporation; 1.3c: Courtesy of IBM; 1.3d: Courtesy of Apple Computer, Inc.; 1.3e: Courtesy of Princeton Graphic Systems; 1.3f: Courtesy of Hewlett-Packard Company; 1.3g: Courtesy of CalComp/Richard Stehr; Page 15 top left: © Mark Antman/The Image Works; top right: Courtesy of Hitachi; bottom: © Bob Coyle

Chapter 3   Fig. 3.4 a,b: © James L. Shaffer; 3.4c: AT & T Laboratories

Chapter 4   Page 107: © Bob Coyle

Chapter 5   Page 149: © Will and Deni McIntyre/Photo Researchers, Inc.

INDEX

star network, *97f,* 98
statistical analysis, 160, 165*t,* 166*t*
stress assessments, 128, 153–56
supercomputer, 4
supervisory or control unit, 10
switch network, 94, *97f*
synchronous, 92, 94
syntax errors, 19
system software, 16, 17

T

tables, 68, 70–71
telecommunications, 80, 93, 99–103

time shared word processing systems, 48
transaction auditing, 180
transistor, 7
transmission characteristics, 89
trends for health education, 168
tutorials, 106

U

unauthorized access, 178
upload, 103
user, 10

V

Visicalc™, 8, 20
voice recognition, 20
von Neumann, John, 6

W

What If Projections, 61–63
wide area networks (WAN), 93
word processing, 32, 48–58
word processing software, 48
workstations, 16
future trends, 191–94
Wozniak, S., 8